Peter Lucantoni

Cambridge IGCSE®
English as a Second Language

Coursebook

Fourth edition

CAMBRIDGE
UNIVERSITY PRESS

CAMBRIDGE
UNIVERSITY PRESS

University Printing House, Cambridge CB2 8BS, United Kingdom

Cambridge University Press is part of the University of Cambridge.

It furthers the University's mission by disseminating knowledge in the pursuit of education, learning and research at the highest international levels of excellence.

Information on this title: education.cambridge.org

First published 2014
3rd printing 2015

Printed in Poland by Opolgraf

ISBN 978-1-107-66962-8 Paperback

Additional resources for this publication at education.cambridge.org

Cambridge University Press has no responsibility for the persistence or accuracy of URLs for external or third-party internet websites referred to in this publication, and does not guarantee that any content on such websites is, or will remain, accurate or appropriate. Information regarding prices, travel timetables, and other factual information given in this work is correct at the time of first printing but Cambridge University Press does not guarantee the accuracy of such information thereafter.

....

IGCSE® is the registered trademark of Cambridge International Examinations

The questions, example answers, marks awarded and/or comments that appear in this book were written by the author. In examination, the way marks would be awarded may be different.

DEDICATION
As always, this book is dedicated to three wonderful people: Lydia, Sara and Emily. Thank you!

Contents

Menu

PART 1 Leisure and travel

U1: Focus on reading skills	In this unit, you will: talk about leisure activities, practise reading strategies, read adverts, talk about preferences, make suggestions	Language focus: adjectives + noun
U2: Focus on reading skills	In this unit, you will: discuss television programmes, read graphs, read about young people, read about Kuala Lumpur, talk about things you would/ wouldn't do	Language focus: adverbs
U3: Focus on writing skills	In this unit, you will: talk about your favourite foods, read about fast food, write an informal letter, express opinions, read about a shellfish found in Oman	Language focus: more adjectives and adverbs
U4: Focus on listening skills	In this unit, you will: talk about transport, listen to people talking about different forms of transport, read about cycle safety, read information in a table, use expressions of surprise	Language focus: tenses – present continuous, present perfect simple, past simple, 'will' future

PART 2 Education and work

U5: Focus on reading skills	In this unit, you will: read and talk about a language school, look at prefixes and suffixes, give advice, read about getting up in the morning	Language focus: prefixes and suffixes
U6: Focus on reading and writing skills	In this unit, you will: talk and read about different jobs, look for details in a text, make notes, write a summary, give advice, read an advertisement	Language focus: giving advice
U7: Focus on writing and speaking skills	In this unit, you will: learn about British English and American English spelling, read about spelling, write a formal letter, act out a job interview	Language focus: spelling
U8: Focus on listening skills	In this unit, you will: talk about CVs and résumés, listen to a radio interview, write a CV, listen to a job interview, take part in an interview, read about jobs for teenagers	Language focus: question forms

PART 3 People and achievements

U9: Focus on reading skills	In this unit, you will: talk about record-breaking, read about sports and athletes, read about Scott of the Antarctic, rank reasons and write paragraphs	Language focus: superlatives; adjectives; vocabulary
U10: Focus on reading and writing skills	In this unit, you will: read about famous people, make notes, talk about twins, write a summary	Language focus: adverbs; vocabulary
U11: Focus on writing skills	In this unit, you will: talk and read about activity/adventure holidays, write an informal letter and paragraphs, read about Girl Guides and Girl Scouts, write an article	Language focus: *either, neither*
U12: Focus on listening skills	In this unit, you will: talk about the nursing profession, listen to a talk about Florence Nightingale, complete a form, talk about the ICRC, listen to talks about traffic	Language focus: future in the past

PART 4 Ideas and the modern world

U13: Focus on reading skills	In this unit, you will: read and talk about social media, create and describe a graph, talk and read about mobile phones, read and create a presentation about computer games	Language focus: vocabulary
U14: Focus on reading and writing skills	In this unit, you will: discuss and read about global warming and the North Pole, read and talk about climate problems, write a summary, discuss, research and design a presentation about water issues	Language focus: vocabulary
U15: Focus on writing skills	In this unit, you will: talk and read about chewing gum, write an article, discuss and read about foods that are bad for the planet, research food types	Language focus: *effect* and *affect*
U16: Focus on speaking skills	In this unit, you will: talk and read about fashion, talk about people discussing fashion, plan and write a competition entry, research, design and prepare a fashion presentation	Language focus: varying vocabulary

Introduction

This fourth edition is for students who are following the International General Certificate of Secondary Education (IGCSE) English as a Second Language (E2L) syllabus, and follows on from *Introduction to English as a Second Language*. However, this Coursebook can be used independently of the introductory volume.

It is assumed that most of you who use this book will be studying English in order to improve your educational or employment prospects, so it includes topics and themes relevant to this goal. You will find passages and activities based on a wide variety of stimulating topics and about people from all over the world, which I hope you will enjoy reading and discussing.

The book is divided into four themed parts: Leisure and travel, Education and work, People and achievements, and Ideas and the modern world. Each themed part is sub-divided into units based on the specific skill areas of the IGCSE E2L syllabus: reading, writing and listening. Exam-style questions are provided at the end of Units 1–15. Speaking skills are practised through discussion activities and pair and group work, which occur in every unit. At the end of each unit, there is a selection of 'Further practice' exercises, so that you can do extra work at home or without a teacher.

Appendix 1 contains some examples of topic cards, similar to those used in speaking-test examinations. However, these could be used to practise your speaking skills, whether you will be taking a speaking-test examination or completing speaking coursework.

The material becomes progressively more demanding, with longer and more advanced texts used in the second half of the book. This progressive step-by-step approach, including Top Tips throughout the book, will help to build your confidence in all the necessary skill areas, while also developing your techniques for success in examinations.

I hope you enjoy using this book, and I wish you success in your IGCSE E2L course!

Peter Lucantoni

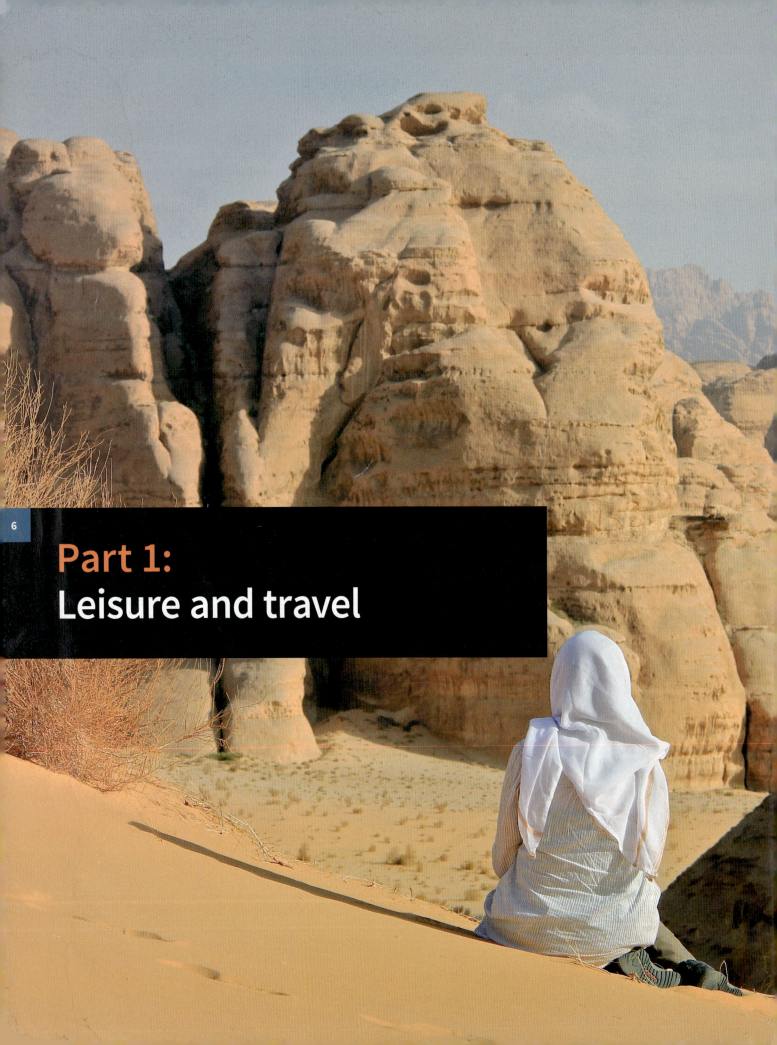

Part 1:
Leisure and travel

Unit 1: Focus on reading skills

In this unit, we will concentrate on skimming and scanning reading skills. These skills are important when you need to identify and retrieve facts and details, and to understand and select relevant information from a short text, such as an advertisement, brochure, notice, guide, report, manual or set of instructions, which may include pictures or a diagram.

In this unit, you will also:

- discuss things you do in your free time, and talk about preferences and suggestions
- answer questions about different types of texts
- look at adjective + noun combinations
- answer some exam-style questions.

A 🗨 🅰ª Speaking and vocabulary

1   What do these pictures show? Discuss your ideas with a partner and write down **at least five** words or phrases that you think of.

Example: *people relaxing*

2   What do you enjoy and not enjoy doing in your free time? Use the pictures and your ideas from Activity A1 to help you. Make a list by copying and completing the table. Compare your list with your partner's. Are they the same or different?

Enjoy	Don't enjoy
watching films on TV	tidying my room

LANGUAGE TIP

Remember that the verbs *enjoy* and *dislike* are both followed by *-ing*.

Example: I **enjoy** watch**ing** movies on TV, but I **dislike** tidy**ing** my room.

B Reading

1 Discuss these questions with a partner.

   a When you want to find something quickly in a text, what do you do? Which reading skills do you use?

   b When you read something for pleasure, such as a book or a magazine, do you read it in the same way as you read a school Chemistry textbook?

   c What other ways are there to read a text?

TOP TIPS

Skimming and scanning reading skills are very important when looking for information in a text. We **skim** to get a general picture of the text – to touch the surface. Think of a stone skimming the surface of water. When we **scan**, we go deeper into the text, looking for more details. Think of an airport x-ray machine looking inside a suitcase. It may not be necessary to read and understand every word in a text to find the answers to questions.

2 Look at the advertisement for Datasource products on page 9. Answer these two questions. You have ten seconds!

   a How many different products are advertised?

   b Which product is the most expensive?

3 Which reading skill or skills did you use to answer Activity B2? Did you read every word in the text? Did you read quickly or slowly?

4 Answer the following question. Do **not** write anything yet.

   ■ Which product has the biggest percentage reduction?

5 Which of the following is the best answer to the question in Activity B4? Is more than one answer possible? If so, why?

   a Datasource Trainer has the biggest percentage reduction.

   b The product with the biggest percentage reduction is Datasource Trainer.

   c It's Datasource Trainer.

   d Datasource Trainer.

   e Trainer.

6 With your partner, ask and answer the following questions. Do **not** write anything yet.

   a How many products have a normal download price of less than $5?

   b How can you save an additional $5?

   c Which product offers the smallest cash saving?

   d How many Datasource Puzzle Finder apps were sold in a month in the USA?

   e Give **three** advantages of joining the Datasource loyalty scheme.

   f Which product offers you 60 minutes free of charge?

   g Which product is available in different languages?

7 Write the answers to the questions in Activity B6. Exchange your answers with a different pair and check them. Use the Top Tips on this page to help you.

TOP TIPS

Often, you do not need to write full sentences for your answers. Sometimes a single word, a few words, or even a number, will be enough. However, you must show that you have understood the question and you must provide all the information required. If you are writing numbers, be careful to spell them correctly. Also, if the answer is a quantity, make sure you include a symbol or a unit of measurement – for example $35, 10 **kilometres**, 2 **hours**.

New apps available to download now from **Datasource.com**!

Datasource Puzzle Finder – special discount price of $1 (normal download price: $2 – save 50%!)

This amazing app is the one that sold a million in a month in the USA! If you're a puzzle lover, now's your chance to get the most up-to-date app for finding literally hundreds of online puzzles.

Datasource Photo Squeeze – discount price of $2 (normal download price: $6 – save 66%!)

Now you can create your own amazing images using Photo Squeeze! Take a pic using your smartphone or tablet and then squeeze it into something awesome.

Datasource Trainer – amazing price – it's FREE! (normal download price: $2 – save 100%!)

If you are into keeping fit, you need this incredible app right now! Download onto your smartphone and keep track of your fitness level. This app will even tell you when you're not running fast enough!

Datasource NewsFeed – discount price of $6 (normal download price: $8 – save 25%!)

Keep in touch with what's going on in the world by using this fantastic app! NewsFeed will keep you informed about whatever you choose – sports, entertainment, music … for up to 60 free minutes every day!

Datasource My Movies – discount price of $3 (normal download price: $6 – save 50%!)

This incredible app stores a list of your favourite movies and lets you know about new releases. My Movies also lets you share your list with your friends.

Datasource Comic Fun – discount price of $1 (normal download price: $4 – save 75%!)

Everyone loves comics and this delightful but simple app gives you access to a huge number of titles. And for all you language learners, there are **five** languages to choose from!

$5 OFFER!

You can save even more by signing up to the Datasource loyalty scheme. Download a minimum of **three** apps today and get a voucher for **$5** to use on your next purchase. You also get a 21-day money-back, no-questions-asked guarantee on all our apps, a monthly digital newsletter, and a membership card and number.

9

www.youwrite.eu

The amazing online webzine for teenagers who want to share their writing!

Send us your writing by 30th June for a chance to see it in the next issue (publication date 31st July) of **You Write!**

Choose which section you want your work to appear in: **MY STORY**, **MY POEM**, **MY OPINION**, **MY REPORT**

MY STORY:
For those of you with a story to tell, this is the section for you! We will consider your funny, or serious, original, creative stories up to a maximum of 275 words.

MY POEM:
What has inspired you to write a poem? An interesting person? An unusual place? A funny pet? Extreme weather? Send us up to 25 lines of your inspired writing in order to be considered for this section.

MY OPINION:
Use this section if you want to get something off your chest! Has something annoying happened that makes you want to put pen to paper? If you are feeling particularly angry, upset, or even happy about something, share your opinion by writing no more than 200 words.

MY REPORT:
Seen or heard something interesting locally that you want to tell others about? Perhaps a new cinema has opened in your town, or your local team won its most recent match? Maybe you want to write about something that you were personally involved in, such as a music or drama festival? Send us your report, up to 275 words.

What do I do next?

Complete and submit the form below. You **must** do this electronically. Do not forget to attach your piece of writing!

UPLOAD YOUR ARTICLE   **SUBMIT**

First name: _____   Family name: _____

Email: _____   Age last birthday: _____   Name of school: _____

Which section are you writing for? Please select.

My Story ❑   My Poem ❑   My Opinion ❑   My Report ❑

Title for your writing (maximum **FIVE** words): _____
Number of words: _____

I have my parent's/guardian's permission to submit my writing to **You Write!** Please select **YES   NO**

Data Protection Act: Sometimes we may wish to send you information about other products that we feel may be of interest to you. Select this box if you do **NOT** wish to receive such information ❑

Need to contact us? **Click here** or email us: info@youwrite.eu

8   Have a quick look at the second text, *You Write!*, on page 10. Where might you find a text like this? Why? Choose one or more from the list.

> a dictionary   an email   a newspaper   a comic
> a TV magazine   a children's magazine   a blog
> a shop window   a leaflet   an encyclopaedia   a website

9   What is the best strategy for addressing short-answer questions? Put the following points into a logical order. Be prepared to explain your order.

  a   Search likely sections of the text.

  b   Read the question.

  c   Underline the key word/s.

  d   Ask yourself what information the question is asking for.

10   Look at these questions based on the *You Write!* webzine on page 10. Do **not** write anything yet. Find and note down the key word/s in each question.

  a   Who is *You Write!* for?

  b   When can you read the next publication?

  c   How many sections are there in the webzine?

  d   What is the maximum number of words for a creative story?

  e   If something has made you angry, for which section should you write?

  f   Which section does **not** tell you how many words to write?

  g   After you have finished your writing, what do you have to do?

  h   How long can the title for your writing be?

  i   If you select the final box, what will you **not** receive?

TOP TIPS

Notices, leaflets, signs, advertisements and timetables can contain a lot of information in various formats. The best strategy for answering questions on sources like these is to decide which word or words in the question will lead you to the place in the text that contains the answer. These words are called *key words*.

Was it possible to identify key words in every question in Activity B10? Sometimes you may not be able to decide, but usually there are one or two words that will help you to identify where in text you can find the answer.

11   Now write the answers to the questions in Activity B10. Keep your answers short, but remember to include all the information that the questions ask for. Exchange your answers with a partner and check them.

C ⊕ Language focus: Adjective + noun

1 Notice the use of adjectives in the two texts you have read in this unit:

amazing app   *up-to-date* app   *amazing* online webzine   *creative* stories

   a Copy and complete this sentence.

   Adjectives are used to provide … about … . In English, adjectives usually come … the noun.

   b What happens in **your** language? What is the usual order for adjectives and nouns?

2 Quickly read through the two texts on pages 9 and 10 again. Find **at least three** more examples of adjective + noun combinations in each text. Compare your examples with a partner's.

3 Adjectives can often be formed from other parts of speech. Copy and complete the table with the correct words. You may not be able to fill in all the gaps.

Adjective	Noun	Adverb	Verb
amazing	amazement	amazingly	amaze
special	…	…	…
incredible	…	…	…
delightful	…	…	…
funny	…	…	…
serious	…	…	…
original	…	…	…
creative	…	…	…

4 Look back at the two texts in this unit and find **at least five** more adjectives. Add them to your table and then complete the other parts of speech (noun, adverb and verb) where possible.

5 Notice that there are different possible endings for adjectives in English. Using the words from Activities C3 and C4, list some of these possible endings. Then think of **three** more examples for each ending.

   Example: *-ing: interesting, amazing   tiring, fascinating, boring*

6 Choose **eight** adjectives from Activity C5, then combine them with nouns and use them in sentences of your own.

   Example: *That webzine was full of **interesting stories** and **ideas**.*

D 💬 Speaking: Showing preferences and making suggestions

1 🔊 Listen to Maria and Christos talking. How many different ways do they use to show a preference or to make a suggestion?

2 Look at the audioscript on page 188 and check the meaning of the phrases that are underlined.

3 Think of more ways to show a preference and to make a suggestion. Copy the table below and add more phrases. Compare your answers with your partner's.

Showing a preference	Making a suggestion
I'd rather go …	Why don't we go … ? Let's go …

4 Usually when we **show a preference** for something or **make a suggestion**, we also give a **reason**. What reason does Maria give for wanting to go to the shopping centre later? What reason does Christos give for wanting to go to the shopping centre at the weekend?

LANGUAGE TIP

Look at how **preference** and **suggestion** phrases are followed by infinitive, 'to' infinitive or -ing forms of the verb.

+ infinitive	+ 'to' infinitive	+ -ing
Why don't we … + do? Let's + do I suggest we + do Can't we … + do? I think we should … + do I'd rather + do	Would you like … + to do? I'd like + to do I('d) prefer + to do	What/How about … + doing? What do you think about … + doing? I suggest + doing

---

5 Work with your partner. For each of the following examples, one of you makes a suggestion and the other gives a preference. Use a variety of phrases from the Language Tip, and support your suggestions and preferences with reasons.

Example: *Buying new trainers or a birthday present for someone.*

> ***Maria:*** *Why don't you buy those new trainers we saw in town?*
>
> ***Christos:*** *No, I don't think so, Maria. It's my mum's birthday next month and I'd prefer to save my money for her present.*

a Going on holiday to Australia or Iceland.

b Eating Italian or Japanese food in a restaurant.

c Watching a movie at the cinema or on TV.

d Playing basketball or going swimming.

6 A competition has just been announced. An area of land near your school is going to be developed. For the competition, you need to make a short speech to your schoolfriends, giving your preferences and reasons for the development of the land. Plan your speech. It might be helpful to write down some ideas, like this:

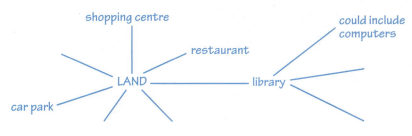

TOP TIPS

Making suggestions and expressing preferences about a particular topic are important aspects of speaking effectively. Although it is important to speak accurately (and using set phrases like the ones in this unit will be very helpful), in order to ensure that no misunderstandings take place, the most important thing is to talk communicatively and effectively in a fluent manner. Also, try to avoid using slang expressions and vocabulary, say 'yes' not 'yeah' and try to use full sentences whenever possible (rather than single-word answers to questions).

E ⊕ Further practice

Read and answer

1   Read the leaflet about the Achileas Sports Centre and answer the questions.

Welcome!

Welcome to the new Achileas Sports Centre and Swimming Pool Complex monthly newsletter! We offer a wide variety of activities for you and all your family and friends. Whether your interest is fitness, football, tennis, basketball or swimming, we can offer you an excellent range of activities to suit all your needs. We hope you will enjoy your visit to the new Achileas Complex and take advantage of the many facilities available.

Opening hours

Swimming Pool

Monday–Friday	07.00–22.00
Saturday–Sunday & public holidays	08.00–21.00

Sports Centre

Monday–Friday	06.00–22.00
Saturday–Sunday & public holidays	09.00–20.00

Achileas Restaurant

Monday–Saturday	12.00–15.00 & 19.00–23.00
Sunday & public holidays	12.00–15.00 only

Membership

	Children (6–17)	Adults (18+)	Couples (2 adults)	Family (2 adults + 2 children)
Annual	$250	$400	$350 each	$1000
6-monthly	$130	$210	$180 each	$600
3-monthly	$70	$110	$100 each	$330
Monthly	$25	$45	$40 each	$120
Weekly	$20	$40	$35 each	$105
Daily	$10	$20	$15 each	$45

Facilities

Five fitness and special-focus gyms, one children's gym, Olympic pool and children's starter pool, four squash courts, four badminton courts, two basketball courts, eight outdoor tennis courts, two all-weather football pitches, Achileas Sports Shop, Achileas Restaurant.

Focus on gyms

Whatever your fitness level, whatever your age and whatever your fitness goals, we have something to offer you in one of our special-focus gyms! If you would like to lose weight, tone up, increase your strength or improve your health, we have highly qualified staff on hand to motivate you in one of our focus gyms.

Whether you wish to work out once a week or every day, for ten minutes or an hour, after an initial consultation, our staff will design your own personal-fitness programme, tailored to suit your individual needs. You will also benefit from regular reviews, where your progress will be monitored and your programme updated or adjusted accordingly.

All of this takes place in one of our five focus gyms: cardiovascular, resistance training, free weights, general and sports injury. All our focus gyms offer state-of-the-art machines and excellent user-friendly equipment, catering for all your health and fitness needs.

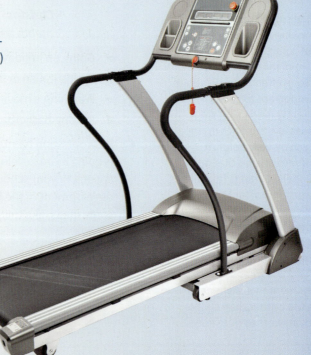

   a   What time does the sports centre close on public holidays?

   b   What is the cost for a family for a six-month membership?

   c   How many swimming pools are there?

   d   What non-sport facility does the complex offer?

   e   How many different 'fitness goals' are mentioned?

   f   What do you need to do before the staff can design your personal fitness programme?

   g   How is your progress assessed?

   h   What two things do all the 'focus' gyms offer?

Investigate and write

2   Find some examples of advertisements, leaflets, brochures or timetables and choose **two**. Study them carefully and then write **five to six** questions about each text for your partner to answer. The questions should require your partner to find factual details and to write short answers (a single word or phrase).

Speak

3   You are going to the cinema with two friends. There are three films to choose from: a comedy, a romantic drama and a sci-fi film. With two partners, say what your preferences are, suggest which film to see and give your reasons. Then make arrangements about when and where to meet.

Read and write

4   Look at the African Safari advertisement on page 16. Find the key word/s in the questions. Then write your answers to the questions below in your notebook.

   a   What is the minimum price for the African Safari?

   b   Name an activity included in the African Safari.

   c   How long is the African Safari?

   d   How far is the Victoria Falls Hotel from the airport?

   e   What can you see from the hotel?

   f   Where will you sleep on Day 2?

   g   Which hotels offer swimming facilities?

   h   Which hotel is said to be among the best in Africa?

   i   When will you get the chance to see animals living in their natural environment?

   j   On which day are you offered the chance to go shopping?

   k   What meals are included in the basic price?

   l   Which airline will fly you to Africa?

Weekly News Special Readers' Offer

AFRICAN SAFARI

A night in the African rainforest, camping under the stars, right next to the mighty Mosi oa Tunya (Victoria Falls) in Zimbabwe, is just one of the many never-to-be-forgotten experiences of our latest offer to *Weekly News* readers. Six nights of pure African luxury in Zimbabwe's best hotels, with 5-star class and total comfort.

Day 1: The 5* Koningin Hotel will cater for all your needs during your first day in Africa after the 30-kilometre drive from the new international airport. Located only minutes from Victoria Falls, the hotel has splendid views of the breathtaking waters, and is surrounded by jacaranda trees and beautifully tended gardens. This hotel is regarded as one of the best on the African continent and has been voted the best in Zimbabwe by our panel of regular visitors.

Day 2: Your night under the stars, within a few minutes' walk of the cascading waters of Victoria Falls. Our purpose-built campsite retains the comfort and luxury of the main hotel, whilst offering our guests a chance to savour the atmosphere of the rainforest. Your evening starts with a sumptuous barbecue cooked by our head chef, followed by a programme of African music and dance. Then, as the moon rises and the stars shine, you retire to your tent to sleep or to listen to the fascinating sounds of the African rainforest. An experience never to be forgotten!

Days 3–4: The 5* Zimbabwe National Hotel will accommodate you in the heart of the Zimbabwean wilderness. By jeep from your campsite near the Falls, you arrive at midday via the Zambezi river. The hotel complex offers you every amenity you would expect from a 5* luxury hotel, including golf, tennis, squash, badminton, swimming in one of three open-air pools, bowls and full use of our health suite. In the evening, enjoy our international menu, or relax in the gardens.

Days 5–6: Arrive by helicopter at the 5* Plaza Hotel, only 20 minutes' drive from the airport. The Plaza is located near to the Zimbabwean National Game Reserve, and Day 5 includes an amazing safari to see some of the world's most exotic animals in their natural habitats. Your final day can be spent in the luxurious surroundings of the hotel, or you can make a shopping trip into town. The hotel itself offers a full range of 5* facilities, including its own cinema, as well as a pool complex with diving boards.

Included in this special offer: six nights in 5* hotel accommodation. Depart from London Stansted Airport. B & B meal basis (for HB add $250). Price is per person based on two people sharing (add $450 for single room). Scheduled flights with Air Zimbabwe.

From only $1999 per person

17

Read and answer

5   Look at the ESRB Ratings Guide below and answer these questions.

   a   What is the purpose of the guide?

   b   There are six different age-rating categories. Match each one with the correct description a–f.

   c   What do the following words and phrases in the text mean?

      (i) concise and objective, (ii) consumers, (iii) informed choices

ESRB Ratings Guide

The Entertainment Software Rating Board (ESRB) ratings provide concise and objective information about the content in video games and apps, so consumers, especially parents, can make informed choices.

Rating categories suggest age appropriateness

1   **a** Content is generally suitable for ages 17 and up.

2   **b** Content is generally suitable for all ages.

3   **c** Content is generally suitable for ages 13 and up.

4   **d** Content suitable only for adults ages 18 and up.

5   **e** Content is intended for young children.

6   **f** Content is generally suitable for ages 10 and up.

6   Look at the next section: *Interactive Elements*. Answer the following questions in your notebooks.

   a   Apart from *email address*, think of **three** other examples of *personal information*.

   b   What does *third parties* mean?

   c   Give another word or phrase for *location*.

   d   What does *exposure* mean?

   e   Which is the best meaning of the word *via*:
(i) using, (ii) with, (iii) across, (iv) through?

Interactive Elements

   Shares Info: indicates that personal information provided by the user (email address, phone number, credit card info, etc.) is shared with third parties.

   Shares Location: includes the ability to display the user's location to other users of the app.

   Users Interact: indicates possible exposure to unfiltered/uncensored user-generated content, including user-to-user communications and media sharing via social media and networks.

Adapted from http://www.esrb.org/ratings/ratings_guide.jsp

Exam-style questions

1 Read the following advertisement and answer the questions.

The E-Scoot rechargeable battery-operated electric scooter

ONLY £79.95 inc. p&p, for beating traffic or just having fun!

This new, ultra-lightweight (just 7.35 kilograms), folding electric scooter can be great fun for all the family (minimum recommended age 10 years) – and you don't need a licence to use it.

Its rechargeable on-board batteries, built in under the floor, will provide power to the engine up to a maximum distance of 15 kilometres and at a maximum speed of 12 kilometres per hour. Each full charge of the batteries takes approximately 4–5 hours, using the AC/DC charger provided.

The E-Scoot incorporates a foot-safety cut-off switch, as well as handlebar brakes. There's even a built-in stand to avoid having to lean it up against something when not in use.

E-Scoot is available in a choice of three great colours (blue, red and yellow), requires virtually no maintenance, can be used without battery power, if and when required, and is available at only £79.95 each, including postage and packing.

Adapted from an advertisement in *The Independent on Sunday*.

a How much extra do you need to pay for postage and packing? [1]

b What can the scooter be used for? [1]

c Who should not use the scooter? [1]

d Where are the batteries located? [1]

e How far can you travel on the scooter? [1]

f How long do you need to wait for the batteries to recharge? [1]

g What can stop the E-Scoot from falling over? [1]

Extended

h In what **two** ways can the scooter be stopped? [1]

i What can you do if the battery runs out of power? [1]

[Total: 9 Extended, 7 Core]

2 Read the text and answer the questions that follow.

Somewhere for the weekend ... Bilbao

This artistic city celebrates its heritage with a flamboyant fiesta, set amidst Spain's most dramatic new architecture.

Now is the time to head south-west to see Bilbao at its most active, as celebrations of the city's heritage reach a climax with the Aste Nagusia festival. This is one of Spain's liveliest fiestas, comprising eight days and nights of processions, parades, concerts, dances, demonstrations of rural sports (including stone-lifting, log-chopping and hay-bale tossing) and bullfights. There are also nightly firework displays, best viewed from the city's bridges. Bus stops and street crossings are repainted gaudily, and bright scarves are draped around the necks of the city's statues.

Bilbao was founded in 1300 and is Spain's fourth biggest city (after Madrid, Barcelona and Valencia). Straddling the Nervion river, it is Spain's largest port. There are two official languages, Spanish and Euskara (the Basque language); most signs are bilingual.

The main tourist office is at Calle Rodrigo Arias (www.bilbao.net). It opens 9 a.m.–2 p.m. and 4–7.30 p.m. from Monday to Friday. On Saturdays, the hours are 9 a.m.–2 p.m., on Sundays 10 a.m.–4 p.m. A more useful operation is run at the airport (daily 7.30 a.m.–11 p.m.). There is also a tourist office at the Guggenheim Museum at Avenida Abandoibarra 2, open 10 a.m.–3 p.m. and 4–7 p.m. daily, though not on Sunday afternoons.

Many visitors and locals forsake sit-down meals in favour of nibbling at bars. Eating is no trivial matter, however. In the evenings, restaurants rarely open before 9 p.m. Traditional dishes revolve around veal, lamb and fresh fish (especially cod), often in olive-oil sauces.

Adapted from an article in *The Independent Review*.

a Why is now a good time to visit Bilbao? [1]

b How long do the celebrations last? [1]

c Give **three** examples of non-urban sports. [1]

d In what **two** ways is the city of Bilbao decorated during the fiesta? [2]

e How old is the city of Bilbao? [1]

f Where in Spain is Bilbao situated? [1]

Extended questions

g How many of the tourist offices are open on Sunday afternoons? [1]

h How important is eating in Bilbao? [1]

[Total: 9 Extended, 7 Core]

In this unit, we will again concentrate on the important reading skills of skimming and scanning, which are vital for identifying and retrieving facts and details in a text. Some texts will include a picture or a diagram, and you may also need to understand and select relevant information from the graphic.

In this unit, you will also:

- discuss TV and how much you watch
- look at information in graphs
- read about activities for teenagers and about Kuala Lumpur
- study adverbs
- answer some exam-style questions.

A 🗨 🅰ᵃ Speaking and vocabulary

1 Work with a partner. Look at the pictures. What type of television programme does each one show?

Example: *1 = soap opera*

2 What other types of television programme can you and your partner think of? Make a list.

3 Which of the programmes from Activities A1 and A2 do you like and dislike? Why? Copy and complete the table below.

Programmes I like	Programmes I don't like
...	...

4 Take turns to ask and answer these questions with your partner.

a How much TV do you normally watch each day? How much do you watch each week? What does it depend on?

b What about your friends? Do they watch more or less TV than you do, or about the same?

c Which TV programmes do you and your friends like and dislike?

LANGUAGE TIP

Remember the structure *spend time doing something.*

Example:

How much time do you spend watching movies on TV?

I probably spend three to four hours watching movies.

5   Look back at the list you made for Activity A2 on page 7. How much time do you spend doing these activities each week? Copy the table below. Complete the first two columns for yourself, then discuss with your partner and complete the third column.

Activities	Minutes each week (me)	Minutes each week (my partner)
watching films on TV	...	...

6   Look at the graph and answer questions a–e.

   a   What is the title of the graph?

   b   What does the left-hand axis show?

   c   What does the bottom axis show?

   d   Which axis is horizontal and which one is vertical?

   e   What do the small numbers at the top of each shaded column show you?

Time spent by young people on activities.

LANGUAGE TIP

In Unit 1 Section C, you looked at some of the different endings that adjectives can have. When we want to describe the shape or position of something, we often use an -*al* ending, and sometimes an -*ar* ending – for example *horizontal* and *circular*.

Look at the shapes in the pictures. Which adjectives describe them?

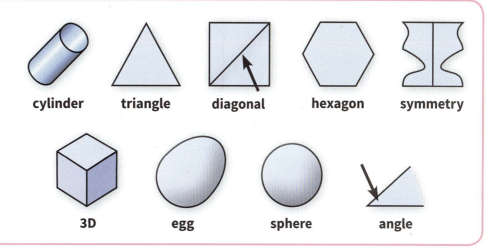

cylinder   triangle   diagonal   hexagon   symmetry

3D   egg   sphere   angle

7   Work with a partner. Which of the following activities do you think are represented in the graph above (A–F)? Write down your answers. Be careful – there are four extra activities that you do not need to use!

doing a hobby   doing voluntary work   doing homework
helping in the home   gardening   playing computer games
doing sport   reading books and magazines
using Facebook or other social media   watching TV

8   Compare your choices with the ones your teacher gives you. Does anything surprise you? Which activities didn't you choose? Why not?

9   Draw a similar graph using information supplied by the people in your class or school. Your teacher will help you to obtain the information and to draw your graph.

TOP TIPS

When writing responses to newspaper/magazine articles or reports, you may need to provide longer answers with more detail than you do for the types of question covered in Unit 1. However, remember that full sentences are not always required.

B Reading

1   Think back to Unit 1. Which reading skills are the most useful in answering questions that require short answers? Copy and complete the sentences.

   a   Skim reading is useful when you want to find ... .

   b   Scan reading is useful when you want to find ... .

2   You are going to read an internet article about holiday activities for teenagers in the city of Denver, USA. Before you read the article, discuss these two questions with your partner.

   a   What activities do you do during your school holidays?

   b   What differences do you think there might be between holiday activities for teenagers in your country and teenagers in the USA?

3   Look at these adjective phrases (a–i) from the first four paragraphs of the article you are going to read. Discuss each one with your partner and try to agree on what they mean. Use paper or digital reference sources to help you.

   a   hard-to-please   d   off-road   g   two-for-one
   b   pulse-pounding   e   heart-shaking   h   state-of-the-art
   c   cutting-edge   f   gravity-defying   i   long-standing

4   What meaning do many of the adjective phrases in Activity B3 have in common? What type of article do you think you are going to read?

5   Match each adjective phrase (a–i) from Activity B3 with one of the following nouns (A–I). Write the complete phrase in your notebook.

   Example: *pulse-pounding rides*

A art museum	**E** attractions	**H** Denver institution
B/C rides (x2)	**F** rollercoasters	**I** teenager
D thrills	**G** trails	

6   Now look at these adjectives taken from the final three paragraphs. Discuss each one with your partner and try to agree on what they mean. Use paper or digital reference sources to help you.

   a   angular   d   creative   g   stimulating
   b   beloved   e   incredible   h   stunning
   c   booming   f   renowned   i   timeless

7   What do you think the adjectives in Activity B6 describe? Work with your partner again and try to guess. Write your answers in your notebook.

   Example: *angular buildings*

8   Read the text opposite and check your answers to Activities B5 and B7.

Denver vacation activities for teenagers

[1] Are you a hard-to-please teenager? Denver offers plenty of things to occupy your time during your stay. From pulse-pounding rides to hip shopping districts, and from cutting-edge art museums to all the sports a teen could dream of, Denver, the Mile High City, is the perfect playground for you, even if you are the choosiest of adolescents! Get the scoop below:

Denver outdoors

[2] As you know, you teenagers have plenty of energy. Well, sometimes anyway! So get out into Denver's legendary fresh air and take advantage of the city's outdoor options. If you're a skateboarder, head straight to the **Denver Skate Park**. This vast area – one of the most renowned skate parks in the country – is filled with bowls for all levels of skating skill, and – wait for it – admission is free! But helmets are required, so don't forget to bring one.

[3] Biking is also big in Denver. The city is home to a massive network of more than 1300 kilometres of paved, off-road trails, making it a two-wheeled paradise. Bike rentals are available throughout the city, most notably at **Confluence Kayaks** (www.confluencekayaks.com) near the South Platte River bike trail and at **Cherry Creek Bike Rack** (www.cherrycreekbikerack.com).

Denver amusement parks

[4] If you are in the mood for heart-shaking thrills, you're in luck! The Mile High City is the place for you. Choose from gravity-defying rides to challenging climbing walls to wet'n'wild waterslides. **Elitch Gardens** (www.elitchgardens.com) is a can't-miss, two-for-one attraction, with unique, state-of-the-art rollercoasters, as well as a refreshingly fun water park. **Lakeside Amusement Park** (www.lakesideamusementpark.com) is a long-standing Denver institution that features a number of classic wooden rail coasters. Every summer, because of the heat, thousands of Colorado residents flock to **Water World** (www.waterworldcolorado.com) looking to relax in the park's beautifully landscaped and shaded 64 acres, and to ride some serious waterslides.

Denver arts

[5] Are you a creative teenager? Denver has a booming arts world, and you'll find plenty of stimulating attractions. Don't miss the stunning **Denver Art Museum** (www.denverartmuseum.org). The building itself is a work of art, thanks in part to the amazing, angular Hamilton Wing, designed by Daniel Libeskind. Inside, you'll discover an incredible array of art, ranging from masters like Cézanne and Picasso to the brightest new lights on the scene.

Denver sports

[6] Denver is a professional sports paradise, with no less than eight professional sports teams that thrill sell-out crowds year-round. Basketball, baseball, football, soccer, lacrosse, hockey, rugby – Denver's got it all, with some of the world's best athletes playing in the teams. For baseball, head to Coors Field for a **Colorado Rockies** game (http://colorado.rockies.mlb.com). The season runs from April to September. The unbelievably enormous Sports Authority Field at Mile High is the NFL's **Denver Broncos'** (www.denverbroncos.com) home – with a season that runs September to January. **The Colorado Rapids** (www.coloradorapids.com) play Major League Soccer from March to October. The NBA's **Denver Nuggets** (www.nba.com/nuggets) rule the court at the Pepsi Center in Downtown Denver, October until June. The Pepsi Center is also the home of Denver's beloved hockey team, the **Colorado Avalanche** (http://avalanche.nhl.com) – called the 'Avs' by fans. Their season runs from September to June.

Denver performing arts

[7] You probably love the Internet, television and movies, but there's nothing quite like the timeless thrill of seeing a musical, a ballet or a concert performed live. The **Denver Center for the Performing Arts** (www.denvercenter.org), located downtown, offers all these events and more on a regular basis. Expand your horizons by going to a performance by the **Colorado Symphony Orchestra**. Go to New York City without the hassle and see a Broadway musical, such as *Jersey Boys*, *Phantom of the Opera* or *The Lion King*. Catch a performance by the renowned **Colorado Ballet**. You'll find that all of these are immediately accessible, engaging and exciting. Check out future performances on the Denver Center's YouTube channel. There are clips from shows, peeks behind the curtain and interviews with cast members.

Adapted from www.denver.org

9 Read the following questions and note down the key word or phrases in each one. Do **not** write any answers yet.

   a What **four** activities does Denver offer you in paragraph 1?

   b Name **two** outdoor activities that Denver offers.

   c How much do you have to pay to use the Denver Skate Park?

   d What must you use while skateboarding?

   e Why do people who live in Colorado visit Water World in the summer?

   f How many different professional sports are played in Denver?

   g Which **two** sports can you watch during July and August in Denver?

10 Look at the article again and try to find the key words and phrases you wrote down in Activity B9. Can you find exactly the same vocabulary?

11 You may find that you need to write more than just a few words in an answer. Choose the best answer from the list below for Activity B9e. Give reasons for your choice.

   e Why do people who live in Colorado visit Water World in the summer?

     (i) Because it's hot.

     (ii) To beat the heat.

     (iii) To beat the heat, relax and enjoy the rides.

12 Now write complete answers to the questions in Activity B9. Exchange answers with your partner and check each other's responses. What should you be looking for?

TOP TIPS

Notice that words and phrases in texts are often rephrased in questions. For example Activity B9c above says: *How much do you have to pay to use the Denver Skate Park?* In the text, there is no mention of having to pay; instead it says: *admission is free!* Look out for these connections between the text and the questions.

C 🌐 Language focus: Adverbs

LANGUAGE TIP

Adverbs can describe verbs, adjectives and other adverbs. They are used to describe how, where, when, why and how often something happens.

Example: *Maria worked **quickly**, but wrote **very** carefully during the test.*
        *When she was **nearly** ready to finish, she re-checked everything.*

In this example, *quickly* tells us how Maria worked (verb), *very* tells us how carefully (adverb) she wrote, *nearly* tells us to what extent she was ready (adjective).

Look at these phrases taken from the article you have just read:

refreshingly fun water park
beautifully landscaped and shaded 64 acres
unbelievably enormous Sports Authority Field
immediately accessible, engaging and exciting

The italic words are all *adverbs*. What is the role of each adverb?

1 Work with a partner. Choose any ten consecutive letters from the alphabet. Think of an adverb that begins with each of the ten letters and list them.

    Examples: *F, G, H, I, J, K, L, M, N, O*

            F – fabulously, G – greatly, H – horrendously, I – interestingly …

2 Use paper or digital reference sources to check your adverbs. Then compare your list with other people in your class.

3 Complete each sentence below with a suitable phrase containing either an adverb + adjective or an adverb + verb. Choose from the adverbs in the box. You may be able to use some adverbs more than once.

> amazingly   completely   extremely   incredibly
> interestingly   really   unexpectedly

Examples: *Mario's brother wasn't injured in the accident and the police were* <u>*incredibly helpful*</u>.

Look at Mario's car. It's been <u>*completely destroyed*</u>.

a Elena thought the new café would be cheap, but ....

b Siphiwe usually plays well, but today he's ....

c When Rasheed and Ranya arrived at their hotel, they were surprised to see that everything was ....

d The mountains in the interior of the island were ....

e The room had been painted in a strange way: the walls were ....

f George did not tell anyone that he was going to visit us. He arrived ....

g The film was much too long and was ....

h Only Sayeed agreed with Fiona. Everyone else ....

i The results of the survey showed that older people ....

j Tutaleni tried to be independent, but his elder sister Nangula ....

4 Write **five** sentences of your own. Each sentence must include either an adverb + adjective or an adverb + verb.

D ○ Speaking: Would/wouldn't do

1 Read this paragraph about the amount of pocket money that young people need. Use paper or digital reference sources to check any unknown words or phrases.

Do teenagers need more or less pocket money to meet their daily expenses?

Pocket money allotted daily or weekly by parents is the main source of cash for today's teenagers around the world. Depending on where they live, teenagers have different financial needs. They usually use pocket money to pay for public-transport fares, cinema tickets, entrance fees, or to buy some snack while at school. As the living standards in many developed and developing countries are constantly increasing, teenagers need more and more pocket money to meet their daily expenses. In countries that are experiencing a state of financial instability and currency fluctuations, teenagers need more cash every day simply to make up for the rampant inflation. The money they had yesterday could buy fewer things today.

Adapted from www.financialized.ca

25

LANGUAGE TIP

When you want to ask for something in a polite or formal way, you might use expressions such as:

Is there any chance/possibility I could have (something)?

Do you think it would be possible (for me) to have (something)?

Would you mind if I had (something)?

Might I have (something)?

Could you let me have (something)?

Notice the verb forms before (something).

2 Work in small groups. Ask and answer these questions.

a Do you think you receive enough pocket money?

b What do you buy with your pocket money?

c What phrases would you use to ask your parents or a family member for more pocket money?

d Would you need to give a reason for asking for more?

3 Copy the table and add the phrases below in the correct columns.

Cleaning the car is fine by me   ~~Cleaning the car is something I'd never do~~
Cleaning the car is the last thing I'd do   I can't imagine myself ever cleaning the car   I certainly wouldn't ever clean the car   ~~I would be prepared to clean the car~~   I would enjoy cleaning the car   I wouldn't have a problem with cleaning the car   I wouldn't mind cleaning the car   I'd be quite happy to clean the car   There's no way I'd ever clean the car

Would	Wouldn't
I would be prepared to clean the car	Cleaning the car is something I'd never do!

4 Suppose you urgently needed some extra money. Would you be prepared to 'earn' it instead of just asking for it? What would you be prepared to do to earn it? What wouldn't you be prepared to do? Discuss your ideas with your partner and try to use some of the phrases from Activity D3.

Examples: **would:** *I'd be quite happy to do the washing.*
wouldn't: *I certainly wouldn't empty the bins.*

E 📖 Reading

1 You are going to read a newspaper article about Kuala Lumpur. Before you read, work with a partner to ask and answer these questions.

a What type of holiday do you enjoy most: in the city, on the beach, in the mountains or staying at home? Why?

b If you have a city holiday, what do you like to do when you're there?

c Are there any large cities in your country? If so, what would you recommend a visitor to see and do? If there are no large cities in your country, think about a city in another country.

d What are the advantages and disadvantages of living in a large city?

2 The following words appear in the article. Work with your partner to decide what they mean. Use paper or digital reference sources to help you.

a bustling

b cosmopolitan

c temperate

d awed

e immense

f stunning

g luxury

h bargain hunter

3 Scan the article and find the words from Activity E2. Do the meanings you decided on with your partner make sense?

The KL Experience

Kuala Lumpur, the capital of Malaysia, has transformed itself into a vibrant, bustling, cosmopolitan city that is home to more than 7 million people. Visit this city and you can discover wonderful hotels, fantastic shopping, incredible food options and endless entertainment opportunities. KL is the destination that has so much, it's difficult to choose the best places. Because of its temperate climate, KL is a great destination at any time of the year.

The Towers

At more than 450 metres tall, the 88-storey Petronas Twin Towers used to hold the world record for the tallest building in the world. It is a major tourist attraction, especially at night, when both towers are fully illuminated. A skybridge between the two towers is 170 metres above the street and gives a fantastic bird's-eye view over the city.

Mystical Batu Caves

When you've had enough of the bustling city, a trip to the Batu Caves is a must. Located in Selangor, about 20 minutes from KL city, the caves are the site of a Hindu temple and shrine that attract thousands of visitors. On arrival, you'll be greeted by monkeys hoping for peanuts! You'll be immediately awed by the large statue of Lord Murugan at the entrance. From here you can climb 272 steps to see the immense cathedral caves with their 100-metre-high ceiling, and view the stunning KL skyline.

Shop Shop Shop!

KL has every shopping experience imaginable, from exciting street markets to luxury shopping centres. The main shopping district is Bukit Bintang, located in the Golden Triangle area, which is just a ten-minute drive from KL city centre. Here, along the roads and streets, you'll find a mix of shops and bigger stores, as well as major shopping complexes, such as Pavilion Kuala Lumpur. Outside Bukit Bintang, you'll find more great shopping malls, and if you are a bargain hunter, you should head for the Central Market in Chinatown.

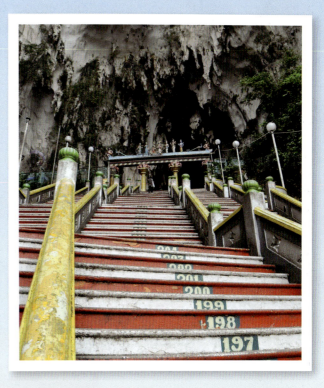

Delicious Cuisine

Malaysians take their food very seriously, which is why dining opportunities in KL are nothing short of spectacular. If you are looking for authentic Malaysian food, make sure you try out some of KL's famous street food in Jalan Alor and the Pudu Markets. If fine dining is more to your taste, you will be spoilt for choice – Neo Tamarind and Lai Po Heen to name just two. If you prefer something fast and tasty, Feast Village at Starhill Gallery is the place for you.

Adapted from 'The Kuala Lumpur Experience' in *Weekender Bahrain*.

4 Answer these questions in your notebook. Remember to identify the key word/s in each question first.

   a How many inhabitants are there in Kuala Lumpur?

   b Why is it difficult to know what to do in KL?

   c How many floors does each of the Petronas Towers have?

   d How high is the bridge that joins the two towers?

   e Which animal will you see at the Batu Caves?

   f What types of shopping can be experienced in Kuala Lumpur?

   g Why are there so many amazing food experiences available?

5   Copy and complete the 'KL fact form' with information from the text.

> **KL fact form**
> **The Petronas Twin Towers:** 88 storeys and … , at night, both towers …
> **Skybridge:** …
> **Things to see at Batu Caves:** monkeys, … and …
> **Places to shop:** … and …
> **Food:** Malaysian food in Jalan Alor, fast food in …

6   Write a short paragraph (no more than about 80 words) about the thing or things in the article that you would you most like to experience. Give reasons for your choices. Before you write anything, use paper or digital reference sources to find out more about the things you would most like to experience.

F ➕ Further practice

Write

1   Copy and complete the table below. You may not be able to fill all the gaps. All the words appear in this unit in some form.

Adjective	Noun	Adverb	Verb
…	…	…	occupy
challenging	admission	…	…
professional	…	…	…
…	…	…	…
…	enormity	…	…
…	performance	…	…
…	…	increasingly	…
…	…	…	finance
…	…	usually	…
…	activities	…	…

Write

2   Imagine you are on holiday with friends. Write a short email to someone in your family in which you:

   ■   describe the place where you are staying

   ■   ask for more pocket money and say why you need it.

Write in complete sentences and limit your email to about 75 words.

28

Analyse and write

3 Write a short paragraph describing the information in your graph in Activity A9 on page 21. Write about 60 words.

Read and answer

4 Read the leaflet about Stonehenge, then carry out the following activities.

    a Find at least **ten** adjectives in the leaflet.

    b Copy the table and fill in your adjectives. Then try to complete the columns for *antonyms* (opposites) and *synonyms* (similar). You may not be able to provide antonyms and synonyms for all your adjectives. Use paper or digital reference sources to help you.

Prehistoric Wonder of the World

Discover one of the world's greatest prehistoric monuments!

As old as the great temples and pyramids of Egypt, Stonehenge exerts a mysterious fascination.

Our complimentary audio tour in nine languages (subject to availability) will tell you all you need to know about the most intriguing and remarkable monument in the British Isles.

Make time to explore the extensive prehistoric landscape around Stonehenge. Some of these mysterious remains of ceremonial and domestic structures are older than the monument itself. Situated nearby is Old Sarum, where you can discover the remains of an Iron Age hill fort, royal castle and cathedral. You can also visit the well-stocked gift shop or sample the delicious refreshments at the Stonehenge Kitchen.

See www.english-heritage.org.uk/daysout/properties/stonehenge to find out more.

Source: © English Heritage.

Adjectives	Antonyms	Synonyms
greatest	worst	best
…	…	…

Exam-style questions

1 Read this text about lightning, then answer the questions that follow.

What is lightning?

The action of rising and descending air within a thunderstorm separates positive and negative charges. Lightning results from the build-up and discharge of electrical energy between positively and negatively charged areas in the storm. Most lightning occurs within the cloud or between the cloud and ground.

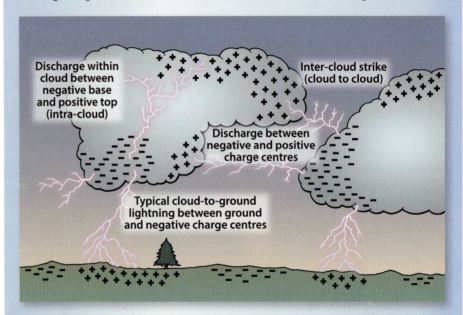

Discharge within cloud between negative base and positive top (intra-cloud)

Inter-cloud strike (cloud to cloud)

Discharge between negative and positive charge centres

Typical cloud-to-ground lightning between ground and negative charge centres

Amazingly, the average flash of lightning could turn on a 100-watt light bulb for more than three months and the air near a lightning strike is hotter than the surface of the sun. Thunder, which accompanies lightning, is the result of the rapid heating and cooling of air near the lightning channel. This causes a shock wave that results in thunder.

Can lightning ever strike in the same place twice?

The popular saying 'Lightning never strikes twice' is meant to put people's minds at rest when something bad has happened to them, such as dropping something valuable, failing a test or losing something important. It reassures them that something bad can't happen to the same person twice. But should people really be reassured by this? Does lightning really not strike in the same place twice? Unfortunately, the answer is no: lightning can strike in the same place twice. In fact, a lot of the time we actually want it to and some tall buildings are built in such a way that they attract lightning. But why?

Lightning will often strike the tallest thing in its immediate area, whether it's a telegraph pole or a tower on a building. Very tall buildings, such as the Empire State Building in New York City, get hit by lightning dozens of times every year. Lightning can do a lot of damage, for example by destroying roofs and starting fires. To avoid this damage, tall structures have lightning rods built into them, which attract the bolts of lightning and give them a path to travel along to reach the ground.

What is a lightning rod?

Lightning rods were invented in 1752 by the famous American statesman and inventor, Benjamin Franklin. Franklin did a lot of work to prove that lightning was actually electricity. He attached a rod, made of metal connected to an electrical wire, to the chimney on his roof. He ran the wire all the way down the house to the ground. To this, he attached an electric bell. Every time the rod was struck by lightning, the bell would ring, thus proving that electricity was passing from the top of the rod down through the wire to the ground, ringing the bell as it went.

How can I stay safe from lightning?

Your chances of being struck by lightning are estimated to be 1 in 600,000, but those chances can be reduced by following basic safety rules. Most lightning deaths and injuries occur when people are caught outdoors and most happen in the summer. Many fires in the western United States and Alaska are started by lightning and, in the past ten years, it has been the cause of more than 15,000 such events.

People on golf courses get hit by lightning more often than people just about anywhere else. If a storm has gathered and lightning is ready to strike, someone out in the open, swinging a metal gold club, or even holding a metal umbrella, is behaving just like a lightning rod. So how can you keep yourself safe from being hit by lightning? If you are outside when a storm hits, lie on the ground and stay as low as possible. Keep away from tall objects like trees, especially if they are the only tall objects in your immediate vicinity.

Perhaps the popular saying should really be: 'Stand in the open with an umbrella during a storm and there is a good chance lightning will strike you. Do the same thing the next time there's a storm and there's a good chance that lightning will strike you again!'

Adapted from *Actually Factually, Mind-Blowing Myths, Muddles and Misconceptions*, (Buster Books, 2009) and www.factmonster.com

a Where does most lightning happen? [1]

b Give **two** amazing facts about lightning from the text. [2]

c What causes the shock wave that leads to thunder? [1]

d Can lightning ever strike in the same place twice? [1]

e According to the diagram, what is an inter-cloud strike? [1]

f How often is the Empire State Building struck by lightning each year? [1]

g In what **two** ways can lightning cause damage? [1]

h What does a lightning rod do to prevent damage to a tall structure? [1]

i How did Benjamin Franklin show that lightning is electricity? [2]

Extended

j Give **four** pieces of information about staying safe from lightning. [4]

[Total: 15 Extended, 11 Core]

Unit 3: Focus on writing skills

In this unit, we will concentrate on writing an informal letter. Informal letters require a different style and layout from more formal letters and, as a consequence, the vocabulary and grammatical structures you use will also be different. An effective letter will communicate your ideas clearly, accurately and appropriately, and use a variety of grammatical structures and vocabulary in order to convey information and to express your opinions. Paragraphing, punctuation and spelling are also important. Remember that with any type of writing, you should keep in mind the purpose (why you are writing), the format (what the layout and organisation is) and the audience (who is going to read it).

In this unit, you will also:

- talk about your favourite foods
- read about fast foods
- write a letter about a restaurant you have visited
- look at how to express your preferences
- answer some exam-style questions.

A ◯ Speaking

1 In small groups, discuss the following questions.

   a What is your favourite food? Why? Is it because of the person who cooks it for you or the place where you eat it?

   b What is fast food? Why do we use the term 'fast food'? Do you like fast food? Why, or why not? Think about smell, taste, texture, and so on.

   c What would you call food that is not 'fast'? 'Slow food'?!

   d Non-fast food is often referred to as 'traditional' food. Put the following foods into two groups: 'fast food' and 'slow (or traditional) food'. (There are no right or wrong answers).

   > hot dog goulash sandwich vegetable pie rice moussaka
   > onion soup falafel samosa chicken schwarma

   e Think of some more types of food that could go in each group.

2 On page 33, you will read an internet article called *Eight things your fast-food worker won't tell you*. What do you think are some of the things that your fast-food worker won't tell you? Discuss this in your group.

3 Before you read the article, discuss with a partner whether you think the following statements about fast-food restaurants are true or false. Give your reasons. You will find out which ones are true later in this unit.

a A dirty eating area can mean a dirty kitchen.

b A lot of fast food is reheated until it's sold.

c A salad with dressing is not always the healthiest choice.

d Asking for 'extra' means you have to pay more.

e At the end of the night, food that is not sold is thrown away.

f The black grill marks on a burger are not from cooking it.

g Workers don't wash their hands often enough.

h You don't have to accept the food on display – you can ask for something to be cooked fresh.

B Aa Vocabulary

1 **Student A:** Work alone. Find these four words and phrases in the article. What do you think they mean? Use the context and paper or digital reference sources to help you.

a cabinet (paragraph 1)   c batch (3)

b the timer goes off (1)   d register (4)

Student B: Work alone. Find these four words and phrases in the article. What do you think they mean? Use the context and paper or digital reference sources to help you.

a sachet (paragraph 5)   c neglected (8)

b donate (6)   d in the back (8)

Eight things your fast-food worker won't tell you …

These surprising secrets about your favourite fast-food restaurants might make you think twice next time you're waiting in line or at the drive-thru.

[1] After we cook something, we put it in a cabinet and set a timer. When the timer goes off, we're supposed to throw out the food. But often, we just reheat the food. If you want the freshest meal, come between 11 a.m. and 1 p.m. or between 6 p.m. and 8 p.m. More people are in the restaurant then, so we're constantly cooking and serving new food.

[2] Those grill marks on your burger? Not real. They were put there by the factory.

[3] Most of us will cook something fresh for you, if you ask. If you want to make sure your fries come right out of the fryer, order them without salt. Providing you are polite, that forces us to cook you a new batch. Then you can add your own salt!

[4] Avoid asking for 'extra' of something, like cheese or sauce. As soon as you say 'extra', we have to add it to the register and charge you for it. Instead, just say you want us to 'put a good amount on there' and we'll load you up.

[5] It makes me laugh when someone comes in and says she's trying to be healthy – and then orders a salad. Some of those fast-food salads have more calories than you think. Supposing you want a small order of fries: that probably contains fewer grams of fat than a sachet of salad dressing.

[6] Most of us do not donate our leftovers. I can't believe how much food we throw out every day, especially at the end of the night.

[7] Most of us don't wash our hands as much as we should, even though there are signs everywhere reminding us that it's the law.

[8] Look around to see how much rubbish is in the car park, and if the bathrooms and dining room are dirty. When things that are so publicly visible are neglected, it's likely that even more is being neglected in the back and in the kitchen where the customers can't see.

Adapted from www.rd.com

LANGUAGE TIP

Notice these different ways in the text to say *if*:

Providing *you are polite, that forces us to cook you a new batch …*

As soon as *you say 'extra', we have to add it to the register and charge you for it …*

Supposing *you want a small order of fries …*

2 With a partner, discuss the meaning of the words and phrases in Activity B1. Make sure you understand your partner's words and phrases as well as your own.

3 Scan the text and check your answers to Activity A1.

4 Choose **six** words and phrases from the eight you have discussed. Use each of your choices to write a complete sentence in order to show its meaning.

C 📖 🅰ª Reading and vocabulary

1 You are going to read a text about fast food in Italy. Answer the following questions on your own. You can use paper or digital reference sources to help you. Write your answers in your notebook. Then work with a partner to check your answers.

a Find **five** words or phrases in **paragraph 1** that have a similar meaning to the following:

(i) 10 years, (ii) company division, (iii) increase, (iv) possibility for something to happen, (v) use something to an advantage.

b Look at the **five** underlined words and phrases in **paragraph 2**. What do they mean?

c Use these **five** words and phrases to complete the gaps a–e in **paragraph 3**.
(i) market share, (ii) sector, (iii) target, (iv) workforce, (v) worldwide

d Look at the **five** words from **paragraph 4** in the table below, then copy and complete the table. You may not be able to write something in every gap.

Noun	Verb	Adjective	Adverb	Noun translation/s
…	…	financial	…	…
investment (thing) … (person)	…	…	…	…
…	…	cultural	…	…
… (thing) … (person)	provide	…	…	…
… (thing) … (person)	dine	…	…	…

e Fill in the gaps f–j in **paragraph 5** using suitable words or phrases **of your own choice**.

f What do the following numbers in the text refer to?

(i) Paragraph 1: 30%, €350 million, 3000

(ii) Paragraph 3: 450, €1 billion, 10%, 2%, 3%

(iii) Paragraph 5: 5000

Example: *Paragraph 1: 100 = the number of new restaurants that McDonald's is opening*

Fast-food giant tries to convert Italy's pizza-lovers to burgers

[1] US fast-food giant, McDonald's, believes recession-hit Italy will be one of its higher-growth areas in the coming decade and is opening more than 100 new restaurants to convert pizza-lovers to its burgers. In a country where foreign investment has fallen by almost 30% since 2007, the McDonald's Italian arm plans to spend €350 million and hire a further 3000 people in the coming years to boost its market share. 'We believe in Italy and we are convinced that the Italian market has a potential we can exploit,' McDonald's Italian chief executive Roberto Masi told Reuters in an interview.

[2] The American McDonald's group, which first <u>set foot</u> in Italy nearly 30 years ago and was initially met with <u>suspicion</u> in the land of pizza and pasta, has launched an advertising <u>offensive playing to</u> Italians' patriotism. 'We will create 3000 more jobs. This is our way to show we believe in Italy,' it says. In the TV version of the <u>commercial</u>, shot by Oscar-winning Italian director, Gabriele Salvatores, three young staff members in trademark uniforms tell how good it is to work for the chain's fast-food restaurants.

[3] Annual sales at the 450 McDonald's Italian restaurants are estimated at around €1 billion and its local **(a)** … is nearly 1% of its **(b)** … staff. But while in Spain and food-conscious France, McDonald's has a **(c)** … of more than 10% of the 'informal eating out' **(d)** … , which excludes top restaurants, its share in Italy is just 2%, with a **(e)** … of 3% in the coming years.

[4] Masi said that since the start of the **financial** crisis, McDonald's had won customers in Italy by localising its offering, making sandwiches with crusty bread stuffed with Parmesan cheese and sliced ham. Still, the McDonald's **investment** pledge met with scepticism in some quarters, showing the group still has a **cultural** hurdle to clear in Italy. Roberto Burdese, chairman of Italy's Slow Food Association, which strives to preserve traditional and regional cuisine, said McDonald's menus could not **provide** a balanced diet on a daily basis. 'We accept it, however, as a sort of theme park where you can go and **dine** every so often,' he said.

[5] The **(f)** … of Big Macs is no stranger to cultural snobbiness. Recently, Milan city council forced McDonald's to **(g)** … its restaurant in the Galleria Vittorio Emanuele II, a tourist-packed shopping arcade 50 **(h)** … from the Duomo cathedral, to make way for a new **(i)** … of luxury fashion brand Prada. McDonald's attracted more than 5000 takers for its last-day offering of free **(j)** … , fries and drinks.

Adapted from www.reuters.com

2 Work on your own. Read the questions and find the key word/s in each one. Then read the article again and find and underline the answers to the questions. You do not need to write anything yet.

   a Who does McDonald's want to encourage to buy its burgers?

   b What **three** things does McDonald's plan to do in Italy?

   c How did Italians react to the fast-food company 30 years ago?

   d Which country has the smallest market share of 'informal eating out': France, Italy or Spain?

   e What has McDonald's done to localise its menu in Italy?

   f What does Roberto Burdese compare McDonald's to?

   g Why did the city council close a McDonald's restaurant in Milan?

3 Work with your partner and compare your answers to Activity C2. When you have agreed, write complete answers for each question.

D Writing: Informal letters

1 What is your opinion about fast food taking over from more traditional food? What are the advantages and disadvantages of each type of food? What about the places where you can buy fast food **and** traditional food? It might help if you concentrate on **two** restaurants that you know. Copy and complete the table below, listing the advantages and disadvantages of fast-food and traditional restaurants.

Fast-food restaurants		Traditional restaurants	
Advantages	**Disadvantages**	**Advantages**	**Disadvantages**
quick service	…	…	more expensive

2 Look at these words from an exam-style question: *explain*, *describe*, *write*, *say*. Discuss them with your partner and try to decide what they mean.

3 Look at the exam-style question below and complete the gaps with the words from Activity D2. Discuss your ideas with your partner. Do **not** write anything yet.

You have recently been to a new fast-food restaurant in your town. **(a)** … a letter to a friend, telling him or her about your visit. In your letter you should:

- **(b)** … where the restaurant is, when you went there, and why
- **(c)** … the restaurant and its atmosphere
- **(d)** … what you ate and what you thought of the food.

The pictures above may give you some ideas and you should try to use some ideas of your own.

Your letter should be 150–200 words long (Extended) or 100–150 words long (Core).

4 What would be the best way to begin and end an informal letter like the one in Activity D3? With a partner, make a list of possible opening and closing phrases.

Opening phrases	Closing phrases
Hi Satish!	Best wishes

TOP TIPS

If you are writing an informal letter to a friend or family member, you may be asked to describe something or say what you think about a suggestion or a plan. Often, the question may give you some ideas and there may be a picture to help you. The main things it to show that you can write in an informal style.

5 Look at these two letters written by two students in response to the question in Activity D3. With a partner, decide which of the two letters – A or B – is better. Give your reasons. Think about:

■ the language (the vocabulary and structures)
■ the information (the ideas) contained in the letter.

You do **not** need to rewrite the letters.

Letter A (197 words)

Hello friend

I have got your letter some days ago. How are you? I hope your well. I am well and I am enjoying my holydays which have started before two days. My family are well and I am busy getting ready for to go away on the weekend on the mountains. I have taken good marks in my school tests, but my mum and dad as usually they tell me that I must to work more hard the next year because it is my finally year at school. I enjoy the school, but I think the next year is going to be hard for me because I will have to work hard all the year. Guess what? A new burger restaurant was opening in my town and I went there with Marco and Jasper the last night. We stayed there until very late at night and we had to walk home because there were no buses! We had food and the atmosphere too was good. We will go back there next time you will visit me and I hope to do very soon. Write to me back when you will have free time.

Yours faithfully

Felipe

Letter B (164 words)

Dear Adriana

How are you? Thanks very much for your letter – I was happy to hear that you and your family are all well. We are all well here too!

I know you will be visiting here soon, so I wanted to tell you about a new fast-food restaurant we must to visit when you come here. It's downtown near the bus station, so it's very convenient if we take the bus. It opened last weekend and we went there together with my class friends for Cornelia's birthday party.

Inside, they have fantastic music, so the atmosphere is fabulous too. I know that you're going to like it like I do. Also, they have amazing pictures on the walls and really good furniture – very comfortable! You know I don't eat meat, but there were loads of choice for other food with no meat. It was totally delicious and not expensive like some other places.

Can't wait to take you! See you soon!

Maroulla

TOP TIPS

When you write, use your imagination as much as possible, but remember that your answer must always be relevant to the question. Think about how to improve your writing by using more adjectives and adverbs. Check your work carefully for language errors, and count how many words you have written. Make sure that you follow all the instructions very carefully and write the required number of words.

6 One way to improve your writing is by using more adjectives and adverbs. With a partner, talk about how to improve Felipe's letter by using more adjectives and adverbs, where appropriate. You do **not** need to write anything yet.

Example: *We had food and the atmosphere too was good.*
We ate really delicious food and the atmosphere was fantastic!

7 You are going to write your own full answer to the exam-style question in Activity D3. Before you start, make a draft plan. Think carefully about the question and what information it asks for. Draw a 'mind map' like the one you did in Activity D6 in Unit 1.

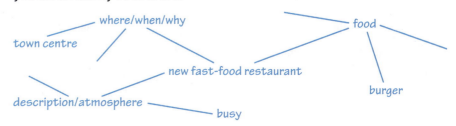

37

TOP TIPS

Remember that when answering questions, you need to think about both content and language. 'Content' refers to the relevance and development of ideas; 'language' refers to style and accuracy. So, you need to make sure that your writing is relevant, with a good development of ideas, and that the language you use is accurate and appropriate.

8 Now write your letter using the draft plan and mind map you created in Activity D7. If you are taking the Extended syllabus, aim for between 150 and 200 words; if you are taking the Core syllabus, your target should be between 100 and 150 words. Exchange your writing with your partner's. Check their letter. What should you be looking for?

E ◯ Speaking: Expressing opinions

1 🔊 Listen to Anna and Terry talking. In how many different ways do they express their opinion?

2 Look at the audioscript on page 188 and focus on the underlined phrases. In small groups, list other phrases that you could use to express your opinion.

Opinion phrases
I strongly believe that … .
I honestly don't agree with that.
I can't imagine … .
I'm not so sure about that.

3 Earlier in this unit, you made a list of the advantages and disadvantages of fast-food and traditional restaurants. Now imagine that you have to discuss these advantages and disadvantages with your teacher. What is your opinion? Using some of the phrases from Activity E1 and your ideas from Activity D1, write notes to prepare for your discussion.

TOP TIPS

When speaking in English, try to focus on the following:
1 Structure – using spoken language (sentences and phrases) accurately.
2 Vocabulary – using a wide range of words.
3 Fluency – having a **two-way** conversation.
Look at some of the speaking-test cards on pages 186–9 and you will see how the phrases you are practising in this unit will help you with more or less any topic.

F ➕ Further practice

Read and answer

1 Read the text *Hospitality with dates* and answer the following questions.

   a What **two** things are offered to guests in Saudi homes?

   b How many dates does Saudi Arabia produce every year?

   c What percentage of the world's date production is outside Saudi Arabia?

   d Apart from the nutritional value, what is another benefit of eating dates?

   e Why are date palms so common in Saudi Arabia?

   f How could eating a date help to relieve a headache?

   g What happens to the vitamin C in a fresh date when it is dried?

   h Give **three** uses of the date palm tree, other than as a source of food.

Hospitality with dates

A visitor to Saudi Arabia will relish the tradition of Arabian hospitality, which is symbolised by a small cup of Arabian coffee, made with lightly roasted coffee beans and cardamom, and served with a variety of fresh dates carefully arranged on a plate. This offering of coffee and dates is a welcome in almost every Saudi home, as well as most Arabian homes in the Arabian Gulf region.

After Egypt, Saudi Arabia is the second largest producer of dates in the world, with an annual output of more than 1.1 million metric tonnes of dates. The Kingdom has considerable experience in date cultivation and it offers a quality selection, including both soft and dried dates. In fact, there are more than 300 types of date in Saudi Arabia, each having its own taste and texture. These different types of date can be seen in shops and markets, but also in oases, where date palm trees stand tall with their branches outstretched towards the sky and their roots anchored deep into the earth. Saudi Arabia has the highest number of palm trees in the world, with more than 23 million trees accounting for 20% of global date production.

But there is much more to dates … Dates have rich medicinal properties, are highly nutritional, and are considered by many to be one of nature's most perfect foods. Date palms cover 3% of the earth's cultivated surface, giving humans one of the best sources of food, without requiring much effort. Because of this, in Saudi Arabia, palm trees are planted along the sides of every major city street, as well as in every garden and yard. The icon of the beautiful palm tree, representing vitality and growth, is everywhere, including in the national emblem of Saudi Arabia, although it does not appear on the Kingdom's flag.

A number of studies have proved the vital importance of the date fruit in a healthy lifestyle. New research has found evidence that the Ajwa date from Madinah contains active elements useful in the prevention of cancer; furthermore, the fruit contains anti-inflammatory properties, not dissimilar to commercially available painkiller medicines, such as aspirin and ibuprofen. Also, a 100-gram portion of fresh dates is a premium source of vitamin C. However, dates lose their vitamin C content when they are dried. A single date provides about 20 calories and is a good source of carbohydrates, fibre and potassium, as well as some calcium and iron. Dates do not contain significant amounts of fat, cholesterol, protein or sodium and are, therefore, wonderful for normal growth, development and overall well-being.

While everyone appreciates the health benefits of eating dates, let's not forget the date palm itself. The wide branches and leaves provide shade from the strong sun and are also seen as thatching on huts, while the strong trunks are often used as support pillars in buildings.

Adapted from 'Hospitality with dates' in *Ahlan Wasahlan.*

39

Write

2 Write your answer to this exam-style question.

You have recently cooked a meal for some members of your family. Write a letter to a friend, telling him or her about the meal. In your letter you should:

- explain why you cooked the meal
- say where you ate the meal, and with whom
- describe what you ate and what everyone thought of the food.

Your letter should be 150–200 words long (Extended) or 100–150 words long (Core).

The pictures on the left may give you some ideas and you should try to use some ideas of your own.

You will receive up to 10/7 marks for the content of your letter and up to 9/6 marks for the style and accuracy of your language.

Write

3   Write a description of your favourite restaurant – or imagine one. Refer to its location, the layout of the furniture, the music and décor, and the types of food. Give it a name. Write 150–200 words (Extended) or 100–150 words (Core).

Read and answer

4   Read the article *Shellfish in Oman* and answer the questions below.

    a   Why is Oman's fishing industry continuing to expand?

    b   Why was the abalone shellfish originally important?

    c   Where is the only place that the abalone is obtained from?

    d   In what way is the abalone different from other shellfish?

    e   How do the habitats of young and adult abalone differ?

    f   What type of water do abalone need to live in?

    g   What **two** pieces of equipment do the abalone divers always use?

    h   What extra piece of equipment do some divers use?

Shellfish in Oman

The diverse riches of the sea have always played a significant role in Oman's economy and the lifestyle of her people. The nation's fishing industry continues to increase in importance, as research into its marine life grows stronger.

An animal that is of enormous importance to the south-eastern coast of Oman is the abalone, a shellfish that has become the centre of a multi-million-dollar industry.

Once, abalone shellfish were brought to the surface in the hope that the soft tissue contained beautiful pearls. Today, the shellfish are caught for a different reason – restaurant menus! The fresh white shellfish has a distinctive and much admired flavour and is the most highly valued product from Omani waters. It is fished exclusively along the shores of Dhofar.

This distinctive shellfish has only one shell, unlike other shellfish, which have two. The shell is extremely beautiful. Light is diffracted by geometrically arranged crystals within the shell, creating a wonderful shine. The shells of several abalone can be used for decorative purposes, and to make jewellery and buttons.

Abalone live in shallow marine waters with rocky-bottom conditions. Young abalone shelter in small groups, holding on to the undersides of medium-sized boulders, whereas the adults live grouped up to a dozen together in rocky cracks. They can only survive successfully in areas where cold, nutritious water rises from the sea bed. There, in the shallow, brightly lit conditions, the abalone shellfish live.

The environmental requirements for cool water conditions are rarely met and, as a result, the geographical occurrence and extent of abalone fisheries worldwide is extremely restricted. Until recently, there was a three-year ban on abalone fishing in Oman and now fishing is only permitted from October 20 to November 15 each year.

The coast of Dhofar in Oman is one of the special environments that support abalone populations. The southern shore of Oman experiences monsoon winds across the surface of the sea from April to September. As these winds skim the surface, the rich cold water from the depths of the Arabian Sea can easily rise and move towards the shore.

Abalone are harvested after the monsoon period, between October and March. Fishermen dive to a depth of 10 metres, assisted only by a face mask and, perhaps, fins. Groups of up to ten men search the sea bed for abalone-encrusted boulders and deftly remove the shells using a knife, before coming up for air. A good diver searches for large adults and will collect up to 600 specimens per day. In order to do this, the diver may have to cover an area in excess of 100 square metres.

Adapted from 'Marketing the mollusc' by Dr Karen Millson, in *Tribute*.

Exam-style questions

1 You have recently been on holiday. Write a letter to a friend or someone in your family telling them about your holiday. In your letter you should:

- explain where you went on holiday and name the people who went with you
- say what you did on holiday and whether or not you enjoyed yourself
- say if you would recommend this type of holiday.

Your letter should be 150–200 words long (Extended) or 100–150 words long (Core).

The pictures above may give you some ideas and you should try to use some ideas of your own.

You will receive up to 10/7 marks for the content of your letter and up to 9/6 marks for the style and accuracy of your language.

 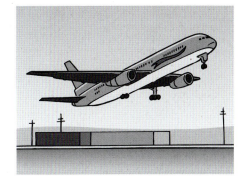

2 You have won a scholarship to study abroad for a year. Write a letter telling a member of your family about it. In your letter you should explain:

- where you will go to study and why
- what you are most looking forward to doing
- the advantages this year abroad will bring.

Your letter should be 150–200 words long (Extended) or 100–150 words long (Core).

The pictures above may give you some ideas and you should try to use some ideas of your own.

You will receive up to 10/7 marks for the content of your letter and up to 9/6 marks for the style and accuracy of your language.

Unit 4: Focus on listening skills

In this unit, we will concentrate on some of the listening skills you may need when listening for specific information in short, separate statements or announcements (for example on the radio, at train stations, at airports). We will also focus on listening for factual details (for example in news reports, weather reports, travel reports).

In this unit, you will also:

- talk about methods of transport
- listen to people talking about different methods of transport
- read some statistics about road accidents
- use expressions of surprise
- answer some exam-style questions.

A 🗨 🔊 Speaking and listening

1   How many different methods of transport can you and a partner think of? Make a list. Use the pictures on this page to help you.

2   There are ten different methods of transport hidden in the word snake. How many can you find? Are any the same as the ones you thought of in Activity A1?

bustaxiballooncampervanmotorbikeplanecartraincoachbicycle

3   Which method of transport do you think is the best for going on holiday? Why? Does your choice depend on the type of holiday? Discuss your ideas with a partner.

> **LANGUAGE TIP**
>
> Remember to use a **comparative** form when you are discussing two things and a **superlative** form when you are discussing more than two things.
>
> **Examples:** *I think flying is **better than** going by train.*
> *Don't you think that flying in a balloon would be **the best way** to travel?*

4   Copy and complete the table. Make a list of the advantages and disadvantages of some of the methods of transport from Activity A2.

Method	Advantages	Disadvantages
car	stop when and where you like	traffic jams

5 In Activities A3 and A4, did you consider the cost of each method of transport? With a partner, rank the methods from 1 to 10, with 1 the most expensive and 10 the cheapest. What factors do you need to think about when deciding on the cost of each method?

6 You are going to listen to four people talking about their experiences of different methods of transport. Which of the following methods do you think you will hear about? Why?

bus	car	motorbike	balloon	train	ferry	camel
bicycle	coach	campervan	cab	quad bike	horse	

7 Listen and write the answers to these questions in your notebook.
  a Which methods of transport are being talked about?
  b Which of the people enjoyed themselves?
  c Which speakers do not mention the name of a country or town?

8 What helped you to answer the three questions in Activity A7? What information did you focus on as you were listening. Context? Vocabulary (key word/s)? Something else?

9 Listen carefully again to each speaker. As you listen, write the answers to the following questions in your notebook.

Speaker 1
  a Where exactly did the speaker wait for the train?
  b How many people were with the speaker?
  c How did the family feel before 8.30?
  d What made the speaker and his family become anxious?
  e What did the speaker do at 9.00?
  f What mistake had the speaker made?

Speaker 2
  a Why was the speaker going up in a balloon?
  b How old is the speaker now?
  c Why did the speaker feel uncomfortable about the balloon trip?
  d How long was the balloon trip?
  e How did the speaker feel once the balloon had taken off?

Speaker 3
  a What **two** advantages convinced the speaker to travel by coach?
  b How many disadvantages of travelling by coach does the speaker give?
  c How often does the coach stop?
  d How long did the coach journey last?

Speaker 4
  a At what time of day did the speaker depart?
  b What was the weather like?
  c Who was the speaker with?
  d How fast did they travel?
  e What **two** things amazed the speaker?

43

10 How much can you remember? With a partner, copy and complete the table of information below (not all the gaps can be filled).

	Speaker 1	Speaker 2	Speaker 3	Speaker 4
Departure time	8.30 a.m.	…	…	…
Length of journey	…	…	…	…
Arrival time	…	…	…	…
Weather / time of year	beautiful summer day	sunny, May	…	…
Speaker's feelings	…	…	…	…
Speaker with who?	wife and three children	…	…	…
Cost	…	…	$275	…

11 Read the audioscript on pages 188–9 and check your answers to Activities A9 and A10.

12 Choose a method of transport and write a short paragraph similar to the ones in the listening activity. You can include information about the time and length of the journey, the weather and/or time of year, the speaker's feelings and so on. Do not mention the method of transport. Write four or five questions about your paragraph for your partner to answer. Read your paragraph to your partner, then see if they can guess the method of transport and answer your questions.

B 💬 🔊 Speaking and listening

1 You are going to listen to a Ugandan police officer talking about Uganda's famous motorbike taxi, the *boda-boda*. Unfortunately, there are many traffic accidents involving *boda-bodas* and many people are injured as a result.

  a Work with a partner and answer the following questions.

    (i) What type of taxis do you have in your country?

    (ii) Who do you think rides the *boda-bodas* in Uganda?

    (iii) What could be the result of having too many *boda-bodas* on the roads?

    (iv) How could Uganda help young motorbike riders to be safer?

b Work with a different partner. Read the following information and decide if it is true or false.

(i) About 40% of trauma cases at the hospital are from *boda-boda* accidents.

(ii) 62% of young people in Uganda do not have a job.

(iii) The death toll on Uganda's roads is twice the average across the rest of Africa.

(iv) There were 3343 road deaths in 2011.

(v) A national scheme has trained 1800 *boda-boda* riders in basic road safety.

c Work with the same partner. One of you looks at the words in column A in the table below and the other looks at the words in column B. What do the words mean? Using paper and digital reference sources to help you, make notes and then explain the words to your partner.

A	B
ubiquitous potholed livelihoods swelled strain trauma	catastrophic fatalities campaigns initiatives participant slogan

2 🔊 Listen to the police officer talking about the *boda-boda* taxis. As you listen, check if the information in Activity B1b is true or false.

3 🔊 Use the numbers in the box to complete the information below from the listening text. Write your answers in your notebook, then listen again and check your answers.

20	25	100	1960s	20,000	250,000	300,000

a Since they appeared on the streets of Uganda in the **(i)** ... .

b One recent news report estimated that there were more than **(ii)** ... bikes operating.

c There are up to **(iii)** ... *boda-boda*-related cases every day.

d Ali Niwamanya, **(iv)** ... , a *boda-boda* driver ...

e A monthly fee of **(v)** ... Ugandan shillings paid by the city's **(vi)** ... motorbike taxis.

f A one-day workshop for **(vii)** ... riders.

LANGUAGE TIP

In the text you have just listened to there are some examples of nouns ending in -*ion*, for example *collision, organisation*. The verb forms of -*ion* nouns follow various patterns:

collision ⟶ collide

organisation ⟶ organise

Look at the audioscript on page 189. Find **three** more -*ion* nouns in the text and write the verb form for each one.

C ✛ Language focus: Tenses

1 Look at these sentences from the information you have just listened to. What **verb time** (e.g. present) is being referred to by the verbs in blue in each sentence?

   a For many years, *boda-bodas* have been called Uganda's silent killers.

   b Since they appeared on the steets of Uganda in the 1960s, …

   c They are also injuring and killing thousands every year …

   d Some people are warning that in the very near future, the death toll from Uganda's roads will be higher than that from diseases such as malaria.

2 Complete the rules for each of the four tenses in Activity C1. What is the function of the tenses in each sentence? The first one has been done as an example.

   a present perfect simple   *have/has* + past participle
   Function = *to link the past to the present*

   b past simple   …
   Function = …

   c present continuous   *am / … / … + …*
   Function = …

   d 'will' future   … + …
   Function = …

3 Complete these sentences, putting the verbs into the correct tense.

   a I'm certain that traffic chaos in big cities … (get) worse in the next ten years.

   b This week I … (see) four accidents on the roads in town.

   c Some friends of mine … (think) of selling their car because the roads are so dangerous!

   d When I was at the police station, a policeman … (tell) me that road cameras … (catch) a lot of speeding drivers last month.

   e These days, the government … (try) to improve the situation on the roads.

   f In the coming years, there … (be) an even greater increase in the number of road deaths.

   g That's the second time someone … (have) an accident at that junction since the traffic lights were installed.

D ◯ Speaking

1 ◀) Listen to how we can show surprise about something.

2 ◀) Listen again and write down the expressions that show surprise about something.

3 In small groups, discuss the following questions.

   a What information in the listening text from Section C surprised you? Use the expressions in Activity D2 to help you.

   b How does the situation in Uganda compare with the situation in your country? If you don't know, how can you find out?

   c What can be done to reduce road injuries and deaths?

4 Look carefully at these statistics about traffic accidents in the Republic of Ireland, then answer the questions in small groups.

🏠 ◄ ► + 🌐 http://www.   ⟳ Reader

An Garda Síochána

| About Us | Contact Us | Crime Prevention | Publications | Traffic | Careers |

	Jan	Feb	March	April	May	June	July	Aug	Sept	Oct	Nov	Dec
Fatalities	19	14	15	12	17	13	18	19	17	13	16	17
Section 41 RTA – Detention of Vehicles	1540	1503	1213	1816	2036	1966	1712	1914	1779	1762	1738	
Road Transport Offences	335	312	231	368	296	211	353	430	348	367	506	
Dangerous Driving	33	220	196	211	221	207	146	184	186	215	167	
Fixed charge notices												
Seatbelts	734	865	877	1019	1229	1101	1029	1,002	1071	1050		
Mobile Phones	2210	2108	1513	2427	2335	2094	2057	2113	3058	3167		
Speeding	13,641	12,553	12,111	18,589	19,015	19,425	18,620	19,931	16,815	21,790		

Figures for fatalities are current as of 2nd January 2014; all other figures are current as of 5th December 2013 and are provisional figures and subject to change.

Fixed charge notices are reported one month in arrears.

Adapted from www.garda.ie

a At the bottom of the page, what does this phrase mean: *are provisional figures and subject to change*?

b What do *Fatalities* and *Fixed charge notices* mean?

c Find out what *Section 41 RTA – Detention of Vehicles* means.

d What do you think *Road Transport Offences* refers to?

e If you were interested in working with Ireland's national police service, which link on the web page should you click?

f If you clicked on the *Publications* link, what information would you find?

g Use the information in the table to draw a graph. Choose a single month or a particular set of statistics. Your teacher will guide you.

5 Look carefully at the statistics in the table. Ask your partner **five** questions.

Examples: **You:** *In May, how many people got a fixed charge notice for not wearing a seatbelt?*

Partner: *1229.*

You: *What surprises you most about the statistics?*

Partner: *I couldn't believe the number of people caught for speeding!*

6 Does your country, or a country that you know, have a traffic problem? If so, what is being done to overcome the problem? What would you do if you were in charge of solving traffic problems and reducing the accident rate? Discuss in small groups.

E 🔊 Listening

TOP TIPS
When listening, you will be given time to read the questions before you listen. Make sure you use this time well. Read **all** the questions and underline the key word/s in each one. Decide what type of information each question requires, for example a number, a place, a street name.

1   Look at these exam-style questions. With your partner, decide what information each question requires you to listen for.

   a (i) What does Gregory want to order?

      (ii) What is the product number?

   b (i) What will the weather be like during the late morning?

      (ii) What is the highest temperature expected?

   c (i) Where does this conversation take place?

      (ii) What does Marina want to do?

   d (i) For which sport has the price increased?

      (ii) How much does it cost for members to book a court on a weekday evening?

2   Here are the answers to some questions. Which of these answers could fit the questions above? Why?

   a €20   e a shirt

   b a bank   f 25 degrees

   c very hot   g basketball

   d 17 XW 3FG9   h buy something

3   🔊 Listen to the audio and answer the questions in Activity E1 in your notebook.

4   Compare your work with your partner. Then use the audioscript on pages 189–190 to check your answers.

F ➕ Further practice

Read and answer

1   Read the internet article about safe bicycle riding for teenagers on page 49, then answer the questions below.

   a Choose a heading from the box below for each paragraph in the article.

> Protection   Distractions   Maintenance   Laws of the road
> Road position and signalling   Visibility

   b Why do cyclists need to concentrate more than other people on the road?

   c What is the benefit of wearing a fluorescent or reflective jacket?

   d Give **five** pieces of advice to help cyclists with their position on the road.

   e How can you let a driver know that you have seen them?

   f Where can you get information about the correct pressure for tyres?

   g Who do traffic laws apply to?

   h According to traffic laws, what can a cyclist do if they see a sign giving them permission?

Cycle safety

[1] ... Cyclists need to concentrate more than other road users, as you are much more vulnerable. Remember that when you are on a cycle, you have absolutely no protection from dangers around you. Using your mobile phone and MP3 player whilst cycling is extremely dangerous, as you need to concentrate on the road and other traffic.

[2] ... Think about your clothes. Are they bright and visible to others on the road? If bright clothes are not suitable for everyday use, fluorescent and reflective jackets (which will identify you to other users) can be worn until you reach your destination. White front lights and red rear lights MUST be used after dark and in poor light conditions. They will also help you to be seen in the rain.

[3] ... You should always wear a helmet, as this can reduce the risk of head injury in a crash.

[4] ... Keep clear of the kerb and do not ride in the gutter. Give space on the left and don't hug the kerb if a car behind you gets impatient. Don't weave between lanes, or change direction suddenly. Show drivers what you plan to do in plenty of time. Always look and signal before you start, stop or turn. Make eye contact with drivers and let them know you have seen them.

[5] ... Is your bike regularly maintained and checked? If not, why not?! Brakes MUST work well in all conditions: dry and wet. Are lights and reflectors clean and in good working order? Are the tyres in good condition and inflated to the pressure shown on the tyre? Are the gears working correctly? Is the chain properly adjusted and oiled? Are the saddle and handlebars adjusted to the correct height?

[6] ... Traffic laws apply to you as a cyclist, as well as other road users. Cyclists MUST obey traffic signals and signs.

Remember: it is against the law for cyclists to:

- jump red lights, including lights at pedestrian crossings
- cycle on pavements, unless there's a sign showing that cyclists are allowed to do this
- cycle the wrong way up a one-way street, unless there is a sign showing that cyclists can do so
- ride across pedestrian crossings, unless there is a sign saying that cyclists can do so.

Adapted from http://think.direct.gov.uk

Read and decide

2   You are going to listen to a short podcast about some tourist attractions in Turkey. Before you listen, read the questions below and decide what type of information is required in each answer.

   a   Why does Turkey have so many places for people to explore?
   b   When was the Hagia Sophia built?
   c   Why is it so difficult to choose one ancient city to visit?
   d   Apart from watching the marine mammals show, what **two** other things can you do at the Dolphinarium?
   e   What methods of transport are available on the Princes' Islands?

Listen and answer

3   🔊 Listen to the information and write down the answers to the questions in Activity F2.

Plan and present

4   What new attraction would you like to have in your town? Prepare a short talk outlining your ideas and giving your reasons. Be prepared to answer questions from your classmates and teacher.

LANGUAGE TIP

Linking words and phrases are just as important in speaking as they are in writing. Make sure you use a variety of them in spoken language. Think about words or phrases that indicate **when** (for example *firstly*, *subsequently*, *finally*) as well as **contrast** (for example *but, on the other hand, however*) and **in addition** (for example *also, furthermore, for example*).

🔊 Exam-style questions

You will hear four short recordings. Write no more than **three** words for each detail in your notebooks. You will hear each recording twice.

1 (a) What is the name of the cinema? [1]

(b) What time does the cinema open on Tuesdays? [1]

2 (a) What does Daniela want to buy? [1]

(b) Which is the best place she could go to buy one and why? [1]

3 (a) Who is Jason trying to find? [1]

(b) Where exactly should he go to find the room he needs? [1]

4 (a) Apart from visiting the museum, what else does the speaker
suggest the tourists do when they get off the bus? [1]

(b) How long are the tourists allowed to be off the bus for? [1]

[Total: 8]

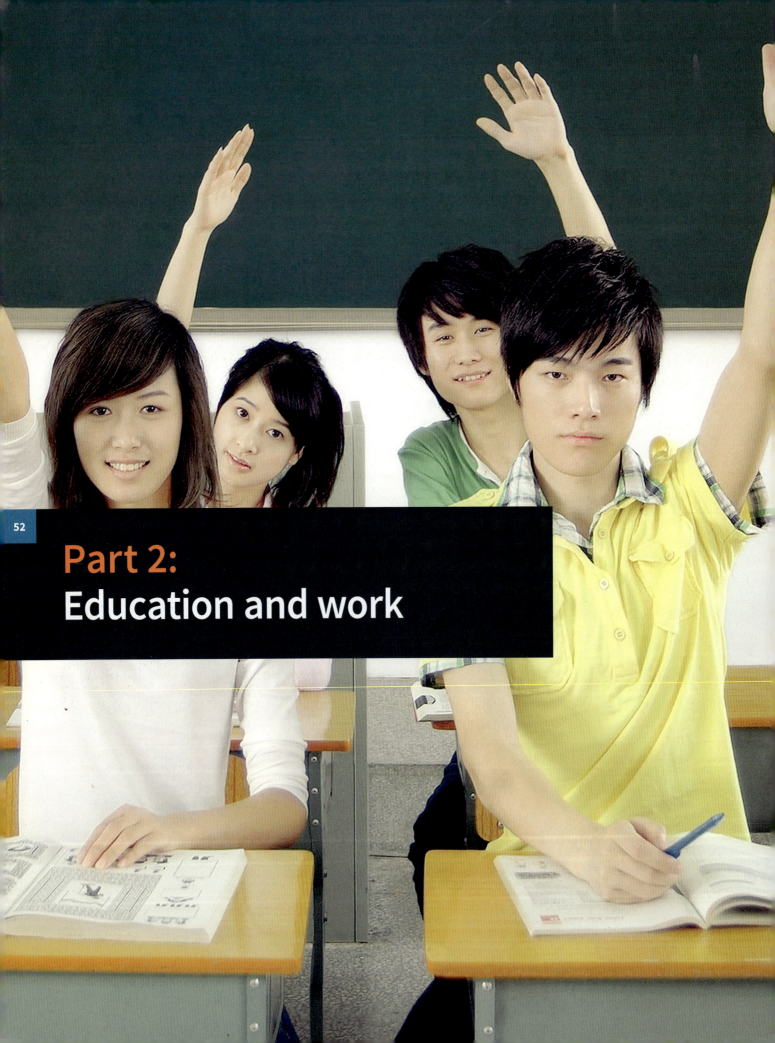

Part 2:
Education and work

Unit 5: Focus on reading skills

In this unit, we will concentrate on the skills required for more detailed comprehension of longer texts, similar to the type found in a report, or a newspaper or magazine article, and which may also include a picture or a graph. We will also focus on showing an understanding of information that is implied, but not actually written.

In this unit, you will also:

- read and talk about a language school
- study prefixes and suffixes
- use expressions for giving advice
- read about getting up in the morning
- answer some exam-style questions.

A 🗪 Speaking

1   Look at the pictures of some facilities in language schools. Work in small groups and answer these questions.

   a   Which **two** facilities do you and your group think are the most important? Why?

   b   Which facilities would you expect a language school to have that are missing from these pictures?

2   On your own, do the following activities.

   a   Make a list in your notebook of the facilities you would expect a language school to have.

   b   Which of the facilities and services on your list are the most important to you? Put them in rank order and draw a graph illustrating the order. Your teacher will help you.

3   Work in small groups. Tell your partners **three** things about the information in your graph and give reasons for your choices.

   Example: *I think a gym is the most important facility because we have nowhere else to play sports.*

4   In your groups, draw up a final list of facilities for a language school. You can include the facilities shown in the pictures. Share your list with other groups. Do you agree or disagree on the facilities?

B 📖 Reading

1 The following words and phrases appear in the text below, which is taken from the website of a language school: LearnFast Language Centre. Discuss the words and phrases with your partner and try to agree on their meanings. Use paper and digital reference sources to help you.

a extensive
b blended learning
c volumes
d on loan
e counselling

f appropriate
g intolerant
h policy
i welfare
j self-catering

2 Skim the text below. Match one of the headings in the box with each of the paragraphs in the text, 1–5. There are three extra headings that you will not need to use.

> Accommodation and welfare   Social and leisure programme
> Banking facilities   Sports centre   Cafeteria   IT centre
> Library and Multimedia Resource Centre (LMRC)   Counselling service

http://www.   Reader

LearnFast Language Centre

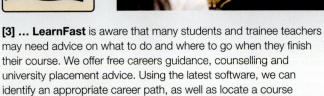

Facilities and Services

[1] ... Our extensive, state-of-the-art IT-centre facilities offer our students a completely new approach to language learning. At **LearnFast**, you can choose between classroom-based lessons with a teacher, computer-based self-study lessons, or a mixture of both: blended learning. The choice is yours! Even if you choose classroom-based lessons, there will still be one weekly timetabled lesson using IT. Our IT facilities are open from 0700 in the morning until 2200 at night (0900–1700 at weekends) for general use and for further practice, with someone always available to help and advise you. We have special software to help you practise: pronunciation, listening skills, grammar and examination skills, as well as the chance to improve your speaking skills. However, if you just want to check your emails or send a message on Facebook, the IT centre facilities – including Internet – are free and available for all **LearnFast** students.

[2] ... If you prefer paper to digital, our Library and Multimedia Resource Centre (LMRC) is the place for you. With more than 10,000 volumes, this is the ideal place for some quiet time, not just for language students, but also for our many teachers and trainee teachers. Students can choose from a wide range of graded reading books, from beginner to advanced, many of which also have MP3 audio files, so you can listen, as well as – or instead of – read. If you want to do some studying at home, most items in the LMRC are available on loan, including audiovisual equipment. The librarian (available from 0900–1900) can advise you on what materials are best for your level. You may also purchase books (digital and print) and audio files, at a discounted price, from the LMRC. Please note that coursebooks are included in your course fees and are yours to keep. The LMRC is open 0900–1900 every day, but is closed at weekends.

[3] ... **LearnFast** is aware that many students and trainee teachers may need advice on what to do and where to go when they finish their course. We offer free careers guidance, counselling and university placement advice. Using the latest software, we can identify an appropriate career path, as well as locate a course suitable for your needs and abilities.

[4] ... Open from 0600 to 2100 every day (0900–1600 at weekends), our cafeteria offers hot meals, snacks, sandwiches, hot and cold drinks and fruit for all types of diet, from vegetarian to lactose intolerant! It is a policy at **LearnFast** to keep our cafeteria prices as low as possible. Generally, a meal will cost less than half the price of a similar meal elsewhere. The cafeteria also offers free access to online English-language newspapers and magazines by supplying its customers with small hand-held tablets!

[5] ... **LearnFast** understands that different people require different types of accommodation, and our three full-time Accommodation and Welfare officers will help you choose the best for you. Staying with an English-speaking family, a short walk from **LearnFast**, is always a popular option, but self-catering in student hostels is a cheaper option. For those who prefer hotel accommodation, we have many for you to choose from, either budget or more luxurious. However, please note that only one of the hostels and none of the hotels are within walking distance of the Language Centre.

3 Skim the text again. What facilities and services are offered by the school? Are any of them the same as the ones you listed in Activity A2? Are there any that you did not list? Are there any facilities that you would like to add to the school? Why, or why not?

4 Look at the text again. Find the words from Activity B1. Do the meanings you and your partner agreed on make sense?

5 Copy the table below into your notebook. Then look at the text again and complete the information about the opening and closing times for the cafeteria, the IT facilities and the LMRC. Remember that there are different times for some of the facilities at the weekend.

Facility	Time	0600	0700	0900	1600	1700	1900	2100	2200
Café		Opens M–F	…	…	…	…	…	…	…
IT facilities		…	…	…	…	Closes wkend	…	…	…
LMRC		…	…	…	…	…	Closes M–F	…	…

TOP TIPS

It is important to show that you can understand information presented in a visual format, such as a graph, table or chart, as well as in a written text. Look out for questions that start with the words: *According to the chart/ graph/picture …* , as these will tell you that the answer is not in the written text itself.

6 Here are the answers to **ten** questions based on the text. Write the questions.

a once a week

b from 0900 to 1700

c pronunciation, listening skills, grammar and examination skills

d about 10,000

e MP3 audio files

f from the LMRC

g the latest software

h small hand-held tablets

i three

j students can walk to LearnFast

7 Compare your questions with a partner's. Are they the same?

8 Write **five** more questions based on the information in the text. Then ask your partner to answer them.

C ⊕ Language focus: Prefixes and suffixes

LANGUAGE TIP

A *prefix* is a group of letters added before a word or base to change its meaning. When a prefix is added, a new word is formed. Two of the most common prefixes are *un-* (meaning *not*, or *the opposite or reverse of*) and *re-* (meaning *again* or *back*).

REMEMBER! The spelling of the word never changes when a prefix is added. Also, the spelling of the prefix never changes, no matter what word you add it to.

Examples: unnecessary, **re**pay, **multi**media

A *suffix* is a group of letters added after a word or base to form a new word. Two of the most common suffixes are *-ing* (for example: *bringing*) and *-ed* (for example: *worked*). A suffix can make a new word in one of two ways:

1 **Grammatical change** – for example changing tense: *climb → climbed*. The basic meaning of the word *climb* does not change.

2 **Changing meaning** – the word + suffix has a new meaning, and often a new part of speech: *teach → teacher* (verb → noun)

55

1 Look at these phrases from the website article on page 54.

… *self*-study lessons
… *facilities including* Inter*net*
… *lactose* in*tolerant*
… *one week*ly *timetabled lesson*
… *from begin*ner *to advanc*ed
… *suit*able *for*

The underlined groups of letters are prefixes and suffixes. Do they change the grammar or the meaning of the words?

2 Work with a partner. Look at these prefixes. For each one, decide what it means then think of more words that contain the prefix.

Example: micro- = *very small, on a small scale:* **micro**chip, **micro**scopic

a self-   e audio-
b multi-   f dis-
c inter-   g pro-
d con-

3 Match each prefix with a suitable word or base from the table below to create a new word. Then say what the new words mean.

Example: *auto + matic = automatic = without human control*

Prefixes	Words and bases
auto-, hyper-, sub-, trans-, equi-, bi-, mono-, anti-, ex-, contra-	marine, distant, annual, dote, president, matic, diction, lingual, market, continental

4 Different suffixes can change words into nouns, different verb tenses or parts of verbs, adjectives or adverbs. For example -*ed* and -*ing* are mostly used with verbs, -*tion* with nouns, -*est* with adjectives and -*ly* with adverbs.

Match the following words and suffixes to make new words, then say what part of speech the new words are. You may need to change the spelling of the word when you add the suffix.

Example: *happy + ness = happi**ness** = noun*

Words	Suffixes
accident, avail, cheap, excite, guide, happy, imagine, love, luxury, say	-ability, -al, -ance, -er, -ing, -ious, -ly, -ment, -ness, -tion

5 Look at the following noun and adjective suffixes. Use each one to create a word. Then choose **five** of your words and use each one in a sentence.

Examples: *comfort + -able = comfortable (adjective)*
               music + cian = musician (noun)
               Marios always chooses the most comfortable chair in the room!
               Stella excelled as a musician.

-able   -ac   -ade   -ary   -cian   -est
-less   -phobia   -sion   -ular

D  Speaking: Giving advice

1 On page 58, you will read an internet newspaper article called *Why can't teenagers get up in the morning?* Work in small groups and discuss these questions.

   a Do you have a problem getting up in the morning? What about your friends or people in your family?

   b Why do you think some teenagers have this problem? Is it laziness or is something else to blame?

   c Do you know any adults who have a problem getting up in the morning? Why do they have this problem? Is it for the same reason that some teenagers can't get up in the morning?

2 Look at these five statements. Do you think they are true or false? Why? What do the others in your group think? Use paper or digital reference sources to help you.

   a During the 'terrible teens' period, most children appear to develop a lazy streak.

   b Evidence is emerging that teenagers are biologically incapable of going to bed at a sensible time.

   c Other studies have shown that sleep-deprived teenagers are more likely to smoke than their well-rested peers and are prone to depression and anxiety.

   d Despite the potentially fatal consequences of a shortage of sleep, just one in five teenagers gets the nightly nine hours recommended to keep them in tip-top condition.

   e Although it isn't known exactly how our body clock controls our sleeping hours, it is thought that teenagers are around an hour out of sync with everyone else.

3 🔊 Listen to these seven expressions for giving advice. Which ones are followed by *to*? Which ones are followed by an infinitive without *to*?

4 What advice would you give to someone who can't get up in the morning? Work with a partner and give each other some advice. Try to use the advice phrases from Activity D3.

   Example: *If I were you, I'd buy a really loud alarm clock and keep it next to your bed!*

5 Team up with another pair and tell each other what advice you gave.

   Example: *Myria advised me to buy a really loud alarm clock …*

E 📖 Reading

1 Look at these words and phrases, which have been removed from the text on page 58. With a partner, quickly discuss the meanings. Use paper or digital reference sources to help you.

   a bleak   e out of sync
   b jeopardises   f sleep deprivation
   c metabolism   g succumb to sleep
   d moan   h trivial matter

LANGUAGE TIP

The words *advice* (noun) and *advise* (verb) are often confused. Look at these two examples:

My advice would be to revise all the units in the book.
The teacher strongly advised us to revise all the units in the book.

advice is an uncountable noun:
~~My advices would be …~~
My advice would be …
~~He gave me good advices~~
He gave me some good advice

advise is a regular verb:
advise, advised, advised

TOP TIPS

When speaking in English, you should try to use a variety of structures and vocabulary. If you use a selection of different words and phrases, your spoken English will sound much more fluent and you will be a lot more confident when you speak.

2 Which of the following phrases do you think you will read in the article? Why?

> a different time zone   chronic jet lag   getting good grades   hormones
> in a car accident   lie in bed for hours   perform very poorly in the morning
> sleepiness   sleeping hours   teenage body clocks

3 Skim the article and do the following. Do not worry about the gaps at the moment.

  a Find out what advice Dr Ralph advised.

  b Check if the statements in Activity D2 are true or false.

  c Check if the phrases from Activity E2 appear in the article.

Why can't teenagers get up in the morning?

[1] They refuse to go to bed at a decent hour, **(i)** … when they have to get up for school and lie in bed for hours at weekends. During the 'terrible teens' period, most children appear to develop a lazy streak. And now it seems that their inability to get up in the morning may not be their fault, with research showing that teenage body clocks may simply be **(ii)** … . A slight shift forward in the body's natural rhythms makes teenagers annoyingly alert late at night and frustratingly groggy in the morning. While this may be irritating for their parents, it could have serious consequences for the teenagers themselves.

[2] *New Scientist* magazine explains: 'Evidence is emerging that teenagers are biologically incapable of going to bed at a sensible time. This is no **(iii)** … . If teens are refugees from a different time zone, then by making them get up and go to school before their bodies are ready, we are not just making school life difficult for them and their teachers, we are also putting them at risk. **(iv)** … **(v)** … their future prospects, their health and even their lives.'

[3] Toronto University psychologist, Professor David Brown, said: 'Adolescents, who are usually evening types, perform very poorly in the morning, which is the time of day that they are usually assessed for examinations. There are some kids whose teachers have simply never seen them at their best and that is a terrible shame.'

[4] However, getting good grades could be the least of their problems, with other research showing that disruptions to our body clock could seriously damage our health. Tests on hamsters* showed that changing their cycle of sleeping and wakefulness had shocking consequences. Dr Martin Ralph, of Toronto University, said: 'Their cardiovascular system was destroyed, they suffered kidney disease and they died much earlier.'

[5] His findings look **(vi)** … for sleep-deprived teenagers. 'These kids are being woken in the night – before their body should wake – and are suffering the equivalent of chronic jet lag,' he said. 'All our animal studies show how harmful this is to health.'

[6] Other studies have shown that sleep-deprived teenagers are more likely to smoke than their well-rested peers and are prone to depression and anxiety. And half of all people who die in a car accident through falling asleep at the wheel are aged between 16 and 25.

[7] Despite the potentially fatal consequences of a shortage of sleep, very few teenagers get the nightly nine hours recommended to keep them in tip-top condition. The situation is so bad that many teenagers exhibit symptoms more usually associated with narcolepsy**, a serious condition in which sufferers can nod off in an instant.

[8] Although it isn't known exactly how our body clock controls our sleeping hours, it is thought that teenagers are around an hour out of sync with everyone else. Our natural cycle is kept in check by two mechanisms – one promotes wakefulness, while the other enhances sleepiness. During the day, the ever-increasing pressure to fall asleep is kept in check by hormones stimulated by light. But, at dusk, our bodies produce the hormone melatonin, which encourages sleepiness. At the same time, the body temperature cools and **(vii)** … slows, and eventually we **(viii)** … .

[9] In teenagers, there are two key changes. The build-up of pressure to fall asleep is much more gradual, making it easier for them to stay up later and be alert later. And their bodies start to produce the hormone melatonin around an hour later than usual. While some researchers are trying to find ways to reset the adolescent biological clock, others favour a more simple solution. Dr Ralph advised: 'Schools and universities should ideally not start before 11 a.m.'

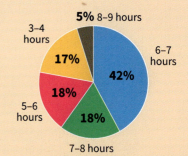

The number of hours spent sleeping by 9–17 year olds according to a survey of 1000 people.

* *hamsters = small animals without a tail, sometimes used in laboratory experiments*

** *narcolepsy = medical condition that makes you fall asleep very suddenly*

Adapted from www.dailymail.co.uk

4 Read the text again and complete the gaps i–viii with the words and phrases a–h in Activity E1.

5 Answer the following questions in your notebooks.

   a Give **three** examples of behaviour during the 'terrible teens' period.

   b What reason is given for children's inability to get up in the morning?

   c What can sleep deprivation put at risk?

   d Why have some teachers never seen their students at their best?

   e What does Dr Ralph's research on animals show?

   f What percentage of people who die in car accidents are aged between 16 and 25?

   g When and where do you think teenagers might show symptoms of narcolepsy?

   h According to the pie chart, how many hours are spent sleeping by the largest percentage of students?

   i Give **two** pieces of information about how the human sleep cycle works, and **two** pieces of information about how teenagers are different.

F ⊕ Further practice

Write

1 Someone you know is having problems getting up in the morning.

   Write a letter to a friend asking them for advice. In your letter you should:

   - explain the situation to your friend
   - describe what problems it is causing
   - ask your friend for advice.

   Your letter should be 150–200 words long (Extended) or 100–150 words long (Core). Do not write an address.

   The pictures on the left may give you some ideas and you should try to use some ideas of your own.

   You will receive up to 10/7 marks for the content of your letter and up to 9/6 marks for the style and accuracy of your language.

Read and answer

2 Read the text *Communicating with the world?* on page 60, then answer the following questions.

   a Which levels of language are the audiomagazines suitable for?

   b What is contained in the magazine that accompanies the CD?

   c How much time is needed for improvement?

   d Where should you go for further information?

   e Which course will provide you with information about cars?

   f What would you expect Vladimir Khruschov's job to be?

   g What is the total cost, including postage and packing, for the Italian course on CD with the study supplement and DVD?

   h How many methods of payment are offered?

3 Look again at the text *Communicating with the world?* Find examples of words with prefixes or suffixes. Are there any words that have both a prefix and a suffix? Are there any prefixes or suffixes that you have not already come across in this unit? Make a list and check using paper or digital reference sources if you are unsure about their meaning.

4 Write an extra paragraph of about 60 words to insert into the LearnFast Language Centre article on page 54, describing a facility not already mentioned. Think carefully about the style and content of your paragraph.

Communicating with the world?

Unsuccessful so far? A foreign language could help!

LanguageLearning audiomagazines have, for many years, helped learners of all levels to develop and improve their foreign-language skills in order to communicate effectively. Available in French, Spanish, Russian and Arabic (and in Mandarin from next year!), each unique edition arrives in your home or office, complete with a CD*, packed with 90 minutes of authentic radio and TV interviews, conversations, and news items about up-to-date current affairs, travel, entertainment, the arts, sports and health issues. As well as the CD, subscribers receive a magazine that includes a word-for-word transcript of everything, a mini-glossary and information about the source of the listening material.

An optional study supplement provides further listening-comprehension practice, and an optional DVD** provides a further source of practice material in each issue. In addition, with each issue, we provide you with a list of online links and resources to enhance your language learning studies.

Each magazine is produced in a country's capital: Paris, Madrid, Moscow or Doha, by a team of professional language trainers working with journalists and businesspeople. You need only spend a few hours each month and you will see your vocabulary and confidence building at an amazing rate. Furthermore, your knowledge of national events and culture will increase dramatically. Visit our website to find out more and see examples of what LanguageLearning audiomagazines offer: www.LanguageLearning.eur

*/** the content of CDs and DVDs is also available to download directly to your tablet or smartphone!

This month's special features!

Bonjour! in French
- The success of French soccer, with interviews with the top football stars and managers.
- Are French chefs the best in the world? A gastronomic look at French cuisine.
- What is the best French-produced road vehicle, and where exactly is it manufactured?

¡Hola! in Spanish
- Holidays in Spain – can you avoid the tourists? We check out the best places to visit.
- What's the most unusual job you can think of? How about clock-tower repairing? This month we have a special feature on this strange but important job.

Привет! in Russian
- The biggest country on Earth – how big is big? Did you know that Russia stretches across **nine** different time zones?!
- The dramatic differences in climate across the country.
- Post-Sochi – what next for sport in Russia? Vladimir Khruschov from the *Moscow Times* explains the plans.

مرحبا! in Arabic
- Sports facilities in Doha – the best in the Gulf?
- The Museum of Islamic Art – a collection spanning more than 1400 years.
- The best places to eat in the Qatar capital – for vegetarians!

Order form
A subscription to any one of the four audiomagazines costs $99, plus an additional $29 on CD. The optional study supplement and DVD are $35 and $39 respectively; p&p is included in the basic price. Please add $5.99 if ordering the DVD.

Name: _____
Address: _____
Postcode: _____
Email (to confirm your order): _____

Payment by CHEQUE   VISA   MASTERCARD   AMEX

If paying by credit card, please supply:
Card number: _____ Expiry date: _____
Signature: _____

For faster service, order via telephone +44 1202 789 1234 or fax +44 1202 798 1289 or online www.LanguageLearning.eur with your credit card details.
LanguageLearning Ltd, Europa House, Summer Lane, Epsom, Surrey, KT16 1JG

Exam-style questions

1 Read the article about hydrogen phone chargers and answer the questions that follow.

Hydrogen phone chargers – batteries need help

African smartphone users will soon have an alternative means to get round the power shortages afflicting much of the continent: a portable charger that relies on hydrogen fuel cells. Hydrogen fuel cells have the potential to replace batteries completely and offer a clean alternative power source for portable devices.

A British company, Intelligent Energy, plans to roll out 1 million of the new chargers, mainly in Nigeria and South Africa, after successfully testing them over the last few months. In countries where the national electricity grid is not reliable, and people are relying heavily on their mobile phones for both work and personal use, it is essential to have a constant source of power. Alternative sources of power are very important because smartphones and tablets need lots of energy, particularly when they are being used throughout the day (and night). For a business that relies on using the Internet and social media, power is crucial, and the technology of normal batteries has not kept pace with the innovations in the devices they power, such as smartphones and tablets.

The new chargers are designed to be compatible with most types of smartphone and tablet, and are small enough to fit into a handbag or pocket. Weighing only 620 grams, they consist of a fuel cell and a non-disposable cartridge that can be detached when exhausted. The hydrogen in the cartridge combines with oxygen in the air to produce electricity and water vapour.

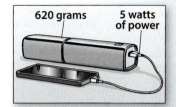
620 grams   5 watts of power

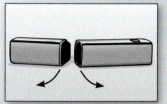

Intelligent Energy says that the device is able to produce 5 watts, the power at which modern chargers operate, and that each cartridge holds 25 Wh, capable of five complete smartphone battery charges before it needs replacing. The cartridge is able to charge devices as fast as a mains electricity connection and provides instant power on the go. A unique element is the Intelligent Auto Shutoff feature, which stops the charging process when the phone or tablet is fully charged. This saves energy and ensures a longer life for the device's battery itself. The entire device, including the fuel cell, will initially cost less than $200 and plans are in place to offer consumers a monthly payment scheme. Users can expect to pay around $5 to 'refuel' a cartridge.

Mobile technology experts predict that smartphones are the key to boosting mobile internet access in sub-Saharan Africa, where only 4% of the population has access. This is some way behind the global average of 17%. It is predicted that smartphone usage in Africa will increase tenfold between now and 2019, when around 476 million devices will be in use.

a Give **one** advantage of using hydrogen fuel cells. [1]

b Why is it so important to have a constant source of power for smartphones and tablets? Give **two** reasons. [2]

c What is the problem with normal batteries? [1]

d According to the pictures, what are **three** aspects of the new fuel cell charger? [2]

e After how many uses will the cartridge need replacing? [1]

f How does the new charger compare with a mains electricity connection? [1]

g What are **two** benefits of the Intelligent Auto Shutoff feature? [2]

h Why are plans in place to offer a monthly payment scheme? [1]

Extended

i Give **four** pieces of information about the differences in internet access between sub-Saharan Africa and the rest of the world. [4]

[Total: 15 Extended, 11 Core]

In this unit, we will concentrate on the skills needed to make notes on a reading text, which are important and necessary skills to develop. If you need to make brief notes on a text, you will be identifying and retrieving facts and details, as well as understanding and selecting relevant information from. This will show that you understand ideas, opinions and attitudes, as well as the connections between ideas.

In this unit, you will also:

- talk and read about different jobs
- practise making notes and writing a paragraph
- study language for giving advice
- listen to a careers advisor
- answer some exam-style questions.

A ○ Speaking

1   Look at the pictures. What jobs are the people doing? Would you like to do any of the jobs? Why, or why not?

2   Work with a partner and answer these questions.

  a   What job would you like to do when you finish your education?

  b   Have you always wanted to do this job, or have your ideas changed as you have grown older?

  c   What in particular appeals to you about this job? Are there any negative aspects to it?

3   Here are seven jobs, but the letters are jumbled. What are they? Use the pictures to help you. The first letter of each job is in **bold**. Write the words in your notebook – be careful of the spellings.

a coat**c**atnun

b itlo**p**

c te**c**hsmi

d dami**c**one

e ra**g**enerd

f **f**loaterlob

g tunar**a**tso

4 What does each person do? Write a short definition for each of the seven jobs you found in Activity A3. Use paper or digital reference sources to help you.

Example: ***d*** *A **comedian** is someone who tells jokes and makes people laugh.*

5 Which job in Activity A4 would you most or least like to do? Why?

B 📖 Reading

1 You are going to read a newspaper article about how to become a cosmetic scientist. Before you read the article, talk with a partner about what you think a cosmetic scientist does.

2 A cosmetic scientist makes perfumes and fragrances. Scientists in this industry also find scents that work well together. With your partner, look at the following information and decide if it is true or false. Try to give reasons.

a Cosmetic scientists usually need a four-year degree in Chemistry or Microbiology.

b It is essential to have a Masters or PhD degree.

c There are plenty of work opportunities for cosmetic scientists.

d 'Formulators' invent and create.

e A résumé or CV is very important when you start looking for a job in the industry.

f You must get a temporary position first.

g Social networking sites can help you find a job.

3 Skim the text and check if the information in Activity B2 is true or false. Give reasons. Correct any information that is wrong.

Seven steps to becoming a cosmetic scientist

[1] You could start your own company, or work for a family member who has started one, but this is not how most people get into the cosmetic industry. If you are following the <u>traditional path</u>, you should get a four-year degree from a college or university. The most common degrees that cosmetic scientists get are Chemistry, Chemical Engineering, Biology or Microbiology. You also find a few Physics majors too.

[2] While a four-year degree is all you need, larger companies <u>tend to favour</u> students who have Masters or PhD degrees in Cosmetic Science. The truth is that most of these degrees do not help make you a better cosmetic scientist. The training you receive on the job is much more valuable. The exception to this is when you enrol in one of the few cosmetic-science-focused programmes in universities.

[3] There are literally thousands of scientists and chemists working in the cosmetic industry. Fortunately, the number of jobs continues to grow. This is an industry that continues to sell its products, even in uncertain economic times. Everyone wants to look good, no matter how much money they are making. There are various types of companies that employ cosmetic scientists and chemists. A great place to find potential employers is through trade journals and magazines.

[4] In college, you are rarely told what kind of job you might get when you graduate. If you are looking to work as a scientist in the cosmetic industry, there is a wide variety of jobs to choose from. Use the list below to see which one <u>best fits your interests</u>:

- **Cosmetic formulator:** If you like inventing and creating, the formulator is where you should be. Most of these jobs are with finished goods and contract manufacturers.
- **Quality control chemist (QC):** If you enjoy chemistry and physics, and more analytical studies, you might enjoy a QC or QA job. Every company in the industry hires these scientists.
- **Analytical services:** This is the closest thing in the industry to scientific research. Most raw material suppliers and finished goods manufacturers have analytical departments.
- **Process engineering (PE):** Do you like building things and engineering? Then this might be the job for you. Almost any cosmetic company with manufacturing facilities will hire PE scientists.
- **Synthesis chemist:** If you love organic chemistry, then raw material synthesis is the place you should be.
- **Regulatory scientist:** For people who like science, but do not want to work in a lab, a job in regulatory is a good place to go. Nearly all companies hire regulatory scientists and (unfortunately) more and more jobs are being added. I say unfortunately because more governmental regulations make it tougher to create innovative cosmetics.
- **Sales:** If you like talking to people, going out for meals with potential customers and negotiating, a job in sales might be right for you. Plus, these are the people in the industry who usually have the most flexible jobs and make the most money.

[5] To actually get a job, the first thing you are going to want to do is put together a résumé or CV. You should be working on this in the early part of your final year at university. The sooner you have a résumé or CV, the sooner you can start sending it to human resources (HR) departments. You can go the <u>old-fashioned route</u> of looking through advertisements in newspapers or in university careers offices, but you can also use the power of the Internet and search numerous websites.

[6] Sometimes you will not be able to find your perfect job right out of school. Large companies often hire people who worked for them first as temporary workers. Get your résumé or CV to a scientist-focused temp agency and see if you can <u>land your first assignment</u>.

[7] Perhaps the most powerful way to get a job in the cosmetic industry is to get involved with social networking sites. But EVERYONE should create a LinkedIn page. This is where professionals hang out and post their career information. But it is even better because you can <u>strike up relationships</u> with people all over the industry of which you want to become part. Another great resource is Facebook. People often list the names of the companies they work for and the jobs they do.

Adapted from http://chemistscorner.com

4 Read the text again. Decide which of the seven headings below goes with each paragraph (1–7). Do not worry about the underlined phrases at the moment.

    a A temporary assignment

    b Get a job

    c Get your science degree

    d Maybe get an advanced degree

    e Network with other cosmetic chemists

    f Pick a job

    g Research cosmetic companies

5 Work with a partner. Look at the underlined phrases in the text and, using paper and digital reference sources to help you, make sure that you understand what they mean.

C Writing: Making notes and writing a paragraph

1 Look at the text again. For each of the seven paragraphs, try to write **two** notes.

    Example: *Paragraph 1: Get your science degree*
               (i) most common degrees are in science areas
               (ii) some students get degree in Physics

2 Compare your answers with a partner's. Did you both include the same information from the text? For example in paragraph 1 you could also have written something about starting your own company or joining a family business. Which information in the text do you and your partner think is the most important? Why?

3 Imagine that you are a journalist. You are going to write a short article about becoming a cosmetic scientist. Copy and complete the notes below, using a few words in each gap. Refer back to the article and the notes you made for Activity C1.

> **TOP TIPS**
>
> When you are asked to make notes about a text, you will generally be given a heading or headings to guide you. All the marks are usually given for the **content** (**what** you write). Usually there are no marks awarded for your language (**how** you write). You should try to keep your notes brief, but still make sure you have included all the relevant information.

Qualifications needed
Science degree essential, **(a)** … or … very useful

Job opportunities
Number of jobs **(b)** …
People always want to look good, even if **(c)** …

Job types
For lovers of chemistry and physics and organic chemistry, two possible jobs: **(d)** … and …
People who enjoy socialising should think about **(e)** …

Applying for a job
Must have **(f)** … , send to **(g)** …
Look through newspaper ads as well as **(h)** … and …

Benefits of social networking
Professionals **(i)** … information
Good place to find **(j)** …

4   Using your notes from Activity C3, write a paragraph about becoming a cosmetic scientist. Do not write more than 80 words.

5   Exchange your writing with a partner and check each other's work. What exactly should you be looking for?

D ◯ Speaking: Giving advice

1   ◀) Listen to the conversation between Sipho and Tendani. Write down any phrases that give advice (for example *if I were you …*). Compare your answers with your partner's. Afterwards, read the audioscript on page 191 to check your answers.

> **LANGUAGE TIP**
>
> Notice that Tendani and Sipho use words and short phrases to introduce the things they want to say. This makes their speech feel more natural and fluent:
>
> *Well, you know me …   Yes, I do too …   OK, but …   Well, for one thing …*
> *Yes, you're right …   Yes, I know …   Hmmm, good idea …   Yes, absolutely …*

2   What structures come after the phrases giving advice that you heard in Activity D1?

Example: *If I were you,* **I + would + infinitive**

a   You ought + ….
b   Why don't you + … ?
c   What about + … ?
d   You should + ….

3   Add some more advice phrases to the list in Activity D2.

4   Look back at the ideas for jobs that you came up with in Activities A1 and A2. Discuss them with a partner and give each other advice about your future jobs. Try to use some of the phrases from the activities above.

5   Working in small groups, each of you choose one of the jobs in the box below. What advice would you give to one another about doing the job you have chosen? What are the advantages and disadvantages of each one? Give reasons for your decisions.

> accountant   teacher   pilot   doctor   comedian

E  Listening and speaking

1   You are going to listen to a careers advisor being interviewed about jobs with NASA – the National Aeronautics and Space Administration in the USA. Before you listen, work with your partner and answer these two questions.

   a   What is NASA? What does it do? What is it famous for? If you do not know, how can you find out?

   b   Decide what type of careers might be available at NASA. Try to give reasons.

2   Here are some of the interviewer's questions from the interview. Work with your partner and try to guess what the answers might be.

   a   So, what does a young woman need to do in order to work for NASA?

   b   But what is an engineer? What does an engineer actually do?

   c   Is there just one type of engineer then?

   d   So is an engineer a scientist?

   e   I've also heard about technicians. What do they do? Is it different from engineers and scientists?

   f   Most of our listeners are still at school, studying hard, so what should their focus be, if these types of careers are interesting to them?

3   Listen to the interview and answer these two questions.

   a   How many careers are discussed in detail?

   b   What does the interviewer say one of his listeners might be doing in the future?

4   Listen again and make written notes about questions a–f in Activity E2.

5   Work with a partner. Interview each other, using the questions from Activity E2 and your notes from Activity E4.

6   Read the audioscript on pages 191–2 and check the answers you gave in response to the questions.

F  Reading and writing: Note-taking

1   You are going to read a text about certified athletic trainers. The text has **four** missing sub-headings. Look at the six possible sub-headings below and decide, with a partner, which four you think will be in the text.

   (i)   Athletic trainer qualifications

   (ii)   Female trainers and pro sports

   (iii) First aid in athletic training

   (iv) Future of women in athletic training

   (v)   Role of athletic trainers

   (vi) Women and athletic training

2   Quickly skim the text. Use an appropriate sub-heading (i–vi) from Activity F1 to fill in the four gaps (a–d).

Females in athletic training

Athletic trainers play a vital role in sports at all levels, from youth athletics to the professionals, and more and more of them nowadays are women. From administering first aid to implementing rehab programmes for injuries, athletic trainers are health-care professionals who are indispensable to any team or individual athlete. But despite making up nearly half of all certified athletic trainers, female trainers still face challenges, including some discrimination and disrespect from other athletes.

(a) …

Athletic trainers are not the same as personal fitness trainers, explains the National Athletic Trainers' Association, or NATA. They do not develop training programmes or prescribe exercises. A Certified Athletic Trainer, or ATC, is a healthcare provider trained to prevent, diagnose, treat and rehabilitate injuries. ATCs work with physicians and other healthcare professionals, and can be found in a variety of work scenarios, including schools, colleges, professional sports, clinics, hospitals, corporations, industry, military and in the performing arts.

(b) …

Founded in 1950, the National Athletic Trainers' Association is a professional association for athletic trainers whose members number more than 35,000, nearly half of whom are women. For the first two decades after its inception, NATA was primarily a boys' club, until the first female trainer passed her board certification examination in 1972. Four years later, in 1976, the first female trainer joined the US Olympic medical staff. In the 1990s, NATA developed a task force to address the subject of professional female trainers. In 2000, NATA elected its first female president.

(c) …

Despite the increased number of female ATCs, they are under-represented in professional sports, according to certified athletic trainer Katie Boushie. In 2002, the NFL (National Football League) hired a woman as an assistant athletic trainer and the NBA (National Basketball Association) employs two female assistant athletic trainers. Female trainers have had better luck in women's pro sports and, in 2011, the Los Angeles Dodgers named veteran trainer, Sue Falsone, as the first female head athletic trainer to a professional men's sports team. But female ATCs face some problems as they strive to work in professional sports.

(d) …

If you are interested in a career as an ATC, you must satisfy academic qualifications and pass a comprehensive test administered by NATA's Board of Certification. You must obtain a Bachelor's or Master's degree from an accredited athletic training programme and, once certified, you must continue to meet continuing education requirements in order to remain certified. More than 70% of ATCs hold a master's degree, according to NATA.

Adapted from www.livestrong.com

3 Work in groups of four: **A**, **B**, **C** and **D**. Each of you should look again at **one** section in the text: Student A looks at Section a, B/b, C/c and D/d. As you read your section, make **two** notes about the information in your section.

Females in athletic training
Athletic trainers are health-care professionals
Many women trainers face problems

Role of athletic trainers
...
...

Women and Athletic Training
...
...

Female trainers and pro sports
...
...

Athletic trainer qualifications
...
...

* Core candidates should make seven different notes for 7 marks, while Extended candidates should make nine different notes for 9 marks.

TOP TIPS
In a piece of formal writing, you should use full words (not abbreviations or short forms) when writing your notes. For example do not use *pro* for *professionals*, *admin* for *administration* or *vet* for *veteran*.

4   Share your notes with the group. Put everything together in note form.

5   Imagine that you have to write a short summary about ATCs for your school webzine. Look at your completed notes from Activity F4 and then write your summary in 70–80 words.

G ➕ Further practice

Read and complete

1   Read the leaflet about trampolines, then do the activity on page 70.

Hi-5 Trampolines

Trampolining is great fun for all ages! It improves coordination, balance skills and spatial awareness. You could be the next Olympic champion trampolinist!

Hi-5 produces three different sizes of trampoline:

CODE #T1 trampoline
$499   300 cm diameter
max. weight 80 kg
cover $29
anchor kit $39 (CODE #AK1)

CODE #T2 trampoline
$700   400 cm diameter
max. weight 120 kg
cover $59
anchor kit $59 (CODE #AK2)

CODE #T3 trampoline
$1199   500 cm diameter
max. weight 140 kg
cover $119
anchor kit $69 (CODE #AK3)
fun ring $399 (CODE #FR3)

STRENGTH   Hi-5 trampolines are guaranteed for ten years against rust causing damage to the steel frames. The top and bottom rails of the frame are specially designed to give extra strength and stability; this prevents twisting and bending.

WEATHERPROOF   The jumping mat is a soft but strong material, held in place by steel springs. It is specially treated to protect it against the harmful rays of the sun, as well as rain. While we do not recommend that your Hi-5 trampoline is left outside in the rain, the mat is 100% weatherproof!

ACCESSORIES   Three optional accessories are available for your Hi-5 trampoline. First, a plastic cover with drainage holes for rain and an elastic rim, so that it neatly fits your trampoline. There are three sizes available. Second, an **anchor kit** to protect your trampoline from high winds. The kit consists of four straps that attach to your trampoline and to stakes in the ground. Third, a **fun ring safety system** for youngsters and trampoline beginners. The fun ring attaches to our #T3 trampoline, providing a secure environment in which to practise and play.

When we deliver, our experts can help you to set up your new trampoline and accessories – FREE OF CHARGE!

For more information about Hi-5 trampolines and accessories, visit our website: www.hi-5trampolines.en, or email us: enquiries@hi-5trampolines.en

You want to order the following items from Hi-5 Trampolines:

- a trampoline for weight up to 110 kilograms
- equipment to protect the trampoline from high winds
- equipment to protect the trampoline from the rain.

You will be at home on Wednesday, but only in the morning. You do not need help in putting the equipment together in your garden.

Copy and complete the order form below in full.

First name: _____ Family name: _____

Address: _____

Delivery day: _____ Delivery time: _____ (morning or afternoon)

Equipment required:

	ITEM	CODE	NAME	DIAMETER	WEIGHT	PRICE
1						
2						
3						
4						

☐ Tick the box if you do NOT require assistance in setting up your new Hi-5 trampoline and accessories.

Speak and write

2   Interview someone you know about his or her job. Find out what the advantages and disadvantages of the job are and what ambitions, if any, the person has. Here are some example questions that you could ask:

What exactly do you do in your job?

How long have you been doing it for?

Can you tell me what you think the advantages and disadvantages of your job are?

During the interview make notes. Then write a paragraph of no more than 100 words.

Read and write

3   You are going to make some notes based on an article about a Saudi man who cycled across Japan. Read the text and then write short notes under each heading below. Some have already been completed for you.

Details about the journey

- *lasted 39 days*
- start/finish dates: **(a)** ... **(b)** ...
- **(c)** ... kilometres

Weather

- **(d)** ...
- **(e)** ...

Accommodation

- *32 nights in a tent*
- **(f)** ...
- **(g)** ...

Examples of Japanese hospitality

- *given space for tent, and dinner*
- **(h)** ...

Saudi man cycles into Japanese hearts

A 34-year-old Saudi national cycled from the northern tip of the mainland of Hokkaido in Japan to the southern tip of Kyushu island in a journey that lasted 39 days.

Omar Al-Omair began his 3152-kilometre trek from Cape Soya on 16th October, arriving at Cape Sata, Kagoshima Prefecture, on 23rd November.

In a newspaper interview, Al-Omair said, 'I love cycling and I love Japan'. He said that he had visited Japan twice before, but this time he wanted to bike through 'to see what I had missed'.

Al-Omair spent 32 nights in a tent, which he had carried with him, to rest from the arduous journey in the cold mountainous regions of Japan. For the remaining nights, he put up at a hotel or a mosque. During his time in Japan, he ate only fish and vegetables, thus making sure he had only halal food. With his limited Japanese, Al-Omair was able to go to a restaurant and say, 'Hara hetta' ('I'm hungry') and 'Watashi buta dame' ('I can't eat pork').

He said that he met many kind people along the way. On a rainy day in Akita Prefecture, he asked the owner of a shop if he could put up his tent under the eaves to shelter from the rain. Not only did the family let him use the space, but they also gave him dinner and in the morning offered him hot water to wash with. They also asked him if he would like some breakfast. When he refused, the lady of the house presented him with an envelope containing a 1000-yen (nearly $10) note. Quoting another example of Japanese hospitality, Al-Omair said that in Shizuoka Prefecture he met a family whose mother gave him 3000 yen.

However, while the warmth and generosity of the Japanese was overwhelming, the weather was freezing cold. In Hokkaido, with nightly temperatures falling to sub-zero, it was difficult to sleep in the tent. Al-Omair said that he wore three layers of everything, including shirts and socks, to keep warm.

This was the first time he had cycled such a long distance outside Saudi Arabia, however Al-Omair is ready to do it again, but in another country. 'Yeah, it's the first time I have done something like this, but it won't be the last,' he said.

Adapted from www.arabnews.com

Read and write

4 Read the article *Females in athletic training* on page 68 again, then answer these questions.

   a What **two** problems do female athletic trainers face?

   b In what way are athletic trainers not the same as personal fitness trainers?

   c Approximately how many members of the National Athletic Trainers' Association are female?

   d What happened in 1972 and 1976 to change the membership of NATA?

   e Why are women under-represented in professional sports?

   f What happened in 2011 to change the representation of female ATCs in professional sports?

   g What **two** things must you do to become an ATC?

Exam-style questions

1 Read the following article about camel breeders in India, then complete the notes.

Indian camel breeders lament* Pushkar fair's** downfall

As dusk falls on the desert town of Pushkar in northern India, turbaned herdsmen huddle around fires and lament the downfall of one of the world's largest livestock fairs. Like many traders, Jojawa has trekked hundreds of kilometres to reach the decades-old cattle and camel fair, a journey that took him seven days from his village in the desert state of Rajasthan. But the way things are going, he expects to go home with his pockets half-empty and some of the 25 camels that he hoped to sell still in tow.

'This year there are fewer buyers and fewer camels,' says Jojawa, who has been coming to the annual fair for 35 years. 'If it goes on like this, in another four or five years, I'll be finished,' adds Jojawa, who uses just one name.

Official figures for the five-day fair, which has long been a major tourist attraction, show that the number of camels on sale has fallen to less than 5000, a sharp drop from the 8000 recorded in 2011, and a fraction of those from previous decades. The Pushkar fair is the only time of year when camel breeders earn a cash income. Camels are normally sold for around 15,000 rupees, or $230 each, and used on farms or as transport.

But as sales decline, breeding is becoming a less viable way to earn a living and, as a result, the traditional values that underpin the market are rapidly disappearing. Rajasthan's traditional Raika farmers are among the most prominent camel herders and they believe it is their religious responsibility to rear these animals. They consider their relationship with camels as sacred and they are unique among camel herders worldwide for not slaughtering the camels they rear. But that is changing.

In the past ten to 15 years, the taboo against the slaughter of camels has changed and now in Pushkar most camels are actually sold for meat. Traditionally, it was also taboo to sell female camels, considered the life-blood of a herd, but these days they are sold for slaughter. But once the females are sold, many camel breeders go out of business.

As modernisation has swept across India, thanks to the economic boom, the country's camel population has dropped by 50% over the last three decades. In 1982, there were more than 1 million camels nationwide, but numbers dropped to just over 500,000 by 2007. Of these, more than 80% live in Rajasthan, where camels

have traditionally been used as work animals on farms or as transport for carrying goods.

But as vehicles and agricultural machinery become ever more accessible and affordable, sons from breeding families see no value in camels. Like tens of thousands of other young Indians, many are seeking a more lucrative income away from the land in India's cities. The herders who are left are mostly from older generations, men like Jojawa for whom life has changed little and is only becoming harder. Most complain about the reduction in grazing areas for feeding their stock, as development spreads to common land and national parks and forests become out of bounds. Another problem is that breeding becomes riskier because a poorer diet makes camels more susceptible to disease and illness.

A government-backed programme in the city of Bikaner in northern Rajasthan is trying to create stronger animals through better nutrition, but herdsmen say that only herders in the large, arid region of the Thar desert benefit. There has been no impact on communities further south. Herders want the government to provide financial help, so that they can invest in camel milk dairies, an industry that has already taken off in the Middle East. It is estimated that the global market for camel milk is worth $10 billion, but India's share is currently just 0.1%.

Adapted from 'Indian camel breeders lament Pushkar fair's downfall', in *Arab News*.

* *feel very sad about something*
** *an outdoor event, with animals or entertainment, or both*

You have been asked by your teacher to prepare a talk about Indian camels and their breeders. Make notes in order to prepare your talk.

Make your notes under each heading in the box.

Information about the Pushkar fair

- …
- …
- … [Extended only]

Raikas and their camels

- …
- …
- … [Extended only]

Impact of modernisation on camel trading

- …
- …
- …

[Total: 9 Extended, 7 Core]

Unit 7: Focus on writing and speaking skills

In this unit, we will concentrate on the skills needed to write a formal letter, which will have a different style and format from an informal letter (see Unit 3). We will also look at some advice and strategies for developing your speaking skills.

In this unit, you will also:

- talk and read about spelling
- listen to students discussing a speaking exam
- practise speaking in small groups
- practise writing a formal letter
- answer some exam-style questions.

A 🗨 Speaking

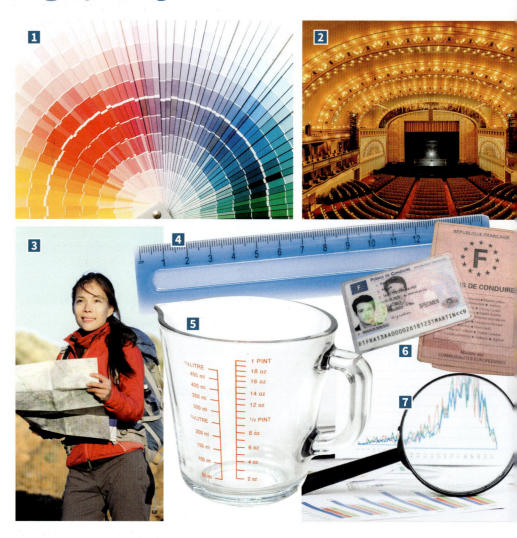

1 Some British English (BrE) and American English (AmE) words differ in their spelling, such as colour (BrE) and color (AmE). With a partner, look at the pictures and decide what they show. Then write a list of the two different versions: British English and American English. Add any other words that you know are different.

Picture	BrE spelling	AmE spelling
1	colour	color

2 Decide if the following words are British English or American English versions. Try to give a reason.

fiber	favour	labor	paralyze	fuelled	defense	dialogue

LANGUAGE TIP

You may come across differences in British and American English other than spelling. Sometimes BrE uses one word for something, while AmE uses a completely different word.

Examples: *pavement (BrE) = sidewalk (AmE)*
underground (BrE) = subway (AmE)
biscuit (BrE) = cookie (AmE)
lift (BrE) = elevator (AmE)

Do you know of any others? It does not matter which spelling system you use, but you must always be consistent. In other words, you cannot write *colour* and then change to *color* later on.

---

3   Work with your partner and correct the spelling mistakes in the following list of words. All the words appear correctly in the text you are going to read on page 76. You can check your answers later.

a	becuse	**e**	literucy	**i**	suprising
b	compleating	**f**	especialy	**j**	extremly
c	desent	**g**	univercity		
d	resonable	**h**	acheeve		

4   On your own, make notes in answer to these questions.

   a Which words do you normally spell incorrectly?

   b What method might help you spell these words correctly?

   c How do you keep a record of vocabulary items?

5   In small groups, discuss your answers to Activity A4.

6   In your group, decide which of the following is the best method for recording vocabulary. Give reasons.

   ■ writing words in alphabetical order

   ■ putting words into thematic groups

   ■ recording words in a sentence

   ■ writing the translation of words

   ■ writing the part of speech and how to pronounce the words

   ■ having a separate book for recording vocabulary.

B 📖 Aa Reading and vocabulary

1   Look at the eight words and phrases below, which have been removed from the reading text on page 76. Work with a partner and decide what they mean. Use paper or digital reference sources to help you.

> a cause for concern   a good impression   crucial
> an effective level   correspond   abbreviations
> fundamental   the vast majority

2 The five paragraphs in the text are in the wrong order. With a partner, work out the correct order. Do not worry about the gaps a–h at the moment. Use the following tips to help you with the order.

(i) To find the first paragraph, look carefully at the title.

(ii) Look at the final words in the first paragraph, and find the opposite in the first sentence of the next paragraph.

(iii) Look at the end of the third paragraph, which mentions the end of a person's school life.

(iv) Use the idea of poor spelling to find the link to the next paragraph.

(v) So the final paragraph must be … ?

Why is learning to spell important?

[1] Despite this, every parent and every schoolteacher knows that being able to spell properly is a **(a)** … skill that young people must grasp as soon as they enter education, although if they can start learning before they enter the classroom, so much the better. But, as every parent and teacher also knows, learning spelling can be difficult for children in the early stages. The problem with English spelling is that the letters do not **(b)** … to speech sounds.

[2] Good spelling skills are an important part of being able to read and write to a reasonable standard. Reading, writing and spelling are important in the first place because they all help to develop **(c)** … of literacy. Without this, school coursework would not be completed satisfactorily and end-of-year exams would be failed. Obtaining good grades in exams, especially towards the end of a person's school life is **(d)** … if they are looking to go on to college or university before entering the employment market.

[3] Learning to spell is important because being able to spell correctly adds so much to your skills and abilities, especially when it comes to finding a college or university place, or entering the job market for the first time. Writing a decent CV and completing the application correctly is vital in the effort to make **(e)** … . It was reported recently that employers rejected **(f)** … of 1000 job applications submitted by graduates simply because of bad spelling.

[4] Could our use of technology be the reason for bad spelling? Although not proven, there have been concerns in recent years that the rise of text messaging and 'chatspeak' used in social media could be leading to a decrease in literacy, as **(g)** … become commonly used by children. Opinions differ on this possibility. Some research suggests that this may not necessarily be true, but other studies have indicated that in some cases it is **(h)** … .

[5] But the end of school education may be too late. Obviously, the prime time for learning is during childhood and most people achieve a reasonable level of spelling to help their overall literacy. But it is perhaps surprising that many adults have extremely poor spelling and struggle with common words such as *embarrass*, *occasion* and *restaurant*.

Adapted from www.vocabulary.co.il

3 How did you decide on the correct order for the paragraphs? What clues did you find in the text, apart from the ones given in Activity B2?

4 Look at each gap in the text more carefully. What type of word or phrase is required to complete each one? For example does the gap need an adjective or a noun phrase? Use the eight words and phrases from Activity B1 to fill in the gaps. Check your answers with a partner.

5 Find the words that you corrected in Activity A3 in the text. Were your corrections right?

6 Find words or phrases in the text that have a similar meaning to the following:

a understand (paragraph 1)

b match (1)

c realistic (2)

d very important (2)

e above average (3)

f how someone feels or remembers (3)

g confirmed (4)

h worry (4)

i complete (5)

j have a problem with (5)

TOP TIPS

For your course, you will probably either have to do a speaking exam or speaking coursework. Section C is designed for those doing an exam, but it may also help with your coursework.

C ○ ◁ᴷ Speaking and listening

1 Work in small groups. How much do you know about the speaking exam? Discuss your ideas and make notes about what you already know.

Examples: *(i) The examiner chooses the topic card.*
(ii) It's not a good idea to answer a question with just 'yes' or 'no'.

2 Join another group and compare your notes. What can you learn from each other?

3 Which of your ideas could be given as information for someone who is going to take a speaking exam and which are general advice? For instance, example (ii) above is general advice, whereas example (i) is information about the exam. Make a table like the one below in your notebook and list your ideas.

Advice	Information
It's not a good idea to answer a question with just 'yes' or 'no'.	The examiner chooses the topic card.

4 ◁ᴷ Listen to twin sister and brother Fatima and Abdullah discussing their speaking exam, then answer the questions.

a Who knows more about their speaking exam?

b Where does Fatima say that they can find plenty of exam topic cards?

5 ◁ᴷ Listen again. As you listen, add information about the exam to your table. Compare your answers with your partner's.

6 Read the audioscript on pages 192–3 to check that you have all the information.

7   In small groups, look at this speaking exam topic card, which contains ideas to help you develop the conversation with an examiner. Each person in your group should choose one or two of the ideas to prepare alone. Remember – you are not allowed to make any written notes.

> **Education as a preparation for work**
>
> Nearly everyone will one day have to earn a living by getting a job.
>
> Discuss with the examiner how the education you have had so far (and any further education or training you intend to take) will, in your opinion, prepare you for the world of work.
>
> Please use the following ideas to help you develop the conversation:
>
> - subjects you are studying that might help you in a job
> - whether the study habits you have will be useful later on
> - whether some of your subjects seem to have little to do with your intended career
> - whether part-time work while you are still at school or college might be a good idea
> - aspects of school life, apart from subjects you study, that help you when you work.
>
> You are free to consider any other related ideas of your own.
>
> Remember, you are not allowed to make any written notes.

8   When you are ready, join the other members in your group and talk through your ideas. Other members of the group should ask questions. Try to keep in mind all the advice and information from the previous activities during the discussion.

Example: *A:* *I think that the science subjects I'm studying now might help me to find a job.*
B: *Why do you think that?*
A: *Well, I've thought about working in the cosmetics industry.*
B: *And do you need science for that career?*
A: *Yes, because I want to work in quality control.*

D Writing: Formal letters

1   What should the layout of a formal letter or email look like? What should be included in the introduction and the conclusion? How should the body of the letter deal with the subject? Discuss your ideas with a partner and try to agree on the best layout.

2   How do you begin a formal letter in English? What can you write after *Dear* … ? Look back at Activity D4 in Unit 3 (pages 36–7). Which endings would be suitable for a formal letter?

3   Look at this email sent to an online newspaper. Does it follow the layout you agreed on in Activity D1?

TOP TIPS

Sometimes you may be asked to write a formal letter. A formal letter may give or ask for information, or it may simply state an opinion about something. Remember – a formal letter is the type you write to someone you have never met before, or to someone with whom you have no personal relationship.

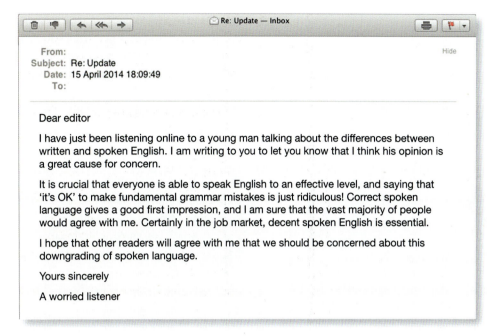

Re: Update — Inbox

From:
Subject: Re: Update
Date: 15 April 2014 18:09:49
To:

Hide

Dear editor

I have just been listening online to a young man talking about the differences between written and spoken English. I am writing to you to let you know that I think his opinion is a great cause for concern.

It is crucial that everyone is able to speak English to an effective level, and saying that 'it's OK' to make fundamental grammar mistakes is just ridiculous! Correct spoken language gives a good first impression, and I am sure that the vast majority of people would agree with me. Certainly in the job market, decent spoken English is essential.

I hope that other readers will agree with me that we should be concerned about this downgrading of spoken language.

Yours sincerely

A worried listener

TOP TIPS

In a letter-writing task, you do not need to supply addresses or a date, unless you are specifically asked to. However, you usually need to write the name of the person you are writing to – there will often be a space provided for this.

4   Which of the following phrases would be appropriate in a formal letter or email?

   a   I would be grateful if you would send me …

   b   Send me …

   c   I want some information about …

   d   I would appreciate it if …

   e   Please tell me …

   f   It would be useful if you could inform me …

   g   How much does … ?

   h   Give me …

5   Look at this exam-style question. What exactly do you have to do? Discuss the question with a partner, but do **not** write anything yet.

Improve your spelling! ✎

Do you want to improve your spelling?

Would you like to be able to stop using your spellcheck or dictionary and not worry any more about making spelling mistakes?

Would you like to help your friends and colleagues with their spelling?

Yes?

Then write for more information about our courses today!

The English Spelling Society – ESS

578 Oxford Street, Birmingham, BS3 8YG

info@ess.en

Write a letter to the ESS in which you:

■   explain why you are interested in getting more information

■   ask for more details about ESS courses (prices, length, materials, etc.).

Write 150–200 words (Extended) or 100–150 words (Core).

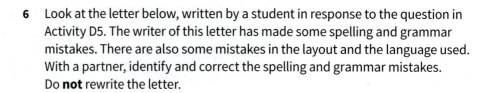

6   Look at the letter below, written by a student in response to the question in Activity D5. The writer of this letter has made some spelling and grammar mistakes. There are also some mistakes in the layout and the language used. With a partner, identify and correct the spelling and grammar mistakes. Do **not** rewrite the letter.

> Dear ESS
>
> January 29
>
> I have seen your advertisement today in my local newspaper magazine and want to get more information from you about the cources you offer people who want to improve their speling. I would like to be able to throw away your dictionary and not worry any more about making speing mistakes. I would like to help your friends and work colleagues with their speling.
>
> I am a student who I am studyng english in college and my speling is not very good so I want to improve and write better english. I need to write compositions in english and I do not have time to use a dictionary all the time at home and at school. Please will you send me some informations about your cources, the prizes and lenth and the materials you will send me and tell me when I can start a cource with ESS. I am look forward to hear from you a.s.a.p.
>
> Best wishes
> Bruno

TOP TIPS

A formal letter will usually contain at least two paragraphs, and will use formal language and no abbreviations. If the letter begins with *Dear Madam* or *Dear Sir*, it should end with *Yours faithfully*. If the letter begins with somebody's name, for example *Dear Mrs Sanchez*, it should end with *Yours sincerely*.

7   Look at the content and layout of the letter. How can they be improved? How can the language be made more formal? Talk about this with a partner, but do **not** rewrite the letter.

8   Look at the following answer to the question in Activity D5. In what ways is it an improvement on the letter in Activity D6? Discuss the letter with a partner.

> 29th January
>
> Dear Sir or Madam,
>
> I have just seen your advertisement in today's 'Daily Courier' newspaper and I would be grateful if you could send me further information and details about your courses for people who want to improve their spelling and their friends' spelling.
>
> I am a 16-year-old student studying English, Geography and History at a college in Botswana. I am currently in my first year at college. My teachers tell me that I need to improve my spelling to make my writing better. Also, I find that using a dictionary at home and at college takes up a lot of very valuable time, and often it is difficult to find the word that I want. Furthermore, as I sometimes study with my classmates, I would also be able to help them when they have problems with their spelling.
>
> I think one of your courses might be of use to me, and I would therefore appreciate it if you could send me some information about your courses, including full details of your prices, the length of the courses and the study materials available.
>
> I look forward to hearing from you in the very near future.
>
> Yours faithfully,
> M. Gaobakwe

9 Read this job advertisement.

VACANCY

Are you aged 16–19 with a school-leaving certificate? Want to join a well-known international sports company? Would you like to influence sports fashion over the next three years? Here's your chance!

We are looking for young, enthusiastic people with a real interest in sport and the sports clothing industry to join our Head Office.

Your role will be to decide which new fashion designs should be sold in Winning Sports shops all over the country.

Why not contact us today for more details?
Winning Sports, 246 Arena Lane, Cairo, Egypt
Tel: 246 1234, email: enquiries@winningsports.int

Write a letter of application for the job in which you:

- describe yourself and your qualifications
- say why you think you are suitable
- say when you are available for an interview and when you would be free to start work.

Write 150–200 (Extended) or 100–150 words (Core). Remember the rules for writing this type of letter:

- use formal language
- no slang
- no abbreviations
- use an appropriate beginning and ending.

You will not usually be required to write any addresses or date for this task in writing exams.

E ◯ Speaking: Job interview

1 You are going to act out a job interview with a partner. Read the following instructions for Student A or Student B – your teacher will tell you which role is yours.

Student A: Your letter of application for the job in Activity D9 has been successful and you are going to have an interview. Your partner is going to interview you. Prepare yourself for the interview. Remember to:

- pay particular attention to the points made in the job advertisement
- be prepared to give details of your exam qualifications
- say why you want this particular job
- think about what experience you already have of sport – are you a player, or a spectator?

Student B: You are the Human Resources Manager at Winning Sports and you are going to interview your partner for the job advertised. Prepare the questions for the interview. Remember to:

- pay particular attention to the points made in the job advertisement
- ask questions about your partner's exam qualifications, their experience of sport and their reasons for wanting this particular job.

Now join up with some other students who have the same role and discuss the type of language you will use during the interview. Write down your ideas. Use the table below to get you started.

Student A	Student B
I've enjoyed studying X at school …	What are your interests?
I think fashion designs these days are …	Have you studied X at school?

2 When you are ready, join up with a student playing the other role and act out the interview.

F ⊕ Further practice

Read and answer

1 Read the text *Are you a poor talker?* opposite and answer the following questions.

  a In what situations can the new technique improve your conversation skills?

  b Where can you get more details about the method for improving your speaking and writing skills?

  c In what **two** ways does the text say that you can influence others?

  d In what ways is conversation like any other art?

  e Why have the publishers printed details of the training methods in a book?

  f How can you obtain more information? Give **three** ways.

Understand and write

2 Using the text *Are you a poor talker?*, give another meaning for each of the following phrases. Use your paper or digital reference sources to help you. Then use each one in a sentence of your choice that makes its meaning clear.

  a pay dividends

  b work like magic

  c radiate enthusiasm

  d make a good impression

Are you a
poor talker?

A simple technique for acquiring a swift mastery of everyday conversation and writing has been announced. It can pay you real dividends in both social and professional advancement. It works like magic to give you added poise, self-confidence and greater popularity. The details of this method are described in a fascinating book, *Adventures in Speaking and Writing*, sent free on request.

Many people do not realise how much they could influence others simply by what they say and how they say it. Those who realise this, radiate enthusiasm and hold the attention of their listeners with bright, sparkling conversation that attracts friends and opportunities wherever they go. Whether in business, at social functions, or even in casual conversation with new acquaintances, there are ways in which you can make a good impression every time you talk.

After all, conversation has certain fundamental rules and principles – just like any other art. The good talkers, whom you admire, know these rules and apply them whenever they converse. Learn the rules and you can make your conversation brighter, more entertaining and impressive.

Then you could find yourself becoming more popular and winning new friendships in the business and social worlds.

To acquaint all readers of this newspaper with the easy-to-follow rules for developing skill in everyday conversation and writing, we, the publishers, have printed full details of this interesting self-training method in a fascinating book, *Adventures in Speaking and Writing*, sent free on request. No obligation. Just email: admin@effectivespeaking.org.sz or visit our website www.effectivespeaking.org.sz for more information.

Write

3   You have seen this advertisement about a new magazine for teenagers. Write a letter to *Teen Weekly* in which you:

- describe why you think you are suitable for the job
- request more details about the job
- ask for information about the application procedure.

Write 150–200 words (Extended) or 100–150 words (Core).

TEEN WEEKLY!
New magazine for teenagers all over the world!

Stories, celebrity biographies, sports gossip, competitions, problem page and lots more!

We are looking for people who are interested in these topics to join our team of young writers.

If you think you can write for teenagers, contact us today for more details.

Teen Weekly, 912 Riddle Road, London, SW16 4RT
vacancies@teenweekly.en

Read and write

4   Read the letter below, which was printed in a weekly newspaper. Write your own letter to the Editor in response, expressing your opinion of young people today and commenting on the views of the writer.

Your letter should be 150–200 words long (Extended) or 100–150 words long (Core).

Dear Editor

I am writing to complain about the crowds of young hooligans who meet outside the 'Café New' in Market Street on a Friday night.

Last Friday, I was walking along Market Street at about 9 p.m. when I noticed a crowd of perhaps ten or twelve of these young troublemakers, standing around talking to each other, smoking and chewing gum. As I approached, they made no effort whatsoever to get out of my way, and I had to go off the pavement into the road to get past them!

Not only is this sort of behaviour totally unacceptable, but it is also an indication of the laziness that we are seeing in young people today. When I was a teenager, we used our free time constructively and we knew how to be polite to our elders and superiors. As for smoking and chewing gum, they were unheard of. These louts should find themselves a responsible job and learn some decent manners.

Yours faithfully

Exam-style questions

1   Imagine that a new cinema complex has opened in your home town.
    Here are some comments that have been made by local cinema-goers

> Considering the cost of the tickets, I was expecting a much better experience.

> Do we really need cafés and restaurants and shops in the new cinema, as well as six different screens?

> Finally, a cinema where we can relax and enjoy a variety of films in comfortable surroundings.

> The new cinema really provides so much more than just films – it's a great place to go for an enjoyable afternoon or evening.

Write a letter to the cinema management explaining your views about the new cinema.

Your letter should be 150–200 words long (Extended) or 100–150 words long (Core).

The comments above may give you some ideas and you should try to use some ideas of your own.

You will receive up to 10/7 marks for the content of your letter and up to 9/6 marks for style and accuracy.

2   You have heard that a new supermarket in your town is offering all its customers a course about healthy eating and preparing healthy meals. You think it would be useful for you and your schoolfriends to attend.

Write a letter to the supermarket, asking for more information:

*   Ask when the course takes place and how much it costs.

*   Ask who can join the course and if there are any age restrictions.

*   Say what you and your friends hope to learn from it.

Your letter should be 150–200 words long (Extended) or 100–150 words long (Core).

Unit 8: Focus on listening skills

In this unit, we will concentrate on general listening and on answering multiple-choice questions, which require different skills.

In this unit, you will also:

- talk about different jobs
- discuss and write your own CV/résumé
- listen to a careers advisor
- take part in a job interview
- read about jobs for teenagers
- answer some exam-style questions.

A ○ Speaking

1 Many teenagers in different parts of the world have part-time jobs, either after school or at the weekend – sometimes both. Look at the pictures of teenagers working. With a partner, answer the following questions.

  a What are they doing?

  b Which job would you most like to do? Why? Which one would you not like to do? Why not?

  c What particular skills or qualifications do you think are needed for these jobs?

  d What skills and abilities do you think the teenagers are learning?

2 What is a CV? Check online or in your dictionary. Note: in some parts of the world, a CV is known as a *résumé*.

3 In small groups, discuss what information you think a CV should contain. Make a list of possible headings – Education, for example.

4 Compare your list with the headings below. In what order do you think these headings should appear on a CV? You can check the order later.

- Education
- Hobbies
- Languages
- Qualifications
- Personal information (name, date of birth, etc.)
- Work experience
- Referees (people who will provide a reference for you).

B 🔊 Listening: Radio interview

1 🔊 You are going to listen to a careers advisor, Janine Mesumo, at a school in Spain being interviewed on the radio. As you listen for the first time, check the order in which the CV areas from Activity A4 appear.

2 Look at the multiple-choice questions and answers below. Read each one carefully and decide which option is correct – A, B or C. Check if your partner agrees. Do **not** write your answers yet.

a Janine Mesumo's main role is to …

   A advise students who have completed their exams

   B give advice on writing a CV

   C deal with students' problems.

b Why should CVs not include too much information?

   A Because students do not have time to write very much.

   B An employer only needs a brief overview.

   C Students cannot write very good CVs.

c What information do some people forget to include in their CV?

   A Contact details.

   B Education and qualifications.

   C Name.

TOP TIPS

With multiple-choice questions, make sure you take time to read **all** the options carefully before you decide which one is the best answer. Usually, at least one of the incorrect options is close to being correct, so watch out!

d The section after 'personal details' is usually …

  A work experience

  B hobbies

  C education and qualifications.

e Why do some students worry about their work experience?

  A Because they don't have any.

  B Because part-time work is not important.

  C Because they work for charities.

f What should students **not** do in the 'hobbies and interests' section?

  A Give details about what they like to read.

  B Give information about playing an instrument.

  C Provide a list of things that interest them.

g The final sections of a CV should include …

  A all the skills already mentioned

  B proficiency in languages

  C anything not already mentioned.

h A referee is someone who …

  A will write positive things about you

  B will check the content of your CV

  C will help you to write your CV.

3 🔊 Listen to the interview again and answer the questions in Activity B2. Were your predictions correct?

4 How much can you remember? Here are some of the things the interviewer said. How did Janine respond? Work with your partner and write notes to answer each point.

  a What areas should first-time CV writers include?

  b So what information would you say is essential?

  c But often students don't have any work experience!

  d What about hobbies and interests?

5 Read the audioscript on page 193 and check your answers.

My CV

Personal details

  Name: Sophie Labane

  Email: labane.sophie@swazimail.com.sz

Referees

  My headteacher

  My Aunt Millicent

Education & qualifications

  2011–today: Manzini High School

  Before 2011: Manzini Primary School

Work experience

  None

Hobbies and interests

  I love reading books and watching my favourite basketball team, the Bosco Steels

Other skills

  I speak Swazi and English, but Swazi is my first language

  I am a member of the Bosco Steels fan club

C 🖊 Writing

1 Look at this CV written by Sophie Labane, an IGCSE student in Swaziland. Unfortunately, she has omitted some important information and has put some other information in the wrong order. Work with your partner and rewrite Sophie's CV. Use the advice in the previous sections to help you.

2 You now know what information should go in a CV and the order in which it should appear. With a partner, talk about the information you would put in your own CV. Think about the details that you would **not** include too!

3 Write your own CV. Use the template below. Make sure that you include information in all the areas: try not to leave anything blank. Read your partner's CV. Has your partner included all the necessary information?

Personal details

Name

Address

Email

Telephone

Education and qualifications

(Put your current school or college first and then the one before, and so on)

(Include any qualifications or certificates with the school or college where you obtained them)

Work experience

(Include part-time or voluntary work, starting with the current or most recent)

Hobbies and interests

(Don't forget to give details)

Other skills

(IT, languages, club memberships, etc.)

Referees

(Give two – not members of your family! A teacher and a doctor?)

D ◀ Listening: Job interview

1 You are going to listen to a student being interviewed for the job advertised in Activity D9 in Unit 7 (page 81). Before you listen, decide with a partner what questions the interviewer might ask the interviewee. Write down your ideas as notes.

Examples: *Tell me in what way you are interested in sports.*
How up to date with fashions do you think you are?

2 What information do you think the interviewee should give the interviewer? Before you listen, decide with your partner and make notes.

Examples: *I love all sports, but, in particular, I really enjoy swimming.*
I think I'm quite up to date – I read online fashion blogs.

LANGUAGE TIP

Notice how the word *interviewer* changes to *interviewee*. When spoken, the stress on these two words is different: *interviewer*, *interviewee*. Other examples are *employer* and *employee*. There are a small number of other 'person' nouns in English that end in *-ee*.

3 🔊 Listen to the interview. What do you notice about the interviewee's techniques in answering the questions? Can they be improved? How? Make notes.

4 🔊 Listen again to four of the interviewer's questions, this time without the interviewee's answers. What would *you* say in response to the questions? Look back at your notes in Activity D2. Discuss with your partner.

E 🔊 Listening

1 🔊 Listen to Bambos being interviewed for the *Teen Weekly* job in Activity F3 in Unit 7 (page 83). Look back at the advert, then, as you listen to Part A, note down **three** positive things that Bambos does or says in the interview.

> **Example:** *He introduces himself politely and gives the interviewer some information about himself.*

2 Compare your notes with your partner's. Did you note down the same things?

3 Before you listen to Part B of the interview, decide what questions you think Bambos will ask Lan Huang. What answers do you think she gives? Work with your partner.

> **Example:** *Question: How much time would I need for this job?*
> *Answer: It's part-time, only five hours a week.*

4 🔊 Listen to the second part of the interview, then work with your partner and check your ideas in Activity E3.

5 Read the audioscript on pages 194–5 and double check your ideas.

6 Do you think Bambos got the job? Why do you think this?

F 💬 Speaking

1   A youth organisation in your home town is looking for young people to join the group. Read the online advertisement and then do the activities that follow.

> # Youth Club
>
> ### WE need YOU to join US!
>
> *Our club is looking for 16–18-year-old volunteers to help us organise weekend activities with three different groups of young people aged 6–9, 10–13 and 14–16.*
>
> *We also need a new name!*
>
> *If you think you have the skills to work with young people in a fun and engaging way and can spare some time at the weekends, drop us an email or click this link NOW!*
>
> *volunteers@weneedanewname.org.zx*

2   Work in pairs.

Student A: You are going to be interviewed by Student B for the job above. Using the CV you have already written and the ideas about interview technique from this unit, prepare yourself for the interview.

Student B: You are going to interview Student A for the job above. Prepare some questions, using the ideas from this unit. Refer to Student A's CV during the interview.

3   When Student B has interviewed Student A, change roles. If possible, record or video your interviews.

G 📖 Reading

1   You are going to read an internet article giving advice to teenagers looking for their first job. Before you read, look at the following pieces of information and decide with your partner if they are true or false.

a   There aren't many jobs available for teenagers.

b   Car washing and helping with the shopping can earn you lots of money.

c   A summer job can help you get a job at other times of the year.

d   Teen jobs help you develop important life skills.

e   It's important to start a résumé or CV as soon as possible.

f   Teen jobs don't usually require you to attend an interview.

g   A part-time teen job can guide your career choices.

h   There are laws to prevent under-16s from working too many hours.

2   Skim the text and check if the information in Activity G1 is true or false. Give reasons for your answers and correct any information that is false. Write your answers in your notebook.

TOP TIPS

Body language is just as important as spoken language! During an interview, make sure you sit in a comfortable position, but don't look too relaxed – keep your back straight and your feet on the floor! This is true for both the interviewer and the interviewee. Also, try to maintain eye contact with the person you are talking to – this not only shows that you are interested in the conversation, but also tells the other person if you have understood.

91

First jobs for teens

[1] For a teenager, finding that first job can sometimes be a scary and difficult process. With no or little real-world work experience, you may be concerned that you won't qualify for many jobs, or that there aren't many jobs available. However, your grades, school activities, club memberships, volunteer activities and many other personal traits can demonstrate qualities that employers look for. An after-school or weekend part-time job can be a good first step into the working world.

[2] When the summer and other holidays arrive, you can work more hours and take on more responsibilities that will help you establish job experience. Now that you're getting older, low-paid jobs, such as car washing and helping your neighbour with their shopping, may not be making you as much money as you'd like.

[3] Summer jobs often open doors for jobs during other parts of the year. Be sure to keep in touch with previous employers, as that may help you get hired again for future jobs. Part-time jobs for teens can also lead to full-time employment and even future careers. Some jobs for teens even include on-the-job training that will help you get started in your new position, or even start to develop a career. Teen jobs help build and demonstrate self-responsibility, reliability, a good work ethic and work experience that will pay off later in life.

Getting a teen job

[4] If this is not your first job, you should start to develop a résumé or CV that shows your job history and work experience. In the early stages of your working life, you can also highlight your achievements at school or college, club memberships and social activities that demonstrate characteristics beneficial to this job. You'll definitely be one step ahead of most of your friends when you walk into a job interview and hand them a résumé including your work history and your current skill set. A current résumé is also a good way to maintain a record of the jobs you've held.

[5] Most teen jobs will require you to go through at least a brief interview before you are hired. For this interview, you should dress neatly, be well-groomed, and be prepared to tell someone:

A Why you want the job

Most employers will understand that you're just trying to make some extra money. After all, there are things that every teenager wants to buy. But if you can explain how getting this job will help you develop yourself, or even benefit others, then you'll be ahead of the game.

B What skills you have that will allow you to perform this job successfully

Are you the one that your friends are always asking for computer help, do you organise and run a club or committee at school or are you just really good with people?

C Why they should pick you over other candidates

Talk about your strengths and explain why you are their best choice for this position.

D When you are available to work

Many jobs will have requirements for a certain number of hours or number of days to work per week.

E How long you intend to stay with this job

Employers understand that teenagers can only work for certain periods of time, such as during the summer, until they leave for university or college, or other factors.

Benefits of jobs for teens

[6] Aside from the extra income, getting a job as a teenager can also help you decide what type of career you would like to pursue. Part-time jobs for teens can help you gain experience and also 'get a feel' for the type of job you'd like to have in the future.

[7] Jobs for teens are primarily part-time, and may allow you to work as many hours as you are legally allowed. Laws restrict the number of hours teens under 16 can spend working during a week. Be sure you understand the requirements of the job and that the employer knows how much time you are willing and available to work.

[8] Employers like to re-hire teens with a good work history. A part-time summer job or holiday job may be temporary work, but it could lead to bigger and better things! Always try to leave on good terms with your employers, so that they can provide a good reference for you to use in your next job search.

Adapted from http://bestcareerlinks.com

3   Find words or phrases in the text that have a similar meaning to the following.

   a be suitable (paragraph 1)   **f** keep (4)

   b characteristics (1)   **g** have an advantage (5)

   c while you work (3)   **h** follow (6)

   d principle, belief (3)   **i** limit, control (7)

   e up to date (4)

4   Read the text again more closely and answer these questions.

   a What are **two** worries that a teenager might have when looking for their first part-time job?

   b Why might a teenager decide to no longer wash cars and do the shopping?

   c What reason is given for staying in touch with previous employers?

   d Give **three** things that a teenager's first résumé or CV should include.

   e Change the **five** statements (A–E) after paragraph 5 into questions.

   f Why might a teenager want to make some extra money?

   g How can a part-time job prepare you for the future?

   h How does the law affect teenagers with part-time jobs?

   i Why is having a good work record important?

H ⊕ Further practice

Write

1   Write a report for your school magazine describing the interview you had in Activities F2 and F3. Include information about:

   ■ the job

   ■ the type of questions the interviewer asked you

   ■ how you replied

   ■ the outcome of the interview – did you get the job?

   Your report should be 150–200 words long (Extended) or 100–150 words long (Core).

Research and speak

2   Work in pairs. Student A is going to interview Student B, then Student B is going to interview Student A. Try to record or video the interviews. Follow these instructions.

   a **Both A/B:** Think of a famous person whom you would like to know more about. Find out as much information as possible about the person, then write their CV. Think about where you can obtain information: the Internet? Your school library? Books and magazines at home?

   b **Both A/B:** Imagine that you have been given the chance to interview the famous person you chose for your school newsletter or magazine. Write a list of about eight general questions that you would like to ask them.

   c **Student A:** Use your questions from to interview Student B.
      Student B: Use your 'famous person' CV to answer Student A's questions Remember to change roles after the first interview.

93

Listen and analyse

3  You are going to hear six people talking about studying in Dubai. For each of the speakers 1–6, choose the opinion they express from the list below (a–g). Copy the list below and write the number in the box. Use each statement only once. There is one extra statement that you do not need to use.

a At first, I was reluctant to study abroad. ☐

b I find the heat difficult to deal with. ☐

c Meeting new people is my aim. ☐

d Making a choice is my biggest challenge. ☐

e I want to see the world. ☐

f Family members told me not to worry. ☐

g I am very busy all the time with my studying. ☐

🔊 Exam-style questions

1 Listen to an interview about tigers in India by a tiger expert Sanjit Roy, and look at the questions. For each question choose the correct answer – A, B or C. You will hear the interview twice.

a Approximately how many tigers remain in India?

A 22,000

B 20,000

C 2000.

b What is the main cause of the loss of tigers?

A Efforts by conservationists.

B Fur-hunters.

C Companies that make cosmetics.

c Where does talcum powder come from?

A Beauty products.

B Tigers.

C Marble and other stones.

d Marble …

A is found where tigers live

B is the only source for talcum powder

C kills tigers.

e Within ten years …

A we will look and smell more beautiful

B Indian tigers will be extinct

C Indian tigers will be protected by laws.

f What is the result of getting marble for talcum powder?

A Waste and forest destruction.

B Waste.

C Forest destruction.

g Because the tigers' hunting area is smaller …

A they now only have 100 square kilometres to live in

B they are being moved to a reserve

C they don't have enough food and water.

h What can be done to save the Indian tiger?

A Nothing.

B Not very much.

C Many things.

[8 marks]

Part 3:
People and achievements

Unit 9: Focus on reading skills

In this unit, we will concentrate on the more detailed reading of texts in order to help you to get a better understanding of the content.

In this unit, you will also:

• talk about world records
• read about some strange Olympic sports
• talk and read about heroes
• answer some exam-style questions.

A 🗨 Speaking

1   *Guinness World Records* is a book that is famous all over the world. What is a 'record'? Do you know the details of any records? Discuss your ideas with a partner.

2   Look at these pictures. What records do you think are being broken?

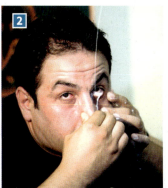

3   What record would you like to break? For example:

■   Would you like to be the tallest person in the world?

■   Would you like to be the person who can eat the most doughnuts without licking their lips?!

■   Or would you prefer to break one of the records in the pictures above?

Discuss your ideas with your partner and be prepared to give feedback to the class.

4   Work alone. Choose the answer that you think best completes the following statements about world records and record-breaking. Then compare your answers with a partner.

a   The fastest serve of a tennis ball was … kilometres per hour by Samuel Groth on 9th May 2012.

183   223   263   303

b   The longest snake held in captivity is … long.

7.67 metres   8.67 metres   9.67 metres   10.67 metres

c The highest waterfall, Angel Falls in Venezuela, has a height of …

379 metres   579 metres   779 metres   979 metres

d Ilker Yilmaz squirted milk from his eye a distance of … on 1st September 2004.

33.8 centimetres   191.4 centimetres   279.5 centimetres   365.1 centimetres

e The fastest time to burst three balloons with the back is … seconds, set by Julia Gunthel on 23rd November 2007.

3   6   9   12

f The record for the longest distance walking over hot plates is … and was achieved by Rolf Iven on 18th April 2009.

25 metres   35 metres   45 metres   55 metres

g Kanchana Ketkaew lived in a glass room measuring 12 metres squared containing 5320 scorpions for … days and nights at the Royal Garden Plaza, Pattaya, Thailand. She was stung 13 times.

11   22   33   44

h The fastest time to enter a zipped suitcase is … seconds, achieved by Leslie Tipton on 14th September 2009 in New York, USA.

5.43   15.43   25.43   25.43

5 Ask your teacher for the answers to Activity A4.

Examples: *How fast was Samuel Groth's tennis serve on 9th May 2012?*

What is the fastest serve of a tennis ball?

6 How many questions did you get right? Which world record surprised you the most? Why?

B 📖 Reading

1 Look at the five pictures on the left. With a partner, answer the questions.

   a What sports do they show? What equipment are the players using?

   b Which do you think are, or have been in the past, Olympic sports?

   c Which one or ones would you like to participate in? Why?

2 Which sports from Activity B1 do you think use the following pieces of equipment? Why?

   ■ a rope

   ■ a walking stick

   ■ roller skates.

3 With a partner, choose who is Student A and who is Student B. Then look at your words in the list below, which come from an article you are going to read about sports. Decide what the words mean and what parts of speech they are (for example verb or noun). Use paper and digital reference sources to help you. Share your ideas with your partner.

Example: *decades = periods of ten years, plural noun*

STUDENT A	braided debut ignoble misleading precise
STUDENT B	precursor premise resemble sabre slain

4 Skim the text and complete the gaps a–j using the words from Activity B3.

The ten strangest Olympic sports

Basketball, track and swimming have been important events at the Olympics for decades, drawing thousands of spectators. But solo synchronised swimming or live pigeon shooting? They are among the strangest events that have, at one time or another, taken place at the Games. Here are the ten oddest sports that have graced the modern Olympics

Solo synchronised swimming This sport features one female swimmer synchronising with herself. The sport made its **(a)** … in the Los Angeles Games in 1984, with US swimmer Tracie Ruiz winning the gold medal. Similar to the group event, a swimmer performs a kind of water ballet. Despite the seemingly **(b)** … title, organisers of the sport say the swimmer is actually in sync with the music. The solo event was discontinued after 1992.

Club swinging Club swinging first appeared in the 1904 Olympics. The athlete stands up straight, holding clubs that **(c)** … bowling pins in each hand. He then twirls and whirls them around. The more complicated the routine, the more points he wins. Historians say the sport was the **(d)** … to rhythmic gymnastics events that use ribbons and hoops. Club swinging was only in the Olympics twice, ending in 1932.

Tug-of-war Once a very competitive Olympic sport, tug-of-war employs teams (originally called 'clubs') that struggle and strain to pull a rope past a certain point. Great Britain actually won the most medals in this event, historians say. A country could enter more than one team, making it possible for one country to win multiple medals. Tug-of-war was an Olympic event from 1900 until 1920.

Live pigeon shooting

The 1900 Olympics in Paris had the great distinction of being the first Games where women competed. It also wore the **(e)** … badge for the sport of live pigeon shooting, where athletes aimed to bring down as many pigeons as possible. Nearly 300 birds were **(f)** … , historians say, leaving a bloody, feathery mess. The winner shot down 21 pigeons. The 1900 Games in Paris was the only time live pigeon killing took place in the Olympics.

Swimming obstacle course As strange as this sport may seem, the obstacles swimmers had to overcome are even more unusual. In the 1900 Games in Paris, swimmers crawled over boats, swam under them and climbed a pole, all the while swimming 200 metres in the River Seine. The sport has not been repeated at subsequent Olympic Games.

Roller hockey Roller hockey debuted at the 1992 Barcelona Games. The game follows the rules of ice hockey, but with roller skates. Argentina took the gold. The Barcelona Games was the only time that roller hockey was in the Olympics.

La canne OK, think fencing. Now take away the **(g)** … and replace it with a cane. You know, the walking stick type of thing? Now you have the French martial art *la canne*, which debuted at the 1924 Olympics, but has never appeared since.

Rope climbing This activity debuted as an Olympic sport in 1896. Just like in your gym class, the climbers were timed to see how quickly they could reach the top of a **(h)** … rope. In 1896, the rope was 15 metres long, but was then shortened to 8 metres. After 1932, the Olympics left rope climbing behind.

Trampolining Despite seeming like an activity you did in your backyard when you were ten, trampolining debuted as an Olympic sport in 2000. Gymnasts take to the trampoline, somersaulting and flipping as stern-faced judges keep score. '**(i)** … technique and perfect body control are vital for success, with judges delivering marks for difficulty, execution and time of flight, minus penalties' Olympic officials say. Both men and women trampolinists still compete in the Olympics.

Race walking In this sport, competitors try to outrace one another – without actually running. Even though the **(j)** … seems a little strange, race walking has actually been an Olympic sport since 1904. To ensure that athletes do not run, race walkers must have one foot on the ground at all times, or risk disqualification. Men compete in 20-kilometre and 50-kilometre races; women only race 20 kilometres.

Adapted from http://edition.cnn.com

99

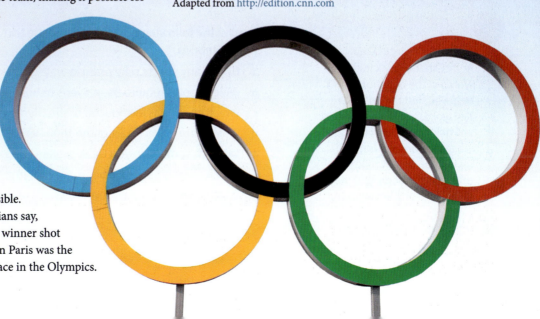

LANGUAGE TIP

Look again at the final sentence of the text: *Men compete in 20-kilometre and 50-kilometre races; women only race 20 kilometres.* Notice that the word *kilometre* is singular in the first half of the sentence, but plural in the second half. This is because it is being used as an **adjective** before *races* – in other words, it is **describing** *races*.

Remember that in English, adjectives only have one form; they do not change for singular or plural, or masculine or feminine nouns (for example *Maria is a very interesting woman, James and Davic are very interesting men*). In the second half of the sentence, the word is being used as a noun, which is why it is plural *kilometres* after *20*.

5   Read the text carefully, then copy the table in your notebook and complete it with the necessary information. You may not be able to fill in all the gaps. An example has been done for you.

Sport	Olympic debut (where + when)	Final Olympic appearance	Equipment	Other information
Solo synchronised swimming	Los Angeles + 1984	1992	None	Swimmer performs 'water ballet'
Live pigeon shooting	…	…	…	…
…	… + 1904	…	…	…
…	…	1932		…
…	…	…	Clubs	…
…	Barcelona + 1992	…	…	…
…	…	…	Boats	…
…	… + 2000	…	…	…
La canne	…	…	…	…
…	…	…	…	Country could win multiple medals

TOP TIPS

Remember to look for key words in the questions to help you find the answers. Key words are the words that will help you to find the place where the answer is in the text. If you do not read the question properly, you may give the wrong answer.

6   Answer the following questions about the text. Write the answers in your notebook.

a   How many sports take place in water?

b   Which sports require the player/s to hold a piece of equipment?

c   Which sport was introduced to the Olympics most recently?

d   Which sports were part of the 1900 Paris Olympics?

e   In which sport/s do you think players are part of a team? Why?

f   Which sport/s has/have been in the Olympics the longest?

g   Which **two** sports mention the length of the race?

TOP TIPS

It is unlikely that you will know what every word means in a reading passage, but don't let that put you off! It is never necessary to understand **everything** in a text. If there are words you need to check, look them up in a dictionary or on the Internet.

There are also strategies you can use to work out what a word means. You can try to work out its meaning from the context: the other words around it. For example look at *and he* **struggled** *on* in the middle of paragraph 1 in the text on page 102. If you look at the information before and after the word *struggled*, it will give you an understanding of what it means. Choose from these options: (i) started an argument, (ii) managed to survive, (iii) continued with difficulty.

Another option is to 'break up' words. Look at this example from the text: *these are the steps of my* **downfall**. This word has two recognisable parts: *down* + *fall*, which help you to understand what the word means.

C 📖 Aa Reading and vocabulary

1   Robert Scott (1868–1912) successfully reached the South Pole, only to find that another explorer (Roald Amundsen) had got there one month before him. Unfortunately, Scott and his team of explorers all perished on their return journey. You are going to read part of a biography about Robert Scott, describing this tragic event. Before you read, match the following words – which appear in the text – with the definitions. There are two extra definitions that you will not need.

Words	Definitions
stumbled	the action of cutting off a person's arm or leg
blizzard	written clearly enough to be read
dissuade	severe snow storm
amputation	full of liquid or gas
rations	a place where food and other things are stored
depot	try to stop someone from doing something
legible	a situation where something cannot continue
	walked unsteadily and almost fell
	a fixed amount of food or water

2   Skim the text on page 102. Find the words from Activity C1 and then note **five** more words that you find difficult. Discuss these words with a partner and use paper or digital reference sources to help you understand what they mean.

3   Skim the text again and answer the following questions.

   a   How many explorers are mentioned?

   b   Which explorer survived the longest?

4   Scan the text, then copy and complete the table below.

Date	What happened
16th or 17th March	…

5   Scan the text again and write short answers to the following questions. Remember that your answers should be brief, but must include all the necessary information. Find the key word/s in each question first.

   a   Why did Scott and Bowers have to make camp by themselves?

   b   Why are two dates given for the day when Oates began to struggle?

   c   What was the weather like when Oates left the tent?

   d   Why was Scott worried about his right foot?

   e   What prevented Scott and his team from reaching the food camp?

   f   What did Scott mean when he wrote, 'Have decided it shall be natural'?

   g   What did Scott want to happen to his written notes?

   h   In what condition was the tent when the search team found it?

   i   How many months after the death of the team were their bodies found?

   j   Why was it remarkable that Scott wrote 12 letters?

Robert Scott: The return journey

Things got worse, as the north wind continued to blow in their faces. Wilson was now becoming weak, so Scott and Bowers had to make camp by themselves. The temperature fell to −43 °F. On 16th or 17th March (they lost track of the days), Oates said he couldn't go on and wanted to be left in his bag. The others refused and he struggled on. There was a blizzard blowing in the morning when Oates said, 'I am just going outside and may be some time,' and he stumbled out of the tent. Scott wrote, 'We knew that poor Oates was walking to his death, but though we tried to dissuade him, we knew it was the act of a brave man.' Oates was never to be seen again.

On 20th March, they awoke to a raging blizzard. Scott's right foot became a problem and he knew that 'these are the steps of my downfall'. Amputation was a certainty, 'but will the trouble spread? That is the serious question.' They were only 11 miles from a food camp, but the blizzard stopped them from continuing. They were out of oil and only had two days' rations. 'Have decided it shall be natural – we shall march for the depot and die in our tracks,' wrote Scott. They did not march again and on 29th March, Scott made his last entry: 'It seems a pity, but I do not think that I can write more. R. Scott. For God's sake look after our people.' On another page he scribbled, 'Send this diary to my widow'.

It was not until 12th November that the search party found Scott's tent all but buried in snow. When the tent was opened, the searchers saw three men in their sleeping bags. On the left was Wilson, his hands crossed on his chest; on the right, Bowers, wrapped in his bag. It appeared that both had died peacefully in their sleep. But Scott was lying half out of his bag with one arm stretched out – he had been the last to die.

Remarkably, Scott had been able to find the strength, despite being half-starved and three-quarters frozen, to write 12 complete, legible letters. In one of these he wrote: 'I may not have proved a great explorer, but we have done the greatest march ever made and come very near to great success.'

D 🔵 Speaking

1 Work in small groups and answer these questions.

   a What do you think happened to Oates after *he stumbled out of the tent*? Why do you think this?

   b How did the men react to their situation? Did they all react in the same way? If not, in what ways were they different?

   c What do you think about Scott's achievements? Would you describe him as a hero? Why or why not?

   d Do you agree with the following definition of a hero/heroine? Do you think that Scott fits this definition? Why or why not?

   Someone admired for their bravery or abilities, particularly someone who has acted with great courage under difficult or dangerous conditions.

e Which qualities do you think make someone a hero/heroine? Do they have to be brave? Could a coward be a hero/heroine? Are some heroes/heroines stupid or irresponsible?

f Do you know (or know of) anyone whom you regard as a hero/heroine? What did s/he do? Why? What was the outcome? Does the person fit the definition above?

2 🔊 Listen to two students talking about Scott. The first student thinks that Scott was a hero; the second does not. What do you think? Why?

E 🖱 Writing

1 Read the audioscript for Activity D2 on pages 198–9. Notice the way the two speakers give their general opinion about the question at the beginning (*I really think Scott was a hero because …* and *For me, Scott was not a hero because …*) and then proceed to give specific reasons. How many different reasons does each speaker give to support their opinion? Tell your partner what you think.

2 Choose a famous person whom you consider to be a hero/heroine. Make a list of **at least three** reasons why you have chosen this person. Rank the reasons in order of importance.

3 You are going to write a paragraph of about 100 words in which you give your reasons why you think this person is a hero/heroine and reasons why other people would not think this person is a hero/heroine. Write your introductory sentence in a similar style to the ones in the audioscript: *I really think XXX was a hero because …* and *For other people, XXX was not a hero because … .*

4 Continue your paragraph, giving specific reasons for your opinion.

F ➕ Further practice

Write

1 Write a short piece describing how Scott's widow felt when she received the diary. Use details from the text. Do not write more than 100 words.

Note and present

2 What do you think about people participating in 'extreme sports' (sports that put people in some sort of danger, such as ice climbing or BMX riding)? Do people have the right to do this (as Scott did) in pursuit of their own goals? Make some notes and then give your opinion to the group. (Remember that in the speaking exam you are not allowed to make any written notes when you prepare to talk about your topic.)

Read and analyse

3 Read the newspaper article on page 104 about a teenager who helped to rescue a family of five children from a burning house. Then decide if the statements below it are true or false.

Heroes:

Brave mother and son clamber into blazing house to rescue family of five terrified children

[1] A teenager and his family have been praised as heroes after rescuing five children from a fire. Matthew Robinson, 18, his mother and his father rushed to help when a neighbour's home went up in flames. Jackie Robinson, 40, climbed a ladder to pull 12-year-old Tamara Barlow and her 16-month-old brother from their first-floor bedroom.

[2] Matthew Robinson, 18, has been hailed a hero for his actions after he charged into a burning building to rescue children from a house fire. After their 16-year-old sister Charlotte clambered down, Matthew went up the ladder and into the smoke-filled room to save two more children. He grabbed semi-conscious Jack, 11, and his sister Chantelle, five, and passed them to his father Roy, who carried them to safety.

[3] Last night, fire crews said one or more of the children would almost certainly have died had it not been for the Robinsons, but the modest family denied they were heroes. Trainee mechanic Matthew said: 'Anyone would have done the same thing. I was in the right place at the right time and it was adrenaline that took over.'

[4] Mrs Robinson added: 'The kids are alive and that's all that matters. It all happened so quickly, we didn't really have time to think about our own safety. Matt was very calm, I am very proud of him. He has more guts than I have, considering he is only 18.'

[5] The blaze at the home in Abbotsbury, Dorset, began around 9.30 p.m. on Sunday night. The children's mother, Tracee Barlow, suffered a broken pelvis when she jumped five metres from the property, and her screams of 'Get them out' woke the Robinsons. Matthew smashed his way through the front door, but was beaten back by flames. After his mother helped three of the children down the ladder, he climbed into the bedroom to get the others.

[6] 'I had to feel my way round the room, trying to find the two kids and get them to make some noise, so I could find out where they were,' he said. 'The boy was in a pretty bad state, almost passed out. They were too shocked to say anything.'

[7] He handed Jack to his father Roy, 43, a farm worker, who gave Matthew a damp cloth to put over his face when he went back in to save Chantelle. Matthew added: 'Being in the room with all that smoke, I started to panic, wondering whether I would be able to find them or not. It was impossible to see anything.' He was taken to Dorset County Hospital, suffering from smoke inhalation. There, he was reunited with the grateful family he had just saved.

[8] Steve Isaacs, station manager at Weymouth fire station, said: 'There was some very, very quick thinking on the part of Jackie and Matthew, which certainly helped save some lives. Normally we would never encourage people to go into a burning building but, on this occasion, it all worked out well. We're still investigating the cause of the fire, but we suspect an electrical fault in the living room.'

Adapted from www.dailymail.co.uk

a   Matthew was helped by his parents during the rescue.

b   Matthew has a 16-year old sister called Charlotte.

c   One of the children died in the fire.

d   Matthew is 18 years old.

e   Tracee Barlow was woken by the Robinson family.

f   Matthew easily found the children because they were making a lot of noise.

g   Jack's father is called Roy.

h   The fire service does not want people to enter buildings that are on fire.

Exam-style questions

1 Here is a notice from a hotel. Study the notice carefully and answer the questions that follow.

Royale Hotel
ANSE

Dear Guests,

The Royale Hotel Anse in Seychelles is an environmentally conscious hotel, and is dedicated to the protection of the environment within the travel and tourism industry.

WATER – DID YOU KNOW?

- 97% of Earth's water supply is contained in oceans, and 2% is frozen. This leaves 1% of drinkable water. Wherever you are in the world, it is easy to see that this represents a very limited water supply.
- Showers use 20–30 litres of water per minute. Each toilet flush uses about 15 litres of water.
- After drinking a glass of water, we use up to two more glasses of water to wash it.
- Even a small slow drip from a tap can waste more than 70 litres in 24 hours.
- A running tap uses up to 20 litres per minute. Letting a tap run while brushing your teeth wastes more water than one person needs to drink in a week.

THE ROYALE HOTEL ANSE IS A WATER-CONSCIOUS HOTEL

- Our chefs wash all vegetables with the plug in the sink.
- All water used in the hotel for cleaning and washing is recycled through our water-treatment equipment.
- The hotel gardens are watered using recycled water from the water-treatment equipment.
- All the hotel's taps, pipes, toilets, showers and baths are regularly checked for leaks by our engineers and immediately repaired, if necessary.
- In order to save both water and electricity, dishwashing machines are only switched on when they are full.
- Our staff undergo regular training in environmental issues.

---

a Where is the Royal Hotel Anse? [1]

b How limited is the world's water supply? [1]

c Which uses more water per minute: a shower or a running tap? [1]

d What is the result of letting a tap run while you brush your teeth? [1]

e How do the hotel's chefs save water? [1]

f When would the hotel's pipes or taps need to be repaired by the engineers? [1]

g Why are the hotel staff water-conscious? [1]

Extended

h Name **two** other ways in which the Royale Hotel Anse is water-conscious. [2]

[Total: 9 Extended, 7 Core]

DEALING WITH
asthma triggers

What's a trigger?

People with asthma have what's called a chronic or continuing problem with their airways (the breathing tubes in their lungs), which are swollen and full of mucus. This problem is made worse by asthma triggers, such as animal hair, exercise or smoke.

Triggers are substances, weather conditions or activities that are harmless to most people. But in people with asthma, they can lead to coughing, wheezing and shortness of breath. Triggers don't actually cause asthma (no-one knows exactly what *does* cause it), but triggers can lead to asthma symptoms and flare-ups.

Every person with asthma has different triggers. That's why cats may cause one person's asthma to flare up, but have no impact at all on someone else. Some people have one or two triggers; others have a dozen. Triggers are sometimes seasonal and may even stop affecting a teen with asthma as he or she gets older.

Common asthma triggers include:

- colds or the flu
- allergens (things that cause allergic reactions, such as animal hair and plant pollen)
- irritants in the air (such as perfume, smoke and air pollution)
- weather conditions
- exercise.

Coping with common triggers

Allergens are one of the most common asthma triggers. Allergens include mould, dust mites, cockroaches and pollen, and from animals: skin flakes, saliva, urine and feathers. If you think you might have an allergy, talk to a parent or doctor about getting allergy testing.

In addition to other treatments for allergies, doctors recommend avoiding allergens. It isn't possible to avoid everything, of course, but there are some things you can do:

- Keep your room as clean and dust free as possible – this means vacuuming and dusting weekly and getting rid of clutter. Your old stuffed animals and prize ribbons may need to go into a box in the attic.
- Wash your sheets weekly in hot water and get rid of feather pillows and comforters. You can get covers for your mattress and pillows that will help too.
- Get rid of carpets and curtains. Rugs, carpeting and other heavy fabrics can trap allergens that make you ill.

If you have allergies that worsen your asthma, you might also need to take medication or have allergy injections. Your doctor will let you know. In some extreme cases, it may be necessary to receive treatment in a hospital or clinic, but the number of people who need this has dropped considerably over the past 20 years or so, as these statistics about hospital visits for people in Australia show.

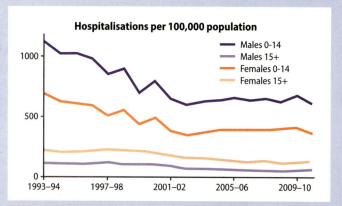

Hospital visits for asthma sufferers per 100,000 of the population

Irritants are different from allergens because they can also affect people who don't have allergies or asthma. For most people, irritants don't create a serious problem, but for people with asthma, they can lead to flare-ups. Common irritants include perfumes, aerosol sprays, cleaning products, wood and tobacco smoke, paint or gas fumes and air pollution. Even things that may seem harmless, such as scented candles or glue, are triggers for some people.

If you notice that a household product triggers your asthma, ask your family to switch to an unscented or non-aerosol version of it. If smoke bothers you, obviously people smoking around you will be a trigger. But a fire in the fireplace or woodstove can also be a problem.

If outdoor air pollution is a trigger for your asthma, running the air conditioner can help. You can check air-quality reports on the news to monitor which days might be bad for you. Then, on days when the quality is especially bad, you can stay in air-conditioned comfort, whether it's at your house or the mall.

Adapted from http://kidshealth.org

2 On page 106 is an internet article about dealing with asthma, a breathing problem. Read the article carefully and answer the questions.

   a What and where are the 'airways'? [1]

   b What actually causes asthma? [1]

   c Why might a cat trigger asthma in one person but not in another? [1]

   d How many asthma triggers do people have? [1]

   e Give **two** examples of allergens and **two** examples of irritants. [2]

   f What advice is given for people who think they might have an allergy? [1]

   g If an asthma attack is particularly serious, what might be necessary? [1]

   h According to the diagram, which age groups are most likely to receive hospital treatment? [1]

   i How are irritants different from allergens? [1]

   j What should someone do if a household product triggers asthma symptoms? [1]

Extended

   k According to doctors, what can be done to avoid allergens? Give **four** pieces of advice. [4]

[Total: 15 Extended, 11 Core]

Unit 10: Focus on reading and writing skills

In this unit, we will focus on the specific reading and writing skills that are required for you to make notes relating to, or to write a summary of, a text you have read.

In this unit, you will also:

- talk and read about famous people
- make notes based on texts you read
- read about adventures on motorbikes
- look at how adverbs are used in English
- write summaries of texts you have read
- answer some exam-style questions.

A 🗨 Speaking

1   Who are the people in the pictures? What do you know about them? What made them successful and famous? Discuss with a partner.

2   Match the name and **two** pieces of information to each of the pictures. If you know any more information about any of the people, tell your partner.

> **Names**
> Sarah Attar   Zaha Hadid   Mark Zuckerberg   Bruce Lee
>
> **Information**
> Iraqi-British architect   competed in 2012 Olympics
> co-founder of Facebook   film actor   Saudi Arabian
> studied at American University Beirut   died 1973   born 1984

3   What qualities or characteristics do you think make a person successful and famous? Talk about this with your partner.

4   With your partner, talk about the following questions. Then join up with another pair and discuss your ideas.

   a   Do you think ambition is important?

   b   Do you think family and educational backgrounds are important? What about money?

   c   What qualities do you think Robert Scott (in Unit 9) had?

B 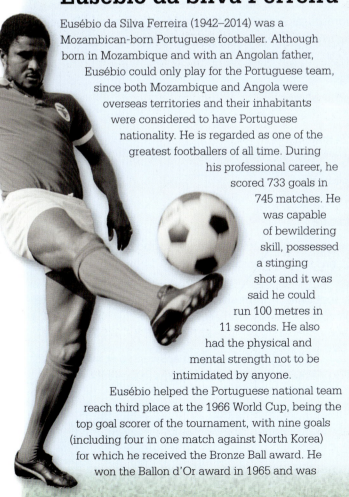 Reading and writing: Making notes

1 You are going to read about the famous Portuguese footballer Eusébio. Before you read, look at these words and phrases from the text and make sure you have a general idea of what they mean. Discuss the list with your partner and use paper and digital reference sources to help you.

> a stinging shot   bewildering   ferocious   homages   humility
> intimidated   prolific   renowned   runner-up

2 Look at these phrases. Which ones do you think you will read in the text? Why?

a A Mozambican-born Portuguese footballer.

b One of the greatest footballers of all time.

c He could run 100 metres in 11 seconds.

d He played for Benfica for 15 out of his 22 years.

e Nicknamed the Black Panther, the Black Pearl or *o Rei* (the King).

f He is considered Benfica's and Portugal's most renowned player.

g Eusébio was an ambassador of football.

3 Skim the text and check your answers to Activities B1 and B2.

Eusébio da Silva Ferreira

Eusébio da Silva Ferreira (1942–2014) was a Mozambican-born Portuguese footballer. Although born in Mozambique and with an Angolan father, Eusébio could only play for the Portuguese team, since both Mozambique and Angola were overseas territories and their inhabitants were considered to have Portuguese nationality. He is regarded as one of the greatest footballers of all time. During his professional career, he scored 733 goals in 745 matches. He was capable of bewildering skill, possessed a stinging shot and it was said he could run 100 metres in 11 seconds. He also had the physical and mental strength not to be intimidated by anyone. Eusébio helped the Portuguese national team reach third place at the 1966 World Cup, being the top goal scorer of the tournament, with nine goals (including four in one match against North Korea) for which he received the Bronze Ball award. He won the Ballon d'Or award in 1965 and was runner-up in 1962 and 1966. He played for Benfica for 15 out of his 22 years as a footballer, thus being mainly associated with the Portuguese club, and is the team's all-time top scorer with 638 goals scored in 614 official games. At Benefica, he won 11 Primeira Liga titles, five Taça de Portugal titles, a European Cup (1961–62) and helped them reach three additional European Cup finals. He was the European Cup top scorer in 1965, 1966 and 1968. He also won the Bola de Prata (Primeira Liga top scorer award) a record seven times. He was the first ever player to win the European Golden Boot, in 1968 – a feat he repeated in 1973.

Nicknamed the Black Panther, the Black Pearl or *o Rei* (the King), he was known for his speed, technique, athleticism and his ferocious, accurate right-footed shot, making him an outstandingly prolific goal scorer and one of the greatest free-kick-takers in history. He is considered Benfica's and Portugal's most renowned player and one of the first world-class African strikers.

From his retirement until his death in January 2014, Eusébio was an ambassador of football and was one of the most recognisable faces of the sport. He was often praised for his fair play and humility, even by opponents. Homages by FIFA, UEFA, the Portuguese Football Federation and Benfica have been held in his honour. Former Benfica and Portugal teammate and friend António Simoes acknowledges his influence on Benfica and said: 'With Eusébio maybe we could be European Champions, without him maybe we could win the League.'

Adapted from http://en.wikipedia.org

4 Read the text again and answer these questions.

   a What was Eusébio's nationality?

   b Why was Eusébio not permitted to play for Mozambique or Angola?

   c Why was Eusébio not afraid of other footballers?

   d In which tournament did Eusébio score four times in one game?

   e What did Eusébio win before anyone else?

   f What particular skills helped Eusébio to score so many goals?

   g What caused Eusébio's opponents to praise him?

5 You have decided to tell your school sports club about Eusébio, but first you need to make some notes in order to prepare your talk. Which **three** of the following headings do you think would be suitable to help you make your notes. Why?

> Home and education   Nationality and family   Physical skills
> Achievements in football   Hobbies and interests

6 The best three headings are *Nationality and family*, *Physical skills* and *Achievements in football*. Make **three** notes under each.

C Reading

1 You are going to read another text, about a different type of person. Look at this list of eight phrases taken from the text and try to guess what type of person you are going to read about. Work with your partner and give reasons for your answers.

   a a dolphin in danger

   b a riotously colourful woman

   c Prime Minister

   d needs to raise £24 million a year

   e severe dyslexia

   f one focus: the children

   g 11,000 volunteers

   h parental love and care

2 Which of the following people do you think the text is about? Discuss with a partner and give reasons for your choice.

> F1 racing driver   footballer   musician
> politician   zoo keeper   charity worker

3 Quickly scan the text on page 111 and check your answers to Activities C1 and C2. Do not worry about trying to fill in the gaps in the text for the moment.

TOP TIPS

You only need to make **brief** notes for each heading. Your notes must be related to the text you have read. In the text about Eusébio, for example, under the heading *Nationality and family*, you could make the note: *born in Mozambique, Angolan father.*

TOP TIPS

Remember that there might be more than three pieces of information in the text for a particular heading, but you only need to make notes for each bullet point. If you write four pieces of information when there are only three bullets (and three marks), you can still only receive three marks!

Fighting for funds
for vulnerable children never ends

[1] … who sits some distance away, behind a closed door, she lets out a curious, high-pitched noise. It is not a particularly nice noise – you instinctively think of a dolphin in danger – but it is effective. She does it twice while I'm in her company and both times her dutiful PA comes running.

[2] … Kids Company, are as remarkable, and awe-inspiring, as the other. Here is a riotously colourful woman, who has given up a private life to help some of the country's most vulnerable children survive and, in many cases, thrive, in a fashion that many can only sit back and admire, but not, seemingly, copy. 'Oh, I've had all sorts of politicians admit to me, privately, that they know that children's social services are not working,' Batmanghelidjh tells me in her office. 'The trouble is, it's not something they want to go near. If you are a Prime Minister coming into power, you suddenly get hijacked by national and international issues, and you have to prioritise. Political life is short. But the fact remains that there hasn't been a real recovery plan for children in this country since Victorian times.'

[3] … to rectify this, she will tell you herself that 'it's hard work'. To keep the organisation ticking over – it works with approximately 36,000 children – she needs to raise £24 million annually, or £2 million a month. The vast majority of money comes from public donations. 'I call myself the Fat Beggar,' she says, laughing. 'Our donations come from 75,000 different sources a year, and I'm sure many of those sources wish I would just go away and leave them alone. But, ha ha, I won't!'

[4] … Her family left Tehran in the late 1970s and settled in the UK, where, despite severe dyslexia, she did well at school. She went on to become a psychotherapist before, increasingly frustrated by the limitations under which social services operates, she set up her charity in 1996. Some 95% of all children who call into one of its drop-in centres in London and Bristol self-refer, drawn to an organisation seemingly unhindered by the bureaucracy that stops governments from operating well.

[5] … she explains, is holistic. It does not have different divisions for different problems. Instead, it simply has one focus: the children. And so it assists with teaching troubled teens, but also provides safe houses and offers hot meals and food vouchers to any family that comes asking. It will even accompany children on appointments to the dentist and doctor. For this, it needs a workforce greater than the full-time staff of 361, which is where the 11,000 volunteers come in.

[6] … is most routinely asked is why a charity has to carry out such clearly crucial work that should be government policy. Her answer is the stuff of headlines. 'This country has a deep wound in relation to its attitude to childhood,' she says, adding that the country is frequently found at the bottom of the league of the 21 wealthiest countries in terms of well-being for its children.

[7] … the next generation to indulge in childhood so much as to simply prepare them for adulthood 'as if childhood were simply a waiting-room'. And, of those children considered troubled, the impulse is to simply label them accordingly and attempt damage control. 'If a child flourishes with parental love and care,' she says, 'then in the absence of that love and care, the state has to find a way to do it. That's the ambition here.'

Adapted from www.independent.co.uk

111

4 The opening words from each paragraph have been removed. Scan the text again and decide which of the phrases from the list below fit the paragraphs. Be careful! There are **three** extra phrases that you do not need to use.

a Although Batmanghelidjh has worked tirelessly …

b However, she believes that …

c Batmanghelidjh and her organisation, …

d Batmanghelidjh is of Iranian and Belgian descent.

e Many have told her this …

f One of the questions Batmanghelidjh …

g She suggests that we don't permit …

h Since that time, …

i The charity's approach, …

j When Camila Batmanghelidjh needs the help of her personal assistant, …

5 Work with a partner and answer the following questions. Use paper and digital reference sources to help you, as well as the strategies in Unit 9 for understanding words you don't know (see page 101).

a Look at paragraphs 1 and 2. What do the following words and phrases mean?

(i) high-pitched noise

(ii) instinctively

(iii) dutifully

(iv) awe-inspiring

(v) riotously

(vi) vulnerable

(vii) have to prioritise

b Look at paragraphs 3 and 4. Find words or phrases that have a similar meaning to the following.

(i) find the answer to

(ii) contributions

(iii) working normally

(iv) unsatisfied

(v) unrestricted

c Look at these words from paragraphs 5 and 6. Copy the table into your notebook, then fill in as many gaps as possible.

Adjective	Noun	Adverb	Verb
different	differently	difference	differ
…	…	divisions	…
safe	…	…	…
…	routinely	…	…
…	…	…	offers
crucial	…	…	…

> **LANGUAGE TIP**
>
> In English, words ending in -*ly* are usually adverbs (for example *differently* and *routinely*), but there are also -*ly* words that are not adverbs – for example *lovely* and *friendly*, which are both adjectives. Other examples are *family* and *apply*, which are a noun and a verb respectively.

d Look at the whole text.

(i) Find all the -*ly* adverbs. What do they mean?

(ii) Do the words have adjective and noun forms? If so, what are they? Write a list.

6 Write answers to the following questions. Find the key word/s first. Remember to keep your answers brief, but include all the necessary information. Check your answers with your partner.

a How does Batmanghelidjh contact her personal assistant?

b Who has told Batmanghelidjh that support for children is not effective?

c How much money is needed each year to keep Kids Company running?

d Where does Kids Company receive its money from?

e Why did Batmanghelidjh create her own charity?

f How does Kids Company help children? Give **four** ideas.

g How many people get paid to work for Kids Company?

h What do you think Batmanghelidjh means when she describes childhood as 'a waiting-room'?

D ✏ Writing: Making notes

1 Look at this exam-style question. What exactly do you have to do? Discuss with your partner. Do **not** write anything yet.

> Read the article and then write notes on Camila Batmanghelidjh.

2 You are going to make some notes about Camila Batmanghelidjh. First, look at the three headings (a–c) for your notes. Then decide under which heading the information (i–iii) should go. Give reasons. Does your partner agree?

a Batmanghelidjh's early years

b Facts about Kids Company

c How Kids Company helps children

(i) 11,000 volunteers

(ii) provides safe houses

(iii) Iranian and Belgian parents

3 Write notes about Camila Batmanghelidjh. Put the information into chronological (time) order, if possible.

4 For each of the notes you have just written, decide if it belongs under heading a, b or c from Activity D2.

5 Compare your notes with your partner's. Have you included the same information? Check that you have both written notes rather than full sentences.

6 Imagine that your teacher has asked you to write a summary of the text about Camila Batmanghelidjh. Using your notes from Activity D4, write the summary. Use your own words as far as possible.

E 📖 Aa Reading and vocabulary

1 You are going to read about an Indian man, Nelson Suresh Kumar, who has ridden his motorcycle on the world's highest motorable (for motor vehicles) road – the Khardung La. Before you read, work with a partner and answer the following questions.

113

a Look at the map and find Chandigarh (Kumar's starting point) and the Khardung La.

b Describe Kumar's route. Which places did he travel through? Use the information on the map.

c How far do you think Kumar travelled? Chandigarh to Shimla is about 120 kilometres. Use this information to roughly calculate the distances between these places: *Shimla to Kalpa, Kalpa to Nako, Nako to Tabo, Tabo to Leh, Leh to Khardung La*. What is the approximate total distance?

d Use paper or digital references sources to check the meaning of these geographical features.

> deserts   glaciers   gorges   gravel   lakes   mountains
> mud   plains   rivers   sand dunes   slush   snow   valleys

e In the text, Kumar mentions many geographical features. Decide which ones from the list above you think you will read about. Give reasons for your choice.

f Kumar mentions only **one** animal. Do you think this will be donkey, bird, snake, camel, lizard or catfish? Give reasons for your choice.

g Kumar mentions **one** other interesting feature. Choose which one you think it will be. Give reasons for your choice.

> the world's highest battlefield   bright orange sand
> a cave village in the mountains   a telecommunications radar

2 The following words and phrases appear in the text. Use paper or digital reference sources to make sure you understand what they mean.

> accessible   biodiversity   en route   entire
> feat   fuelled his passion   resembles

3 Skim the text and check your answers to Activities E1f and E1g **only**. Do not worry about the gaps at the moment.

Riding high

Gareth Kurt Warren talks to motorcycling enthusiast Nelson Suresh Kumar about his Himalayan motorcycle diaries, riding the Khardung La, the world's highest motorable road.

[1] Welcome to the geography of superlatives: the highest mountains, the deepest gorges, and some of the greatest displays of **(a)** … on the planet. Travelling across the Himalayas is truly an adventure and a treat for adrenaline junkies. Even more so for those who decide to do it on two wheels. While motorcycle riders are often misjudged as reckless daredevils, a majority will tell you that they are passionate motoring enthusiasts who live for the joy of the ride. Nelson Suresh Kumar is one of those individuals.

[2] Before leaving his native India, Kumar rode his motorcycle across the **(b)** … country. But he didn't stop there. In 2008, he arranged (and successfully completed) a ride from Argentina to Alaska, making him the only Indian to do a Pan-American solo ride over that distance. And it was a **(c)** … that further **(d)** … .

[3] 'During the 91-day ride from South America to North America, I decided to make my hobby a business,' he says. Once back in Dubai, Kumar's current residence, he partnered with a few of his friends to start a motorcycle touring company and began organising motorcycle tours in India, Nepal and Bhutan, and then in Thailand, Sri Lanka and South Africa.

[4] One of the most popular rides is the Himalayan Mot Adventure – a ride to Khardung La in Leh, Ladakh, the highest motorable pass in the world. This mountain pass is a gateway to the famous Siachen Glacier, the second-longest glacier in the world's non-polar areas, and the world's highest battlefield.

[5] 'This route has the most beautiful valleys along with numerous mountain passes. It is also one of the most remote and thinly populated areas in the world,' says Kumar. The route to Leh is **(e)** … only for four months in a year, from June to September, since the entire area is covered in snow for the rest of the year.

[6] We start in Chandigarh and then head through Shimla. We then get off the highways and onto smaller narrow roads to Kalpa. The next day, we ride through the Spiti Valley and visit the Moon Lake Villages of Nako and Tabo, and Buddist monasteries **(f)** …', explains Kumar. The route continues through the Moree Plains. After a stop at the Leh Palace, the riders continue on to Khardung La, reaching a height of more than 5000 metres above sea level.

[7] 'You have paved roads, gravel, mountain tracks and about 30 water crossings, riding in mud, slush and snow, through deserts, valleys and lakes,' he adds. 'I have ridden half of the world, but nothing compares to this place.'

[8] Sometimes riders do not stop at Khardung La, and travel as far as the Nubra Valley in Jammu and Kashmir, about 100 kilometres from Leh. Kumar says this valley is a site worth seeing due to the sand dune deserts at 5000 metres above sea level. The Nubra valley has white sand that **(g)** … sugar and travellers can see the extremely rare and critically endangered double-humped Bactrian camels as well.

[9] When asked to describe how it feels to complete the ride to the top of the world, Kumar replies, 'I have ridden motorcycles all over the world and this place is entirely different from any place I have ever seen. It is truly amazing. I can guarantee anybody that this is the ride of their lifetime.'

Adapted from Gulf Life.

4   Read the text in more detail and check your answers to Activity E1e. Then fill in the gaps a–g using an appropriate word or phrase from Activity E2.

5   Answer the following questions about the text.

   a   Where was Kumar born?

   b   How long did the solo ride take?

   c   When did Kumar decide to start his tour company?

   d   What happened on the world's second longest glacier?

   e   Give **four** geographical features of the Himalayan Moto Adventure.

   f   Apart from geographical features, what other things can be seen on the Himalayan Moto Adventure? Name **three**.

   g   Why is the Himalayan Moto Adventure only possible during four months?

   h   What is unusual about the animal in danger of extinction?

F Writing

1   Look at this exam-style question. What exactly do you have to do? Do **not** write anything yet.

> Read the article and then write a summary of the geographical features that Kumar describes on the Himalayan Mot Adventure.

2   Scan the text on page 115 and find the relevant information to answer the question. Make written notes. Notice that the first three paragraphs do **not** refer to the Himalayan Mot Adventure, so your summary will be based on the information in the remaining paragraphs. For example:

Example: *Khardung La is highest motorable pass in the world.*
              Gateway to Siachen Glacier, second longest glacier in the non-polar world.
              Beautiful valleys with many mountain passes.

3   Discuss what you have found with your partner. Do you agree with each other?

4   Think how you are going to join the information together. Remember that you are not writing a composition, but you still need to use 'signpost words'. Which ones might be suitable for this summary (*furthermore*, for example)? Work with a partner to make a list.

5   Read this answer to the summary exam-style question, written by a student. As you read, check how many of your own ideas from Activity F2 are included. Which of the signpost words you thought of in Activity F3 are included?

> There are many geographical features on the Himalayan Mot Adventure. Firstly, Khardung La is the highest pass in the world where you can drive a vehicle and it is the entrance to the Siachen Glacier, the second-longest in the non-polar world. In addition, there are valleys and many mountain passes, but these are only open from June to September, due to the snow at other times of the year. Also, you can see deserts and lakes, as well as mountain tracks and sand dunes more than 5000 metres above sea level. Finally, the weather can be snowy, causing mud and slush. (101 words)

TOP TIPS

Read summary questions, such as F1, very carefully. Make sure you understand exactly what you have to write about. Is the question asking you to summarise the whole text, or only a part (or parts) of it? In the question here, you only need to summarise *the geographical features Kumar describes on the Himalayan Mot Adventure* – **not** the whole text.

6 Using the same text, write a summary of Kumar's ride from Chandigarh to Khardung La. Follow the guidelines below.

   a Make written notes about the key information.

   b Think about which 'signpost' words you should use to join the information together.

   c Use a short introductory sentence to start your summary.

   d Write about 100 words and no more than 120 words.

   e Use your own words as far as possible.

7 Read your partner's summary to see if they have included similar information.

G 🔊 💬 Listening and speaking

1 🔊 You are going to listen to someone briefly describing Khardung La. As you listen, answer these questions.

   a How long does it take to drive from Leh to Khardung La?

   b How is it possible to keep the roads open for vehicles?

   c When was the pass first opened?

   d Where do visitors to Khardung La have their photos taken?

2 Compare your answers with your partner's and then read the audioscript on page 199 to check.

3 Discuss these questions in small groups.

   a Would you like to visit Khardung La? Why, or why not?

   b How do you feel about so many travellers visiting places such as Khardung La? What might the result be?

   c Kumar changed his job from being a financial advisor to an organiser of motorbike adventures. Which job would you prefer? Why?

H ➕ Further practice

Write

1 Write a detailed physical description of someone you know. It could be a family member or a friend. Write 150–200 words (Extended) or 100–150 words (Core).

Read and answer

2 Read the article on page 118, then answer the questions below. Find the key word/s first and remember to keep your answers brief, but include all the necessary information.

   a For how many years have the twins been apart?

   b Why were the twins separated?

   c When did the twins begin to find out the truth about each other?

   d What did the twins find out when they first tried to meet Dr Neubauer?

   e List **two** things that Dr Neubauer tried to do when he met the twins.

   f Why can't the twins find out much information from the study?

   g Why do Paula's brother and husband feel threatened by Elyse?

Twins reunited after 35 years apart

To meet them today, you would imagine that they had known each other all their lives. They share an easy intimacy that gives the impression that identical twins Elyse Schein and Paula Bernstein did not spend their first 35 years in total ignorance of the other's existence. They were given up for adoption to separate families as part of an experiment in the US to discover how identical twins would react to being raised in different family backgrounds.

Neither set of adoptive parents knew the babies were part of a study or that they had been born twins. The research project took place under the guidance of a leading US child psychologist with the cooperation of prestigious New York adoption agency Louise Wise Services. It wasn't until Elyse Schein contacted the agency in 2003 to find out more details about her birth that the truth began to emerge.

When the agency contacted Elyse's newly discovered older sister Paula, the two women were quite quickly in touch and arranged to meet in a café in New York.

When Paula saw Elyse for the first time, she was pleased to see that, as similar as they looked, each was unique.

Having lost 35 years of shared experiences, the twins wanted to confront Dr Peter Neubauer about what had happened to them – although they discovered they had been dropped quite early on from the twins study. At first he refused to speak to them, but eventually agreed to a meeting. 'It was quite surreal,' says Paula, who recalls her twin sister's feelings that 'we were his kind of "lab rats" coming back to see the great doctor.'

'We had all these questions for him. But he was very quick to turn the tables and it was clear that he was seeing this as an opportunity to continue his study,' she says. 'He wanted to see how we turned out and question us about our development.'

Neither Paula nor Elyse feel they have received answers to all the questions they have. And the records of the study are sealed until 2066. 'It was obviously about nature versus nurture,' says Paula. 'But there were other issues that we thought they might have been interested in, one of them being the hereditary nature of mental illness.'

And from their researches, the twins have learned that their birth mother did spend part of her life in psychiatric care. Nor do the women feel that they got what they wanted from Dr Neubauer. 'I really was hoping that he would take responsibility for what he had done so many years ago,' says Elyse.

'He refuses to be open to the possibility that they were wrong,' says Paula. 'No matter what, we can't make up for the 35 years that we lost. We are different people because of being separated. We don't regret the lives we've led, but meeting each other and the difficulties that we faced in our relationship, the absurdity of having to get to know a twin, who was essentially a stranger, is very painful.'

Finding each other has been challenging, as well as joyful. 'For my husband and my brother too,' says Paula, 'you know in some ways I think it was a threat to them. My brother and I were always on an equal footing. We were both adopted and didn't know any biological siblings. And now suddenly I'm a twin. And who could be closer to someone than a twin?'

'What's funny is we've kind of come full circle,' says Elyse. 'We were initially twins, which was a biological bond, and then now I say that we've adopted each other. Now we're family by choice.'

Adapted from news.bbc.co.uk.

The photo shows Elyse Schein and Paula Bernskin, authors of Identical Strangers: A Memoir of Twins Separated and Reunited.

Important dates and times
* separated for 35 years
* ...
* ...

How the twins met
* ...
* arranged to meet in café
* ...

The twins' feelings now
* still want answers
* don't regret their lives
* ...
* ...

Write and present

3 You are going to give a talk about Elyse and Paula to your class. Copy and complete the notes on the left to use as the basis for your talk. Make **six** more points, two under each heading.

Read and summarise

4 Read the article again, then write a summary of how Elyse and Paula came to be together after being separated at birth and how they reacted when they met. Use the notes you made in Activity H3 to help you.

Exam-style questions

1 Read the following article about some of the islands in the Indian Ocean. Then complete the activity on page 120.

It's better in the

Indian Ocean...
The Maldives, Mauritius, Réunion, Seychelles

The Maldives came late to international tourism development, and have attempted to avoid many of the negative effects on the local economy and the environment seen in other parts of the world. There are strict controls on the development of resorts, and only certain of the individual islands may be developed for tourism. This, and the fact that the largest island has an area of 13 square kilometres, means that usually a single resort occupies an entire island, becoming effectively a hotel with a beach instead of walls.

Virtually all food, apart from fish, is imported and this means that prices are comparatively high. The Maldives have aimed for the top end of the tourist market and this could be both good and bad: bad because you may not be able to afford to visit; good because, if you can afford to go there, there will not be crowds of tourists going with you.

The Maldives are more sea than land, so there is an abundance of beautiful diving sites, and the country has a well-deserved reputation as one of the best diving regions in the world. If you want warm water, excellent visibility up to 50 metres and an abundance of sea life, you cannot go wrong.

However, if volcanoes are more to your liking, the volcanic islands of Mauritius and Réunion (both situated about 1000 kilometres to the east of Madagascar) offer the chance to explore beautiful beaches and lunar-like landscapes. The central plateau of Mauritius is surrounded by mountains, including Piton de la Rivière Noire (826 metres). The beaches, fringed by palm trees, offer a range of activities, from snorkelling through the coral reefs to sailing, tennis and volleyball. The climate of both islands is tropical with heavy rains in winter.

Sugar-cane plantations cover extensive areas, along with tea and tobacco on Mauritius.

Seychelles, an archipelago of more than 90 islands, is abundant in coral reefs; 40 of the islands are mountainous, and just over 50 are smaller coral islands. Only the largest islands are inhabited, and the economy depends heavily on tourism, which employs about 30% of the workforce. With the tropical climate, there is heavy rainfall but plentiful vegetation.

Area	Population	Capital
Maldives 298 km²	311,000	Malé
Mauritius 1860 km²	1,190,000	Port Louis
Réunion 2510 km²	733,000	St-Denis
Seychelles 455 km²	80,000	Victoria

Adapted from 'Impressed? It's even better underwater …' by Adam Dudding, *The Independent on Sunday.*

119

You are going to give a talk for a geography project about some of the islands in the Indian Ocean. You have decided to use information from this article in your talk. To help you plan your talk, make short notes under each of the following headings.

a Maldives: development of tourism [3]

b Maldives: scuba-diving [2]

c Mauritius and Réunion: geography [2]

d Seychelles: the islands [2]

[Total: 9]

2 Read the following article about the origins of pizza. Write a summary explaining:

- the development of pizza up to and including 1858

- the popularity of pizza today.

Your summary should be about 100 words long (and no more than 120 words).

You should use your own words as far as possible.

You will receive up to 6 marks for the content of your summary and up to 5 marks for the style and accuracy of your language.

[Total: 11]

120

Pizza, Pizza, Pizza

The origins of pizza can be traced back to the Romans, who baked a type of bread called *picea*. At the end of the first millennium and the beginning of the second, the name *pizza* had already become accepted, although the flat, round thing produced from the early medieval oven still looked very much like an ordinary flat cake. It was a long time before the genuine Neapolitan pizza with tomato sauce, anchovies, capers and mozzarella came into existence.

A recipe from 1858 describes something much more like the popular food we know as pizza today. This early recipe describes a piece of dough (the pizza 'bread') rolled out into a flat, round shape, using a rolling pin or the hands, and covered with any food available, topped with oil and then baked in an oven. The recipe also lists other ingredients, such as chopped garlic, cheese, herbs and thin slices of fish. It even mentions that the pizza dough could be folded over in half to make what we now know as *pizza calzone*, or 'sock' pizza.

For a long time, pizza remained a regional speciality. Other products from the south of Italy spread slowly but surely to the north, but pizza was slower to travel. It first made a detour to New York in the USA, where people bought the dough bread with its delicious toppings from street-vendors and ate it as a snack between meals. The first 'Neapolitan' pizzeria opened in New York in 1905. Sixty years later, pizza had become established not only in the USA, but was also eagerly eaten in northern Europe. It was only in Italy – with the exception of Naples – that pizza remained relatively unknown. This nutritious snack did not make its entrance into Rome and the northern parts of Italy until the 1970s and 1980s.

Today, however, pizza is even mentioned in *Guinness World Records*. The society of pizza-makers regularly organises competitions in which the most talented *pizzaioli* (pizza-makers) are rewarded, not only for unusual creations, but also for their sometimes acrobatic skills when throwing the thin, flat cakes of dough into the air and catching them again.

In the 21st century, pizza is eaten all over the world and has perhaps overtaken spaghetti as our idea of typical Italian food. Even in the most remote towns and villages, there is often somewhere to buy pizza and, in large cities, a whole army of pizza-delivery restaurants advertise their products. Supermarkets sell all types of frozen pizza in a wide price range and, if you want to try your skills as a *pizzaiolio*, your local market is sure to sell all the necessary ingredients. *Buon appetito!*

Adapted from *Culinaria Italy*.

Unit 11: Focus on writing skills

In this unit, we will focus on longer pieces of writing, such as articles, which require a different approach and different skills to the ones already discussed for writing informal and formal letters.

In this unit, you will also:

- talk and read about different types of activity/adventure holidays
- listen to an interview about Girl Guides and Girl Scouts
- practise writing articles and letters
- answer some exam-style questions.

A 🗨 Speaking

1   With a partner, look at the pictures below. Where do you think the people are? What are they doing? Have you ever done this type of thing? If not, would you like to?

2   Look at these icons from a web page advertising activity holidays for teenagers. What do you think the icons mean? Match each one to a picture in Activity A1.

3   Look at the second set of icons for activity-holiday destinations, then answer these questions with your partner.

a   Which continents or regions do the icons represent?
b   Try to name at least **three** countries in each continent or region.
c   Which continent or region do you live in? Where exactly?
d   Have you ever visited any of the other continents or regions? What did you do there?
e   Which continent or region do you think would be best for the holidays in Activities A1 and A2? Why?

B 📖 Reading

1. You are going to read some information about an organisation that arranges summer adventure programmes for teenagers. Before you read the texts, discuss with a partner what you know about these four destinations. If you live in one of them, talk about the others! Use paper or digital reference sources to find out **two** things about each of the four destinations. Make notes on: *location, size, population, climate, geography, fauna and wildlife,* and so on.

   a Galapagos and Ecuador
   b Leeward Islands

   c British Virgin Islands
   d Australia

2. Look at the map and identify the location of each of the four destinations in Activity B1. Hint: **three** are in the western hemisphere and **one** is in the eastern hemisphere.

3. Read this information and decide which of the four destinations each one refers to.

   a Separated from South America by the Pacific Ocean, this group of islands is an extremely important biological area.

   b Positioned right at the top of the Caribbean island chain, this group of 36 small islands is characterised by steep green hills and white-sand beaches. Around them lie the clear blue waters of the Sir Francis Drake Channel.

   c … the sixth largest country in the world. Here, you can find the world's biggest coral ecosystem – the Great Barrier Reef.

   d … scattered from the Virgin Islands, southwards to Antigua. The best-known islands of this group include St Kitts, Nevis, St Barts and St Martin.

4. Work in groups of four. You will each receive a different text about one of the holiday destinations (see page 129). Skim your text, but do not show it to the others in your group. Check your answers to Activity B3.

5   Look at these **eight** questions. You will find the answers to **two** of them in your text. Read your text again in more detail and decide which two questions you can answer. Write the answers in your notebook.

   a   What is the only living organism visible from outer space?
   b   Where can you do a wide range of water sports?
   c   Where can you find over 100 islands?
   d   Which destination includes a distance of 2000 kilometres?
   e   Which islands display both cultural and geological diversity?
   f   Which destination offers both mainland- and island-based activities?
   g   Which islands are good for sailing?
   h   Which islands are ideal for exploring?

6   In your groups of four, carry out the following activities.

   a   Tell your group which of the destinations is yours.
   b   Find out from the group the answers to the other six questions in Activity B5.

7   In your group, answer these questions.

   a   What do you think about organised activity holidays, such as the ones described in this unit? What do you think the advantages and disadvantages might be?
   b   Would you like to visit any of the four destinations described? If yes, which one/s? If not, why not?
   c   Agree with your partners on one or two more places that would be ideal as activity holiday destinations. Give reasons.

8   Find out **two** more pieces of information about the destination in your text and report back to your group. Use paper or digital reference sources to help you.

C ◀)) Listening

1   What do you know about Girl Guides and Girl Scouts (WAGGGS)? What is the purpose of the organisation? Are you a member or do you know someone who is a member of WAGGGS (or the equivalent for boys) or a similar organisation? What do its members do? Discuss with a partner.

2   In 1997, the World Association of Girl Guides and Girl Scouts joined a scheme called HARP – the Health of Adolescent Refugees Project – which is being run in three countries: Uganda, Zambia and Egypt. You are going to listen to someone from the Girl Guides being interviewed about the project. Before you listen, look at these words that are used in the talk. Discuss each word with a partner and try to agree on its meaning. Do **not** look up the meanings yet.

   a   adequate
   b   compromised
   c   counterparts
   d   curricula
   e   discriminate
   f   neglects
   g   nutritional
   h   peer
   i   preferential
   j   prevalent
   k   sanitary
   l   self-esteem
   m   transition
   n   vulnerable

3   Check the meaning of each word from Activity C2 using paper or digital reference sources.

123

4 🔊 Listen to Kigongo Odok interviewing Namono Alupo and briefly answer these questions. You do not need to write anything.

    a According to Namono Alupo, what is an adolescent?

    b How many of her peers is each girl expected to reach?

5 🔊 Listen again. As you listen, write down the words from Activity C2 in the order that you hear them. Compare your answers with a partner.

6 Work with the same partner. Each of you should write **five** questions that relate to factual information in the interview. **Student A** should use the first half of the interview and **Student B** the second half. Your teacher will tell you which part of the interview on pages 197–8 to look at. When you have written your questions, exchange them with your partner and answer each other's questions. Check each other's answers.

LANGUAGE TIP

Either is always paired with *or* and *neither* is always paired with *nor*. Both are used to show that two ideas are linked together. Notice these examples of *neither … nor* from the listening activity:

… **neither** children **nor** adults are adolescents …

… **neither** animal feed **nor** cooking fuel is always readily available.

Sometimes there is confusion about whether to have a singular or a plural verb after *either … or* and *neither … nor*, but there is a simple rule: if one or both elements are plural, use a plural verb (*are* in the first example); if both elements are singular, use a singular verb (*is* in the second example above).

D 🖊 Writing

1 These four key words have been removed from the exam-style question below: *explain*, *describe*, *suggest*, *write*. What do the words tell you to do? Do they all mean the same thing?

2 Read the exam-style question and fill in each gap with an appropriate verb from Activity D1. Then decide what you have to do to answer the question. Discuss with a partner. Do **not** write anything yet.

You have just spent a day with one of the girls involved in the HARP project.

(a) … an article for your school magazine in which you:

(b) … the girl and where she came from

(c) … what you learned during your day with her

(d) … ways in which your school and your friends could help HARP.

Your article should be 150–200 words long (Extended) or 100–150 words long (Core).

You will receive up to 10/7 marks for the content of your article and up to 9/6 marks for the style and accuracy of your language.

TOP TIPS

When writing in English, you may be asked to write an article or narrative, or to give a simple description, or to write something persuasive. It is important that you read the question very carefully and that you express yourself effectively. You should also show that you can vary the style of your writing, depending on the topic. Remember to use formal and less formal styles, as appropriate to the task.

3 Read this answer written by a student in response to the question in Exercise D2.

> The girl I met was named Fatima Jawali and she was aged 17 years old. She came here last week to explain me about the HARP project and the work she is doing there. I learned that she has been doing it for two years now and is using many different techniques as books, songs and poems. She works with girls the same age as she is, but there are different ages groups as well. When she will complete her work she will to get a badge. She is trained by a local refuge leader. When she will get the badge Fatima will to go to see her friends and explain them about the situation. She will take her books and songs and poems with her face and teach them what she learned. When she will teach 25 friends she will to get a gold certificate.

TOP TIPS
In some writing tasks, you may be given a stimulus or prompts to help you. These could be pictures or comments, often written as speech bubbles.

4 The writer of the article has made some mistakes. With a partner, identify the mistakes, but do **not** rewrite the article. Don't just think about spelling and grammar mistakes – also consider whether or not the writer has answered the question.

- Is anything missing from the answer?
- Is the layout correct?
- What about the length?
- Is there repetition?
- Does the writer use a range of vocabulary?

5 Use the notes below to write your own answer to the question in Activity D2. You may add ideas of your own, but try to include all the information the question asks for. Remember that the limit is 150–200 words for Extended (100–150 for the Core curriculum).

- Fatima Jawali, 17, tall, from small village in Uganda, three brothers, two sisters, both parents missing during recent conflicts.
- Works with HARP – learns about problems faced by refugees from Zambia and own country, such as food and hygiene issues.
- Started two years ago; uses posters, songs, poems and role plays.
- Creates flipbook which contains everything learned.
- When finished learning will go to friends and educate them using flipbook.
- Must try to reach 25 friends.
- Richer countries can help by donating funds – maybe book sale at school or sponsored car wash?

6 Exchange your writing with a partner. Use the checklist in Activity D4 to check their work.

E ◯ Speaking

1 What do you think about HARP? Do you think it is an effective way to help people who might have lost their family and belongings? Why?

2 What can you as an individual do to help people who are less fortunate than you? Would you consider joining an organisation such as HARP? Why, or why not?

125

F ➕ Further practice

Write

1   A youth group you volunteer with is trying to raise funds for charity.

Write a letter to a friend telling them about what you are doing to help. In your letter you should:

- tell your friend about your youth group
- explain why the group is trying to raise funds for charity
- describe what you are doing to help.

Your letter should be 150–200 words (Extended) or 100–150 words (Core).

The pictures above may give you some ideas and you should try to use some ideas of your own.

You will receive up to 10/7 marks for the content of your article and up to 9/6 marks for the style and accuracy of your language.

Design and present

2   Give an account of a worthy cause or a worthwhile project with which you have been involved. Explain why you became involved and what role you took. What was the outcome of your participation? Make notes and design an information leaflet about the project to present to your class.

Investigate and write

3   Find as much information as you can about Guides, Scouts or other youth movements in your country. Make notes and then write 100–150 words about one of the organisations.

Read and answer

4   Read the article on page 127 and then answer the questions below.
   a   List the **three** aims of the Soma Akriton organisation.
   b   Who oversees the activities of the organisation?
   c   How are the 150 members of Soma Akriton grouped at the moment?
   d   What particular qualities should the group's leaders possess?
   e   What equipment is used on hiking expeditions and survival excursions?
   f   Which **two** organisations have supported Soma Akriton's efforts to protect the environment?
   g   How is the civilisation of Cyprus investigated?

Soma Akriton – an independent youth group

At the beginning of 1998, a group of concerned people in Cyprus decided to set up a new organisation appealing to today's youth. The organisation's objective was to be independent, democratic and modern.

On 14th March 1998, in the Kaimakli area of Nicosia, Soma Akriton was established – its main aims being to offer knowledge and new ideas to the youth of Cyprus, to reinforce the ideals of good citizenship and to raise awareness of environmental issues. Now a flourishing organisation, whose activities are run by an elected council, Soma Akriton organises youth groups in the Nicosia area. The groups are divided by age: 6–11 years, 11–15 years, 15–18 years and over 18 years. Currently, there are five groups, with more than 150 children and young people participating in a rich and varied programme of events during the months of September to June, when the members meet every Saturday afternoon. Each group is directed by a leader and two or three assistants, all of whom have considerable experience in working with children of all ages. The leaders are all university or college graduates; they are people with high ideals and a desire to give something back to society.

Nature exploration
This involves the search for new areas of physical beauty in the mountains and along the coast of Cyprus with the aid of maps and compasses. Hiking expeditions and survival excursions take place at different times of the year, with a focus on nature study and observation.

Protection of the environment
Raising awareness and campaigning for the protection of the environment is a top priority for Soma Akriton. In recent years, the European Union has given financial support to Soma Akriton to help with its Save the Planet campaign, Recently, a successful campaign against the use of plastic bags was supported by the European Union and a campaign to encourage a more 'green' approach to consumerism was funded by the United Nations.

Civil defence
Members of Soma Akriton are trained to deal with emergencies, such as fires, accidents and earthquakes. There are special emergency teams made up of leaders and children who are equipped with first-aid kits and fire extinguishers.

Quality of life
The exploration of Cypriot civilisation, with regular visits to archaeological sites, traditional villages and museums, is the focus of 'Quality of life'. Comparisons are made with other cultures and societies to increase and improve members' understanding of how other people live. Trips to Germany and Italy, as well as participation in European Union programmes and events, all add to the aims of the 'Quality of life' activities.

General knowledge
From the Olympic Games to healthy eating, from philosophers to inventors, from sport to medicine, from games to projects, Soma Akriton's members are guaranteed a wide range of interests and activities, all designed to broaden and develop their general knowledge.

127

Exam-style questions

1 You recently took part in your school's end-of-year performance. Write a letter or email to a friend telling them about the event. In your letter/email you should:

- tell your friend what the event was and what you were doing in it

- explain what you did to prepare for the performance

- describe what happened at the event and how the audience reacted to it.

Your email should be 150–200 words long (Extended) or 100–150 words long (Core).

The pictures above may give you some ideas and you should try to use some ideas of your own.

You will receive up to 10 marks for the content of your email and up to 9 marks for the style and accuracy of your language.

2 The tourist organisation in your country is trying to encourage people not to take their holidays abroad. Here are some comments that have been made in letters to an online newspaper.

Write an article for your school magazine, giving your views.

> If more of us took our holidays here, it would create more jobs and improve the local economy.

> Staying here does nothing to improve our awareness of the rest of the world.

Your article should be 150–200 words long (Extended) or 100–150 words long (Core).

The comments above may give you some ideas and you should try to use some ideas of your own.

You will receive up to 10 marks for the content of your email and up to 9 marks for the style and accuracy of your language.

Texts for Section B Reading Activity 4

TEXT 1: British Virgin Islands

Situated in the western hemisphere, the British Virgin Islands are the perfect destination for both sailing and diving. Positioned right at the top of the Caribbean island chain, this group of 36 small islands is characterised by steep green hills and white-sand beaches. Around them lie the clear blue waters of the Sir Francis Drake Channel. This stunning environment is perfect for a wide range of water sports – that's why we offer our widest variety of adventure training programmes here.

TEXT 2: The Leeward Islands of the Caribbean

Situated in the western hemisphere, the Leeward Islands are scattered from the Virgin Islands, southwards to Antigua. The best-known islands of this group include St Kitts, Nevis, St Barts and St Martin. Although they cover a small geographic area, the islands reveal great geological and cultural diversity, with a great variety of customs, languages and currencies. Some islands are green and mountainous, others are dry and flat. This adventure programme offers longer-distance sailing for both beginners and experienced sailors, and you'll have many opportunities for exploring!

TEXT 3: Galapagos and Ecuador

Situated in the western hemisphere, the Galapagos archipelago – comprising more than 100 islands – was formed about 4 million years ago. Separated from South America by the Pacific Ocean, this group of islands is an extremely important biological area. Among the amazing animals you can see here are giant tortoises, penguins, iguanas and sea lions. Our adventure is shared between the mainland of Ecuador and the Galapagos islands. The programme includes eco-tours of the rainforest, white-water expeditions and community service projects.

TEXT 4: Australia

Situated in the eastern hemisphere, Australia is the sixth largest country in the world. Here, you can find the world's biggest coral ecosystem – the Great Barrier Reef. Stretching roughly 2000 kilometres, the reef is the only living organism that can be seen from outer space and is the ideal setting for many of our adventure activities. Our Australian Expedition will take you from Sydney in the south to Cape Tribulation in the north. Along the way, you'll enjoy diving, trekking, sailing, surfing and community service.

In this unit, we will focus on the specific skills you need for responding to multiple-choice and note-completion questions.

In this unit, you will also:

- talk about nurses and paramedics
- listen to a discussion about Florence Nightingale
- read about how to become a paramedic
- listen to a talk about the ICRC – the International Committee of the Red Cross/Crescent
- answer some exam-style questions.

A ◯ Speaking

1 This unit focuses on people who work in healthcare, especially nurses and nursing: the job, the history of the profession, and so on. Look at the pictures and, with a partner, make a list of as many words and phrases as possible connected with the topic.

Examples: *injection, looking after people, …*

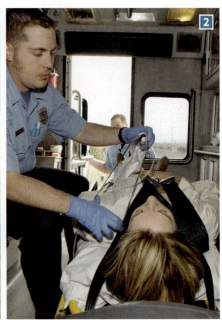

2 Look at this list of phrases that describe what nurses do. With your partner, check the meanings. Use paper or digital references sources to help you.

- **a** provide care
- **b** restore health
- **c** alleviate suffering
- **d** diagnose and treat illnesses
- **e** prescribe and dispense medicines
- **f** perform surgery
- **g** promote health
- **h** prevent illness

3 Quickly skim the paragraph below. Find the phrases from Activity A2 and check that you have understood them correctly.

Nurses care for the sick and injured in hospitals, where they work to restore health and alleviate suffering. Many people are sent home from the hospital when they still need nursing care, so nurses often provide care in the home that is very similar to the care they give to patients in the hospital. In clinics and health centres in communities that have few doctors, nurses diagnose and treat common illnesses, prescribe and dispense medications and even perform minor surgery. Nurses are also increasingly working to promote people's health and to prevent illness in all communities.

4   What do you know about paramedics? What do they do? How does their job differ from what nurses do?

5   Look at the words in the box. Work with a partner and make sure you understand what they mean. Use paper and digital reference sources to help you.

ambulance   care   casualties   emergency   incidents   patient

6   🔊 You are going to hear a brief talk about the work of a paramedic. As you listen, complete the notes using an appropriate word from the box in Activity A5.

> *Paramedics respond to (a) … medical calls.*
>
> *Assess condition of (b) … and give treatment and (c) … before hospital admission.*
>
> *Unexpected situations may include injuries and sudden illness, as well as road (d) … and other (e) … .*
>
> *Some paramedics work alone.*

7   Read the audioscript on page 198 to check your answers.

8   Using words and phrases from the previous activities, talk to your partner about the differences between the job of a nurse and the job of a paramedic.

131

B 🔊 Listening

1   Florence Nightingale is one of the most famous nurses in history. Work with a partner and write down **at least three** things that you know about her. Use the picture to help you.

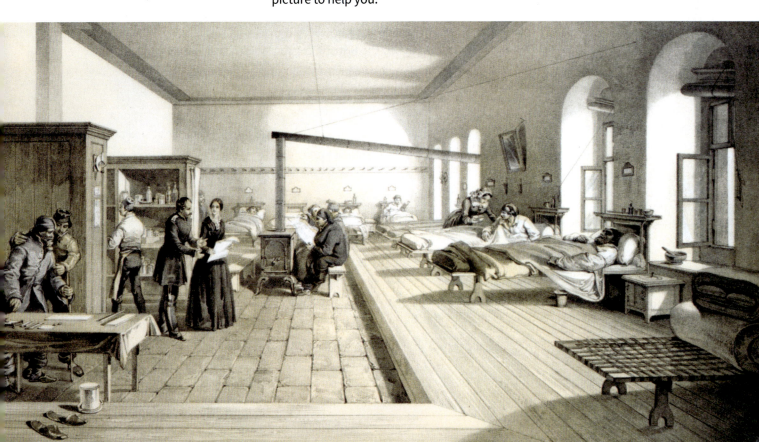

2 Look at the following information about Florence Nightingale. With your partner, decide if the information is true or false.

a Florence Nightingale was born in Florence, Italy.

b Her parents refused to allow her to become a nurse.

c She completed a three-month nurse training course in Germany.

d The British government asked her to work in British military hospitals in Turkey.

e Florence Nightingale received a medal for her nursing work.

f When she died, Florence had been blind for 15 years.

3 You will hear John, a nursing student, asking Dr Mary Winterson, a specialist in nursing, some questions about Florence Nightingale. Before you listen, look at the multiple-choice questions below. With your partner, try to work out which of the three answers is correct – A, B or C. Give reasons for your choices.

a When was Florence Nightingale born?

   A 1812   B 1820   C 1822

b At school, Florence performed …

   A well   B below average   C very poorly.

c Why was Florence not allowed to become a nurse?

   A She was sent to Europe.

   B She wanted to get married.

   C It was not considered appropriate for her.

d Why did Florence travel to Europe with friends?

   A Because of the war.

   B Because of an argument with her parents.

   C She wanted to find a job.

e How many countries did she travel to in 1850?

   A 3   B 4   C 5

f What caused the British Government to send Florence to Turkey?

   A Inadequate medical facilities for soldiers.

   B The number of wounded soldiers.

   C The defeat of the Russians.

g What did the doctors think about the arrival of nurses in military hospitals?

   A They showed their gratitude.

   B They thought the nurses were heroines.

   C They were unsure.

h What did Florence Nightingale do after she received her medal?

   A She retired.

   B She wrote books.

   C She carried on with her work.

TOP TIPS

In multiple-choice questions, there is only **one** correct answer! Usually, one of the other choices is completely wrong and the other choice is there to distract you – it seems as if it could be right, but it isn't! It is a good strategy to guess possible answers to the question in your head and then look at the choices.

4 Now listen to John and Dr Mary Winterson and check your answers to Activities B2 and B3.

LANGUAGE TIP

Look at this phrase from the talk about Florence Nightingale: *the expectation was that she would marry and start a family*. The first part – *the expectation was that* – is about past events (**X**), but *she would marry and start a family* (**X**) moves forward in time:

| Past | Present | Future |

This use of *would* (as the past tense of *will*) is often referred to as 'future in the past'. It is used to express the idea that in the past you thought that something else would happen in the future. It does not matter if you are correct or not. Both *was/were going to* and the past continuous can also be used to express the future in the past:

*When the doctors heard that Florence Nightingale **was going** to work with them, they felt threatened.*

*The doctors felt threatened when they knew she **was coming** to work with them.*

Florence Nightingale

Born: Florence, Italy

School studies: (a) …

Teenage years: visited sick people and investigated (b) …

Nursing in 19th century not (c) …

In 1850, travelled with friends to Italy, (d) …, (e) … and (f) …

Started work in a clinic in London in (g) …

Went to Turkey in 1854 with (h) …

Nurses eventually accepted by Scutari doctors because of (i) …

In 1907, awarded a (j) …

Became (k) … in 1895

5 How much can you remember? Work with a partner and complete the notes on the left.

6 🔊 Listen again and check your answers.

C 📖 Reading

1 How much can you remember about the work of a paramedic? Match the sentence halves.

Example: *3 + e Paramedics provide an immediate response to emergency medical calls.*

1	A paramedic will attend emergencies, including minor injuries, sudden illness,	a	with the other crew member being an ambulance technician or emergency care assistant who helps them.
2	They are usually in a two-person ambulance crew,	b	using an emergency response car, motorbike or bicycle to get to a patient.
3	~~Paramedics provide an immediate response~~	c	and they are responsible for assessing the condition of a patient and providing treatment and care prior to hospital admission.
4	Some will work alone however,	d	and casualties arising from road and rail accidents, criminal violence, fires and other incidents.
5	They are usually the first senior healthcare professional on the scene,	e	~~to emergency medical calls.~~

2 Put the five sentences into the same order as the paragraph in Activity A6. The first sentence is *Paramedics provide an immediate response to emergency medical calls.* Compare your order with your partner's, then look again at the text on page 131 to see if you are right.

3 You are going to read an internet article about the entry requirements and training for young people who want to become paramedics. What would you like to find out? Write **three** questions.

Example: *What subjects do I need to study to become a paramedic?*

133

4   Read the text below. Were your questions answered?

A career as a paramedic

Entry requirements and training

This page outlines the entry requirements and training to become a paramedic. Anyone wishing to work as a paramedic needs to either secure a student paramedic position with an ambulance service trust, or attend an approved full-time course in paramedic science at a university.

Traditionally, staff joining the ambulance service could work their way up, with experience and additional training from care assistant, through ambulance technician to paramedic. However, this route is no longer open to new entrants.

A Entry requirements

Entry requirements for student paramedic positions will vary, depending upon the employer. The range of paramedic science courses at university varies in terms of entry requirements, but a minimum of five GCSEs (including English, Mathematics and/or a science) plus at least two A Levels or equivalent qualifications is typically needed. However, it is essential that you contact each university directly for information on its admissions policy and entry requirements. You can use our course finder to find courses.

You'll also need a full, manual driving licence. Ambulance services use vehicles of different gross weights and staff will be required to hold a driving licence with the appropriate classifications.

B Training

To practise as a paramedic, you must be registered with the Health and Care Professions Council (HCPC). In order to register with the HCPC, you must successfully complete an HCPC-approved programme in paramedic science.

Courses tend to be modular, with flexible entry and exit points, depending upon your academic qualifications and any relevant experience. They last from two to five years, depending on whether you study full- or part-time. It's important to check entry requirements with the university concerned and with the ambulance service trust/s in the areas where you want to work.

C Applying for paramedic training

Students applying for full-time university courses usually need to apply through the Universities and Colleges Admissions Service (UCAS). Those already working as student paramedics (or qualified ambulance technicians where these posts still exist) should speak to their employing ambulance service about applications for part-time courses.

D Funding for paramedic training

Students on full-time courses in paramedic science are not eligible for financial support through the National Health Service (NHS) Bursary Scheme. However, in some cases there may be local funding arrangements between the NHS and some universities, so you are advised to contact universities directly to enquire about these. In many ambulance trusts, student paramedics receive a salary whilst training on the job. For further information on the funding available, please contact the individual ambulance service trust within your region.

Adapted from www.nhscareers.nhs.uk

5   Read the article again, then answer these questions in your notebook. Compare your answers with your partner's.

   a   What does someone who wants to work as a paramedic need to do?

   b   Which route to becoming a paramedic is no longer available?

   c   Which **two** subjects are essential qualifications?

   d   Apart from academic qualifications, what is also essential?

   e   How can you register with the HCPC?

   f   How long does a paramedic science course last?

   g   Who is not eligible to receive financial assistance from the NHS?

D ◯ Speaking

1   Look the picture. What do the letters ICRC stand for?

2   What types of assistance do you think the ICRC provides? To whom? Where in the world would you expect the organisation to operate?

3   You are going to listen to someone being interviewed who works for the ICRC. Before you listen, look at these words and phrases taken from the interview. What do they mean? Discuss them with a partner. Use paper or digital reference sources to help you.

   a   relief workers

   b   victims of famine and drought

   c   instability

   d   insecure

   e   ethnic

   f   foundations

   g   hygiene

   h   veterinary care

   i   priorities

   j   waterborne

4   Here are some of the questions the interviewer asks. What do you think the interviewee's answers might be? Discuss your ideas with a partner.

   a   Can you tell us about how the ICRC assists victims of famine and drought, and other natural disasters?

   b   What about healthcare? Isn't that a priority?

   c   Does the ICRC only assist when there is a crisis?

   d   Is it dangerous working for the ICRC?

E 🔊 Listening

1 🔊 Listen to the interview and check your answers to the questions in Activity D4.

2 🔊 Listen to the interview again and complete the notes below. Write one or two words in each gap.

✚ Number of relief workers: 1200.

✚ ICRC helps victims of **(a)** … and **(b)** … and other natural disasters.

✚ Natural disasters often happen at same time as other problems, for example **(c)** … and **(d)** … .

✚ ICRC help adapts to different contexts: geographic, **(e)** … , **(f)** … and **(g)** … .

✚ In the 'Assistance Pyramid', preference is given to **(h)** … , **(i)** … and **(j)** … first.

✚ Second place **(k)** … .

✚ Third place **(l)** … .

✚ ICRC also gives assistance to both **(m)** … and **(n)** … a disaster.

✚ This is done by distributing **(o)** … and **(p)** … and providing medical help with animals.

✚ Water is often unhealthy and carries diseases, such as **(q)** … and **(r)** … .

✚ ICRC programme of assistance includes **(s)** … and **(t)** … , as well as access to water and hygiene, and environmental protection.

✚ ICRC workers have these qualities: motivated by **(u)** … and can cope with **(v)** … .

3 Check your answers with a partner. If you are unsure, read the audioscript on page 199.

F ○ Speaking

1   What do you know about the ICRC now? Without looking at your notes, tell your partner about the organisation.

2   Answer these questions in pairs.

   a   People who work for the ICRC need to be prepared to leave for any destination in the world at a moment's notice. How would you feel about being in that position? Would you find it exciting or frightening? Why?

   b   Do you think you could work for an organisation like the ICRC? Why, or why not?

   c   What might be some of the advantages and disadvantages of that kind of life?

   d   The ICRC employs people who are mentally mature, motivated and who have potential for personal development. Does that description fit you or anybody you know? Why, or why not?

   e   What motivates people who work for the ICRC? Can you think of anyone who might be suited to work for the ICRC?

G ⊕ Further practice

Write

1   Write a letter to the ICRC, informing the head of the Human Resources department that you would like to be considered as a relief worker. Include in your letter information about your qualifications, as well as your personal abilities. Write 150–200 words (Extended) or 100–150 words (Core).

Speak and write

2   Work in pairs.

   Student A: Give a spoken account of a natural disaster that you have experienced or that you have followed in the news.

   Student B: Listen to Student A's account of a natural disaster and make notes on the important points.

   Now swap roles. Afterwards, write up your notes into a short summary of about 100 words.

Listen and present

3   Listen to the news in English on the radio or television. As you listen or watch, make some notes about **at least two** items of news that interest you. Then design a PowerPoint presentation, using your notes for the content.

Complete

4 Imagine that you want to attend a course leading to a Diploma in Nursing, or a Certificate in First Aid. Copy and complete the application form below.

Application form

1 Personal details

Course applied for: _____

Family name (please write in block capitals): _____

Given name: _____

Sex (please tick box): Female ☐ Male ☐

Date of birth: _____

Full address: _____

Postcode: _____

Email: _____

Mobile tel.: _____

2 Academic background

Is English your first language? (please tick box): Yes ☐ No ☐

If 'No', what is your first language? _____

Schools attended (please list two, starting with the most recent):

1 _____

2 _____

List any certificates or qualifications you hold:

1 _____

2 _____

3 _____

4 _____

Please tell us why you wish to follow this course.

Do not write more than about 50 words.

_____

_____

_____

_____

_____

_____

_____

🔊 Exam-style questions

Listening Part A

You will hear an expert giving a talk about problems with traffic. Listen to the talk and complete the notes in Part A. Write only one or two words in each gap. You will hear the talk twice.

Part A

The cause

Road-traffic accidents are just one problem; the other is … from traffic.

The problem is greatest in … countries.

1.5 billion people suffer from excess levels of pollution daily.

The damage

Young people's health and also … potential affected.

Cars increase problems for poor people, as deaths and injuries occur mainly to pedestrians, cyclists, bus users and children.

Their levels of education, health, water and … , as cars take economic priority over people.

The solution

Reallocation of … in South America has improved lives of poorer people.

Solution should be repeated all over the world.

[5 marks]

Listening Part B

Now listen to a conversation between two students about problems with traffic and complete the sentences in Part B. Write only one or two words in each gap. You will hear the talk twice.

Part B

Information about problems with traffic

In the UK, death from road accidents has fallen by nearly … since 2000.

For every 100,000 people in some … , more than 40 people die on the roads.

Deaths involve … , cyclists and motorcyclists.

These are the … road users who are more at risk.

More emphasis needed on bicycle- and people-only paths and roads.

In many places, banning cars has resulted in more people going … .

[5 marks]

139

Part 4:
Ideas and the modern world

Unit 13: Focus on reading skills

In this unit, we will focus once again on the skills you need when reading texts such as brochures, leaflets and guides, as well as newspaper and magazine articles. These types of texts often require you to skim-read, as well as to read for more detailed understanding.

In this unit, you will also:

- discuss and read about social media sites
- create and describe graphs
- talk about mobile-phone technology
- answer some exam-style questions.

A 🗨 Speaking

1   Look at this graph, which shows the results for a question put to teenagers. Work with a partner and answer the questions below.

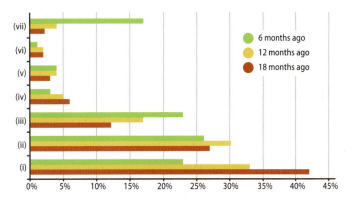

a   Which question (i–iii) do you think the graph shows the results for?

(i) How many types of social networks are there for teens?

(ii) Which social network is best for teens?

(iii) How often do teens use social networks?

b   What do the numbers in the *y* axis represent? And in the *x* axis?

c   What do you think the seven sets of data (i-vii) represent?

d   Why are there **three** coloured horizontal lines in each set of data? What does each colour represent?

2   The seven sets of data represent: Facebook, Google+, Instagram, 'others', Pinterest, Tumblr and Twitter. Discuss the following questions in small groups.

a   Which set of data corresponds to which social network? For example (i) = Facebook and (iv) = Google+.

b   Does this surprise you? Why, or why not?

c   Do you use any of these social networks? If so, which ones and why? If you do not use them, why not?

d   What other social networks do you know for the 'other' category?

e   What are the advantages and disadvantages of social networking?

3   You are going to read an internet article about social networks for teenagers. Before you read the article, work with a partner and decide if these four statements are true or false. Give reasons.

a   Teens rated Twitter the 'most important' social media network, with Facebook and Instagram close behind.

b   Last year, Facebook was rated the most important by 42% of teens.

c   This year, Facebook was rated the most important site by only 23% of teens.

d   Teens told researchers they dislike Facebook because of 'drama', too many adult users and other users 'over-sharing'.

B 📖 Reading

1 Quickly skim the internet article below and see if your ideas about the statements in Activity A3 were correct.

Twitter overtakes Facebook

as the most popular social network for teens, according to study

[1] Mark Zuckerberg admitted it and a new study has proved it: Facebook is no longer cool with teens. The semi-annual 'Taking Stock with Teens' study indicated that Twitter has overtaken Facebook as the most important social media network. Last year, 42% of teens rated Facebook as the most important social media network, while this year only 23% rated it as the most influential. Twitter was rated by 26% of teens as their 'most important' social media site. Not to be outdone, the Facebook-owned Instagram also garnered 23% of votes, up from 12% last year.

[2] The study, by investment firm Piper Jaffray, gathers information relating to teen spending patterns, fashion trends, and brand and media preferences. Another study, Pew's Teens, Social Media and Privacy report, had similar findings. Pew's focus groups said the popularity of Facebook is waning because of parental and adult use of the site, other users 'over-sharing' and 'drama' that can erupt between Facebook 'friends'. According to Pew's research, despite its lack of 'cool', teens continue to use Facebook because 'participation is an important part of overall teenage socializing.'

The study also noted that teens have an average of 300 Facebook friends, but only 79 Twitter followers.

[3] 'I got mine [Facebook account] around sixth grade. And I was really obsessed with it for a while. Then towards eighth grade, things changed. Once you get into Twitter, if you make Twitter and Instagram accounts, then you'll just kind of forget about Facebook. That's what I did,' one teen told Pew researchers.

[4] Zuckerberg himself may concur with teens who think Facebook is no longer cool.

'People assume that we're trying to be cool. It's never been my goal. I'm the least cool person there is! We're almost ten years old, so we're definitely not a niche thing any more, so that kind of angle for coolness is done for us,' he said in September. Instead of being cool, he wants Facebook to be a tool people use every day, 'like electricity'.

[5] 17% responded in the category marked 'other', and this indicates that other niche social media sites, such as SnapChat and Vine, are taking off in a big way with teens.

Adapted from
www.dailymail.co.uk

2 Find words or phrases in the article that have a similar meaning to the following.

    a important or significant (paragraph 1)

    b not wanting to be beaten (1)

    c won or gained (1)

    d fanatical or passionate (3)

    e agree (4)

    f special product (4)

3 What do the following numbers in paragraph 1 refer to?

    Example: *42 is the percentage of teens who rated Facebook as the most important social media.*

    ~~42~~   23   26   23 (again)   12

4 Answer these questions about the article.

a How much more popular in percentage points is Twitter than Facebook this year?

b Which two social media sites are joint second in popularity after Twitter?

c What **four** things does Piper Jaffray collect information about?

d Why is Facebook's popularity decreasing among teenagers? Give **three** reasons.

e Why do teens still use Facebook?

f What does Zuckerberg compare Facebook to?

g Which sites does the article say are becoming more popular now?

5 Look again at the graph in Activity A1. Using only the most recent data (the data in green), redesign the graph. Think carefully about what to put on the *y* and *x* axes.

6 Using your new graph, answer these questions.

a Which social media site is about 10 percentage points less popular than Twitter?

b Which **two** pairs of social media sites (four in total) are similar in popularity?

c Which media sites have a combined popularity of about eight percentage points?

d What is the combined percentage of the first and the fourth most popular social media sites?

e Without Pinterest, Google+ and Tumblr, what would the percentage points for 'other' be?

TOP TIPS

When answering questions that refer to a chart or a table, or some other graphic, make sure that you look carefully at the information in the graphic, including what the two axes represent, as well as the title. Look for questions that start with the words *According to the diagram …*

See the Language Tip on page 145 for more information about *According to …*

C ✏ Writing

1 Which nouns in the box have similar meanings?

> a decrease   a rise   a reduction   a decline   a peak
> a drop   a fall   a dip   an increase

2 All the nouns have the same form when used as verbs – except one. Which one?

3 Which phrases in the box have similar meanings?

> reach a peak   remain the same   fall to the lowest point
> remain stable   remain constant

4 Complete the words to make adverbs.

Example: *sharp… = sharply*

a consider…

b stead…

c slight…

d gradual…

e relative…

5 Now change each adverb from Activity C4 into an adjective.

Example: *sharply = sharp*

6 Use the following data to design a line graph. Think carefully about what to put on the *y* and *x* axes.

Most important social media sites for teens			
	18 months ago	12 months ago	6 months ago
'other'	2%	4%	17%
Instagram	12%	17%	23%
Twitter	27%	30%	26%
Facebook	42%	33%	23%

7 Write **six** sentences describing the information in your graph. Use as many of the words and phrases from Activities C1 to C4 as possible in your description.

Examples: *The popularity of Facebook fell sharply from 42% to 23%.*
'Other' media sites have increased since …

8 Compare your writing with a partner's. Are any of your sentences the same?

D 🗨 Aa Speaking and vocabulary

1 Work with a partner. You are going to read a leaflet about cell (mobile) phones. Before you read the leaflet, make a list of all the things that you can do with a mobile phone. How many different functions can you think of?

Example: *send or receive text messages*

2 Match each verb in column A with a suitable noun or noun phrase in column B. There are several possible answers.

A: Verbs	B: Nouns/noun phrases
chat, get, integrate, keep, make (x2), make and receive, play, send or receive (x3), set, store, use (x2), watch	contact information, email, games, information from the Internet, other devices, phone calls, photos, reminders, task or to-do lists, text messages, the built-in calculator, the MP3 player and GPS receiver, track of appointments, TV, videos, with other users

3 How many of the functions from Activity D2 did you think of in Activity D1?

4 Quickly read the short text below and check your answers to Activity D2.

What can a mobile phone do for you?

Nowadays, for many of us, life without a mobile phone is unthinkable. The thought of being cut off from friends and family, as well as not being able to do all the things that the modern-day phone gives us access to, is frightening for a lot of people. So, if you were without a phone, what exactly wouldn't you be able to do? In alphabetical order … chat with other users, get information from the Internet, integrate other devices, keep track of appointments, make task or to-do lists, make videos, play games, send or receive email, send or receive text messages, send or receive photos, set reminders, store contact information, use the built-in calculator, use the MP3 player and GPS receiver, and watch TV. What have I forgotten? Oh yes, of course: make and receive phone calls!

LANGUAGE TIP

In this unit, you have seen these two expressions: *According to* (Pew's research) … and *Depending on* (the cell-phone model) … . Both can have several meanings, depending on their context.

In *According to* (Pew's research) … , we are being told where the information or ideas have come from (Pew's research). In *Depending on* (the cell-phone model) … , we understand that one thing (in this case the things you can do on your mobile phone) is changed or affected by something else (the cell-phone model).

See the **Top Tips** on page 143 for another example of *According to* … .

---

5 You are going to read a second, longer text from an internet article about the future of smartphones. Before you read, talk to your partner about how you think the next generation of mobile phones will improve.

E 📖 Reading

1 Quickly skim the text below and find out which **two** developments are discussed. Are they the same as any of the ideas you talked about in Activity D5?

Future of smartphones

How will the next generation of mobile phones improve?

[1] The speed of the mobile phone's technological development is scary. Not so long ago, sending a text message was mind-blowing. Now, we can speak directly to our smartphones and ask them for the latest weather forecast, or take a high-definition video and upload it to the Internet in a matter of seconds – and we think nothing of it. So, what are the key areas that the mobile industry is looking to develop in the next generation of phones? Let's look at two …

[2] The next major battleground for all portable computing devices is battery life. All high-end smartphones can now do just about everything we need them to do. Performance is the same, or nearly the same, for all phones, and your operating system of choice will be dictated largely by personal preference and the availability of apps and media, as well as price. But which of us can honestly say they are happy with the battery life of their handset?

[3] Because mobile batteries struggle to last a full day, this results in having to travel with chargers and adaptors and spare batteries (where possible), and rationing use of the phone, which negates the point of having a great smartphone. The trouble is, batteries are measured in terms of the physical size of the cell itself and we all want slim, light handsets. So, although battery capacity will continue to increase, improvement in battery life will come from two other trends.

[4] For one thing, software and processors will continue to become less power hungry. By definition, this should improve battery life. The other trend we can expect is a second tier of smartphones, dedicated to providing the essentials and no more, but staying alive for days – if not weeks. For most people, email, social media and the web are the critical functions of their smartphone. Hardware manufacturers will recognise this and build souped-up feature phones, so you won't own just the one phone. You will carry one device such as this for critical functions – especially when travelling – and use your iPhone or Android as a personal entertainment, communication and navigation device.

[5] Smartphones are an expensive, good-looking and, therefore, highly desirable, piece of kit. And it's this desirability that makes them so attractive to thieves. So what steps can we expect manufacturers to take over the next few years to ensure our devices and our personal details remain secure?

[6] One approach being looked at is a 'kill switch' (an emergency safety switch), which cannot be deleted from the phone's operating system. This will deter phone theft and, because it is becoming such a popular idea, we can expect this option to be included on all handsets very soon.

[7] But what other security features will we see? Most of us (and if you don't, you should) have to input a PIN to access our devices, but manufacturers are looking at alternatives. In the next few years, we can expect to see the widespread use of fingerprint recognition. And, even though we're still in the early days of voice recognition software, it's only a matter of time before this will be extended from asking your handset for directions and searching the web to unlocking your device.

Adapted from www.pcadvisor.co.uk

2 Work in pairs. **Student A** looks at words and phrases in the left-hand box. **Student B** looks at the words and phrases in the right-hand box. Use paper or digital reference sources to help you to understand the meaning of the words and phrases *as they are used in the text*.

Student A	**Student B**
a mind-blowing (paragraph 1)	h second tier (4)
b battleground (2)	i critical functions (4)
c dictated (2)	j souped-up feature phones (4)
d negates the point (3)	k desirable (5)
e trends (3)	l piece of kit (5)
f power hungry (4)	m deter (6)
g By definition (4)	n widespread (7)

3 Exchange ideas with your partner. Make sure you both understand both sets of words and phrases.

4 Read the text in more detail, then answer these questions.

   a How many examples are given of mobile-phone technology that we take for granted?

   b According to the article, what determines our choice of mobile phone? List **three** things.

   c What is the result of mobile-phone batteries having a short life?

   d What do phone users prefer to longer battery life?

   e How will the second tier of mobile phones differ from the first tier?

   f Why are smartphones so attractive to thieves?

   g How do you think a 'kill switch' works?

   h **Two** alternatives are given to PIN as security features. What are they?

F ◯ Speaking

1 Work in small groups and discuss these questions.

   a What do you think about the two developments in mobile-phone technology discussed in the text?

   b Which of the two developments do you think is the most important? Why?

   c If you could only choose one of the two, which would it be? Why?

2 The article on mobile phones goes on to discuss other developments, one of which is *flexible screens* ('a foldable smartphone that doubles as a tablet is a very real possibility'). What would be the advantages of having a smartphone with a flexible screen? What might be the disadvantages?

3 Now that you know about three developments in mobile-phone technology, how do you feel? Excited? Disappointed? Bored? Why? If you could only choose one of the three, which would it be? Why?

4 If you could have any new development on your phone, what would it be and why? Make some written notes and then share your ideas with your group.

G ⊕ Further practice

Listen

1   🔊 In this unit, you have read about developments in mobile-phone technology. Now listen to a student talking about another possible development and then answer the questions. For each question, choose the correct answer – A, B or C.

a   What will wearable devices be powered by?
   A   A heart-rate monitor.
   B   Your smartphone.
   C   A server.

b   What is the current problem with wearable technology?
   A   It is small.
   B   It is expensive.
   C   Meeting power requirements.

c   Why won't wearable devices need cellular connectivity?
   A   Because the phone will provide power.
   B   Because the phone will be the brain.
   C   Because they have their own power.

d   How will a wearable device connect to a smartphone?
   A   Via friends.
   B   Via Bluetooth or Wi-Fi.
   C   Via the cell.

e   As wearable technology develops, so will …
   A   the size of phones
   B   the screen resolution
   C   smartphones.

f   What is the solution to small screens on smartphones?
   A   Make them bigger.
   B   Beam information to a television.
   C   Use a computer.

g   Describe the relationship between the two speakers.
   A   Formal.
   B   Work colleagues.
   C   Informal.

Write

2   Mobile-phone technology is changing rapidly. Here are some comments that you have heard.

> The uses of the smartphone are changing rapidly – soon we really won't be able to live without them!

> New technology will mean our smartphones will be used for many more things, not just the everyday functions we are so used to.

147

Write an article for your school webpage giving your views. Your article should be 150–200 words long (Extended) or 100–150 words long (Core).

The comments on page 147 may give you some ideas and you should try to use some ideas of your own.

You will receive up to 10/7 marks for the content of your article and up to 9/6 marks for the style and accuracy of your language.

Describe

3   In Section C of this unit, you practised describing information in graphical form. Look at the three graphs and charts on this page, then answer the questions for each one.

a   The pie chart shows the results of a school's survey into which device students preferred to play games on.

   (i) Apart from 'other', what are the **two** least popular devices?

   (ii) What is the combined total of the top **two** devices?

b   The bar graph shows the results of a shopping survey to find out what people prefer to buy online.

   (i) Which items have (a) the smallest percentage difference and (b) the greatest percentage difference between online and in-shop purchases?

   (ii) How many items are more likely to be bought in a shop than online?

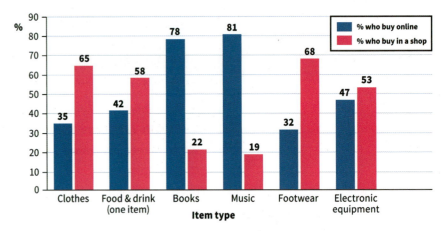

c   The line graph on the left shows global sales of internet devices.

   Write sentences describing:

   (i)   the sales of tablets during the last five years

   (ii) the growth of personal computer sales from 2000 to 2010

   (iii) the sales of smartphones from 2005 to 2009 compared with 2009 to the present day.

Read and present

4   Read the article opposite about the health hazards of computer games, then carry out the following activities.

a   Use paper and digital reference sources to investigate the topic further.

b   Using the information in the article and your own research, create a short PowerPoint presentation with the title: *Computer games – health hazards*.

c   Present your work to the class.

Computer games
health hazards

Doctors are becoming increasingly concerned about the health of children who spend hour after hour glued to computer games. The experts say that young people are exposing themselves to a range of potential hazards, from 'mouse elbow' to 'joystick digit'.

As many as 20% of children have some kind of health problem associated with the overuse of computer games, a recent survey has shown. One in seven children spends so much time in front of video screens that they have black rings around their eyes because of lack of sleep, say the doctors, who interviewed over 1100 children aged six to 11 and their parents. One in five children showed evidence of stiff muscles in their back and shoulders – a result of the strain from the constant use of a computer mouse or video-game joystick.

This study is the most recent in a series of reports that link health problems with excessive use of video and computer

games. All the problems result from repetitive movements and sleep deprivation, and some experts predict that overuse of games could cause long-term heart damage.

'Mouse elbow' is the result of damage to the forearm and elbow. The elbow can also suffer trauma injury if the mouse is moved too vigorously. 'Video eyes' are caused by too little sleep. 'Joystick digit' is a consequence of overuse of the finger on the joystick. 'Vibration finger' is caused by excessive use of computer-game controllers which vibrate. 'Nerve trap' is the result of the neck and head being in the same position for too long.

149

Exam-style questions

1 Read the leaflet below (which is aimed mainly at Western tourists), then answer the questions that follow.

Weekend holiday break
for all the family!

Middle East – Bahrain, Jordan, Kuwait, Lebanon, Oman, Qatar, Saudi Arabia, United Arab Emirates and Yemen

The mysteries of the East are waiting for you: from the ancient cities of Petra in Jordan to the oases in Saudi Arabia, there's always plenty to see and explore, and new experiences to be savoured.

For those seeking a holiday at any time of the year, the stunning beaches of Dubai in the United Arab Emirates are the place to be. Abu Dhabi is a modern city overflowing with wealth and vitality. Look for bargains in the gold market and why not experience camel racing?

Things to do and see

Jordan – Petra, spice route between Petra and Gaza
Oman – National Museum
Saudi Arabia – souks and markets
United Arab Emirates – gold market and souks, fine beaches, camel racing

Muscat is in the heart of Oman, a place to unwind and relax. Explore the fascinating castles, architectural sites, beaches and the old Muttrah souk and discover more about Omani life in the city's National Museum.

Africa – Egypt, Eritrea, Gabon, Kenya, Morocco and Tunisia

The spice and variety of Africa are sure to appeal to everyone.

In Egypt, visit the land of the ancient pharaohs, follow the Nile from Cairo and be sure not to miss the pyramids. Both the resorts of Sharm El Sheikh and Hurghada allow you to relax on the fine beaches. Try scuba diving and experience for yourself the beauty of the underwater world.

Morocco is full of Eastern promise. Go to the markets and bargain for jewellery, carpets and rugs, and a whole selection of beautiful items. Casablanca is a modern city with a traditional Moorish heart, where you won't want to miss the old palaces or peaceful gardens before enjoying the lively nightlife only Morocco can offer.

Kenya is for safaris. Look out for your favourite animals in their natural surroundings. Or shop for gifts in Nairobi.

Tunisia offers the chance for more sightseeing in the ancient walled town of Hammamet. Try the local cuisine or shop for a bargain.

Gabon offers plenty of local colour, with beautiful beaches and vast areas of rainforest full of wildlife. Nightlife is sophisticated with plenty to do, or visit the old quarter for a taste of local, traditional Africa.

Hotels in the Middle East

	Luxury*	Standard*
Jordan	$65	$37
Oman	$62	$38
Qatar	$75	$46
Saudi Arabia	$59	$42
UAE	$67	$47

* Prices are per person per night, based on two adults sharing a room and including breakfast. Single occupancy is charged at double the price per person.

Hotels in Africa

	Luxury*	Standard*
Egypt	$52	$25
Eritrea	$74	$41
Gabon	$60	$30
Kenya	$77	$48
Morocco	$72	$50

* Prices are per person per night, based on two adults sharing a room and including breakfast. Single occupancy is charged at double the price per person, except in Kenya, where 50% is charged.

Call 00 800 22 333 444 and ask for 'Weekend Holiday Breaks', or visit our new website, www.weekendholidays.glo

a Give **two** examples of mysteries of the East. [1]

b When is a good time to visit the beach in Dubai? [1]

c How can you find out more about life in Oman? [1]

d What is the cost of a standard room in a Qatar hotel? [1]

e In which country does the leaflet recommend trying scuba diving? [1]

f In which **two** countries can you see animals? [1]

g Where should you try local food? [1]

Extended

h How can you get more information? Give **two** ways. [2]

[Total: 9 Extended, 7 Core]

2 Read the article below, then answer the questions on page 152.

Gardening in the palm of your hand

The palm tree symbolises everything about tropical climates. It adds beauty to landscapes, lines our roads and grows in our gardens. Many palms are now placed outside front doors, on balconies and inside the home to give an exotic feel to living space.

Palm trees in hot climates are easy to grow and cultivate. You will need a seed, the right soil mix, a fertiliser and plenty of irrigation. There are dozens of books to help you get started, but for those of us who choose not to go this far, there is help close at hand in the form of ready-made palm trees to take home from your local garden centre.

The Green Desert garden centre, which spans more than 5000 square metres of land, contains an impressive collection of over 3000 palm trees. The centre is owned and run by Ali Al Hamsa, who started the business nearly 20 years ago. He explained how to cultivate a palm tree from seed: 'You have to start before the spring. Place the palm seeds under 3 centimetres of special soil for them to germinate; in other words, so that they start to grow. This should be done early in the year, preferably in January or February, or early March, but it depends on the temperature. If you have enough water and good soil, the palm will grow very quickly.'

Palm trees vary greatly in size. You can buy small ones for the house, or grow them larger for planting in the garden. Some will grow as high as 20 metres. There are more than 3000 species of palm tree around the world, with more being discovered all the time. However, most garden centres will only stock a small number of different types because of local climate conditions. The stock will also depend on local demand for different palms. The Green Desert offers three: a palm for the garden which produces dates; a second for the garden which does not have fruit; and the third is a smaller palm that is ideal for growing inside the home or on a balcony.

The price varies enormously and is based entirely on the height of the palm tree. Some palms at the garden centre are small, only 30–40 centimetres in height, but nothing under one metre is ever sold. This is because smaller palms are not yet established.

'Once a palm reaches about 100 centimetres, it will be well established and will be able to survive the move from the garden centre to someone's home or garden,' says Ali Al Hamsa. 'A tree which is not established may suffer during transportation from the garden centre environment, which it is used to, to its new home, whether indoors or in the garden. People who buy palm trees – in fact, any plant from a garden centre – are often totally unaware of how a plant can suffer when it's moved. A common problem is that the plant is banged about in a car, causing the roots to loosen from the soil. This means that the plant can be starved of essential water. Another problem is that the leaves and branches may get knocked and broken, making the plant look damaged and ugly. Some plants may never recover from shocks like this!'

It is no surprise that palm trees have become increasingly popular in the home. Not only do they provide a tropical atmosphere, they have also proved to be tolerant of a wide range of interior conditions, from air conditioning to central heating. They are practically maintenance-free. Surprisingly, an established indoor palm needs only a little sunlight for its leaves to retain their colour; also, it needs only a little water once a week to survive. If the roots of a palm drink a lot of water, the plant will grow, but this is not ideal when the palm is grown indoors. Palm trees in a pot in the home are watered to keep them alive, not to make them grow bigger.

If you are wondering how a palm tree might improve the look of your garden, you should go to an expert for advice and instructions on what to buy and how to plant it. But remember that palm trees are able to grow to great heights in a comparatively small area of land. However, because they have only one branch, palm trees are very easy to control and there are no leaves to clear up. Unlike the leaves on most other trees, palm leaves do not fall, allowing us to enjoy the trees' subtle colours and textures whatever the season.

a Where do palm trees provide an exotic feel to living space?
   Give **three** examples.   [1]

b What **three** items are required to grow a palm tree from seed?   [1]

c In what **two** ways can you get help if you want to grow a palm tree?   [1]

d What determines the month in which a palm seed should be planted?   [1]

e Why do garden centres offer only a small selection of different types
   of palm tree?   [2]

f How is the price of a palm tree calculated?   [1]

g Why are small palm trees not available to buy?   [1]

h In what **two** ways can a plant suffer when it is damaged during transport?
                                                                              [2]

i How many times a week do you need to water a date palm tree in the
   home?   [1]

Extended

j Give **two** reasons why palm trees are becoming increasingly popular in the
   home and **one** advantage and **one** disadvantage of growing palm trees in
   the garden.   [4]

[Total: 15 Extended, 11 Core]

Unit 14: Focus on reading and writing skills

In this unit, you will practise the skills needed to make notes under headings about a text and to develop your summary writing skills.

In this unit, you will also:

- talk about global warming and its causes
- read about the North Pole and the melting ice sheet
- practise note-making and summary writing
- discuss the global shortage of water
- answer some exam-style questions.

A 🗨 Speaking

1 Work with a partner. Look at the pictures and answer the questions.

a What does each picture show?

b What has caused the situation in each picture and what is the result?

c In which part of the world do you think each picture was taken? Why do you think this?

d What can be done to stop these situations becoming worse?

LANGUAGE TIP

Look at these commonly confused introductory phrases that we often use when describing things.

Introductory phrase	+ adjective	+ noun	+ verb
It looks/seems like …		a desert. a disaster.	we are destroying the planet. the ground is completely dry. the bird won't survive. it's too late.
It looks/seems as if/though …			
It looks/seems …	dry.		

2   Answer these two questions about the following.

> the Arctic   the Atlantic Ocean   the Pacific Ocean
> Europe   Canada   Russia   Asia   North America

a   Is it a continent, a country or region, or something else?

b   Where is it on the map below?

3   Decide with your partner whether the following statements are true or false. Give reasons for your decisions. You will have a chance to see if you are right later in this unit.

a   By around 2050, the Arctic ice sheet will be fragile enough for icebreakers to carve a straight path between the Atlantic and Pacific Oceans.

b   A more accessible Arctic could also fuel international disagreements between Europe, Canada and Russia over shipping lanes and the search for minerals below the sea bed.

c   Arctic sea ice has reached a new record low and is due to carry on melting, even if the world manages to cut carbon emissions.

d   The Eocene period, 55 million years ago, was the last time the world's climate grew rapidly warmer.

e   Until recently, thick ice blocked a short cut linking Asia with North America and Europe.

f   Greenpeace is already campaigning to protect Arctic waters from drilling and oil spills.

g   The ice at the top of the world reflects much of the sun's heat back into space and keeps our whole planet cool.

4 Look at these four newspaper and internet headlines (i–iv). Work in small groups and answer the questions.

(i) **Biggest ozone hole over Antarctica revealed**

(ii) **North Pole icecap melts as global warming increases**

(iii) **The seas keep rising, but the world looks away**

(iv) **Shipping lanes could open over the North Pole due to climate change**

a Geographically, where and what is Antarctica?
b Where and what is the North Pole?
c What is the North Pole icecap?
d Make a list of **at least six** things that you already know about global warming.
e What are shipping lanes? Why do they have this name?

5 Copy the table below. Match the ten words on the left (taken from the text on page 156) with the ten definitions on the right. Do not worry about the middle column for the moment. Check your answers with a partner's. If you are not sure, use paper or digital reference sources to help you.

Example: *1 absorbs = i takes in*

Words	Part of speech	Definitions
1 ~~absorbs~~	verb – present tense	a avoid
2 carve	…	b becoming smaller
3 counteract	…	c underside of ships
4 crucial	…	d cut or slice
5 flourish	…	e extremely important
6 fragile	…	f grow well and be healthy
7 hulls	…	g lessen the effect of
8 shrinking	…	h ship or boat
9 skirt	…	i ~~takes in~~
10 vessel	…	j weak

B 📖 Reading

1 Skim the text on page 156. Which of the four headlines in Activity A4 do you think is the most suitable for this article? Why? Does your partner agree with you?

2 Look back at the statements in Activity A3. Scan the text again to find out whether you and your partner made the correct decisions.

Arctic sea ice

will be so thin by the middle of this century that ships will be able to sail directly across the North Pole for the first time, experts have predicted.

[1] By around 2050, the Arctic ice sheet will be **(a)** … enough for icebreakers to **(b)** … a straight path between the Atlantic and Pacific Oceans, the University of California claimed. For the first time in 55 million years, the North Pole is melting. Cargo ships will be able to **(c)** … the North Pole without even using icebreakers because the ice will have retreated so far back.

[2] These predictions, published in the journal *Proceedings of the National Academy of Sciences*, will be welcomed by shipping companies, which would be able to drastically cut journey times and costs. But environmentalists fear wildlife could be destroyed by oil spills and drilling will also come to the area. A more accessible Arctic could also fuel international disagreements between Europe, Canada and Russia over shipping lanes and the search for minerals below the sea bed.

[3] Arctic sea ice has reached a new record low and is due to carry on melting, even if the world manages to cut carbon emissions. Professor Laurence Smith, who led the study, said that by 2050, ships could start going straight over the roof of the world. He said moderate icebreakers will be able to 'go where they please'. 'Nobody's ever talked about shipping over the top of the North Pole,' he said. 'This is an entirely unexpected possibility.'

[4] Researchers had warned that the polar ice cap was **(d)** … by about 6% a year, but nobody expected the North Pole to melt until global warming had become much more severe. The meltdown could also **(e)** … the Gulf Stream, which keeps Britain's climate 2–3 degrees warmer than countries at a similar latitude.

[5] The Eocene period, 55 million years ago, was the last time the world's climate grew rapidly warmer. Fossil evidence shows that it became warm enough for tropical vegetation and animals to **(f)** … in the Arctic and Antarctic Circles.

[6] The scientists studied seven well-established climate simulations for the years 2040 to 2059 to estimate the future thickness of sea ice in the Arctic. They then used a computer programme to look for potential new shipping routes opening up in September, the Arctic's most navigable month of the year.

[7] By mid-century, most common open-water ships will be able, without the help of icebreakers, to cross the Northern Sea Route around the North Pole, hugging the coast of Russia, the forecast shows. The route is about 40% shorter than plotting a course through the Suez Canal. Even the fabled and notoriously treacherous Northwest Passage, which traces Canada's coastline, could be opened up. It is expected to become navigable for Polar Class 6 vessels, which are strengthened against ice, and even some ships with unreinforced **(g)** … .

Current routes
Possible route

[8] Scott Stephenson, who also took part in the study, said at the moment only icebreakers go over the Arctic at certain times of year. 'We're talking about a future in which an open-water **(h)** … will, at least during some years, be able to navigate unescorted through the Arctic, which, at the moment, is inconceivable,' he said.

[9] Until recently, thick ice has blocked a short cut linking Asia with North America and Europe. But, in the past two years, the ice has started to melt in late summer sufficiently to allow ordinary vessels escorted by icebreakers to venture into the Arctic's outskirts. Last summer, a total of 46 voyages were successfully completed along the Northern Sea Route. The Northwest Passage can only be crossed in one in every seven years on average, making it too unreliable for commercial shipping.

[10] A new sea route over the top of the North Pole could make the passage even faster. Sailing directly over the North Pole would provide a passage for icebreakers between the world's two greatest oceans which would be 20% shorter than the Northern Sea Route. Professor Smith said shipping will come to the Arctic, even if carbon emissions are cut now to reduce global warming. 'No matter which carbon emission scenario is considered, by mid-century we will have passed a **(i)** … tipping point – sufficiently thin sea ice – enabling moderately capable icebreakers to go where they please.'

[11] Greenpeace is already campaigning to protect Arctic waters from drilling and oil spills. So far, 2.8 million people have signed a petition 'to create a global sanctuary around the North Pole and ban offshore drilling and destructive industry in the Arctic.'

'For over 800,000 years, ice has been a permanent feature of the Arctic Ocean. It's melting because of our use of dirty fossil fuel energy and, in the near future, it could be ice free for the first time since humans walked the earth. This would be not only devastating for the people, polar bears, narwhals, walruses and other species that live there, but for the rest of us too.'

'The ice at the top of the world reflects much of the sun's heat back into space and keeps our whole planet cool, stabilising the weather systems that we depend on to grow our food. Protecting the ice means protecting us all.'

The melting sea ice will not add to sea-level rise, but could increase warming, as water **(j)** … heat from the sun, rather than reflecting it back into space.

Adapted from www.telegraph.co.uk

3   Scan the text again and check whether any of the things you already knew about global warming are mentioned. Then make a list of **five** more things that you did not know. Compare your list with your partner's.

4   Work on your own. Use the ten words from the left-hand column in Activity A5 to complete the gaps in the article (a–j). Then go back to the table and fill in the middle column (part of speech) for each word.

5   Answer these questions about the text.

   a   What will the condition of the ice sheet be by around 2050?

   b   When was the last time the North Pole melted?

   c   Why will shipping companies feel positive about the predictions?

   d   What **two** things do environmentalists fear?

   e   What keeps the climate in Britain slightly warmer than other countries in the same area?

   f   How do we know that tropical vegetation and animals flourished 55 million years ago?

   g   What is the benefit of the Northern Sea Route?

   h   How much shorter than the Northern Sea Route would sailing directly over the North Pole be?

   i   What have nearly 3 million people done in support of Greenpeace?

   j   According to Greenpeace, how is our planet kept cool?

6   Exchange your answers with your partner's. Check that your partner's answers include all the necessary information. Are there any differences between their answers and yours? Discuss and produce final versions of your answers that you both agree on.

C Writing

1   Look at this exam-style question. With a partner, decide exactly what you have to do. What information is asked for? How many notes do you need to write in total? Do **not** write an answer yet.

You have been asked by your teacher to make a presentation to students about the North Pole and you need to make notes in order to prepare. Make your notes under each heading.

Predictions for 2050	Environmentalists' worries	Greenpeace
• …	• …	• …
• …	• …	• …
• …	• …	• …

TOP TIPS

When you are taking notes, you may be given bullet points to respond to. In these cases, make sure you look carefully at the number of bullet points. This will tell you how many notes you are expected to write.

2 Look at this answer to the question in Activity C1. The student has mixed up the notes. Look at the text again and decide with a partner under which heading each of the notes should appear. Be prepared to say why.

> <u>Predictions for 2050</u>
> • 2.8 million petitioners
> • cargo ships will avoid the North Pole
> • disagreements between shipping countries
>
> <u>Environmentalists' worries</u>
> • ice melting because of humans
> • ice reflects sun's heat and keeps planet cool
> • ice sheet fragile, so icebreakers can cut through it
>
> <u>Greenpeace</u>
> • journey times and costs reduced
> • oil drilling
> • wildlife at risk

TOP TIPS

When you are making notes about a text, remember that they should be brief and must relate to the text you have read. You **cannot** include information that does not appear in the text.

3 Try to find **at least one** more piece of information in the text to make a note about under each of the three headings.

4 Sometimes, the notes you make for a talk, presentation or speech may be used to write a summary. Look at this exam-style question. Identify **at least three** important things that the question asks you to do.

> Imagine that you have given your presentation about the North Pole. Now your teacher has asked you to follow this up with a summary for students. Look at your notes. Using the ideas in your notes, write a summary about the North Pole.
>
> Your summary should be about 70 words long (and no more than 80 words long). You should use your own words as far as possible.

5 Use the notes from Activity C2 to write your summary.

D 🗩 Aᵃ Speaking and vocabulary

1 The following phrases appear in the next text you are going to read. What do you think the text is about?

Forest fires, heavy flooding and confused Lithuanian birds …

Extreme weather events are no longer restricted to far-off, exotic places …

Surveys reveals that half of Danes are worried about their homes flooding …

The EU has released its package of climate measures for 2030 …

2 With a partner, make a list of **ten** more phrases or single words that you think might appear in the text. You will find out later if the words you think of are actually used in the text.

3 Look at these **ten** words and phrases taken from the text. Discuss each one in small groups and try to agree on its meaning.

> ambitious   bloc   curtail   ecology   exotic   vulnerable
> future prosperity   impacts   mild winters   storm surges

E  Reading

1 Skim the text below. Were your predictions in Activities D1 and D2 correct? Do not worry about the gaps in the text at the moment.

REPORT

Europe already feeling climate change impacts

Extreme weather is becoming the new normal across Europe, according to a report from the Climate Action Network

By Sophie Yeo

[1] Forest fires, heavy flooding and confused Lithuanian birds – these are some of the effects that climate change is already having in Europe, according to a new report. The study, assembled by the Climate Action Network (CAN) campaign group, examines how climate change is already affecting Europe, from the points of view of (**a**) … , health and food security. It reveals that countries across Europe are already suffering from the (**b**) … of climate change, which is putting their environments and economies at risk.

[2] 'Europe and the rest of the developed world can no longer ignore the impacts of climate change,' writes Wendel Trio, director of CAN Europe, in the report. 'Extreme weather events are no longer restricted to far-off, (**c**) … places. They are also happening on the doorsteps of the richest, most powerful countries, here in Europe, in our communities, affecting our daily lives.'

Regional impacts

[3] A region-by-region analysis highlights the impacts on different countries across the continent. In Lithuania, for instance, birds are dying because the unseasonably (**d**) … means many decide not to migrate in the winter, leaving them to face the cold when it finally hits.

[4] Low-lying coastal areas across the Nordic region of Europe are already at a high risk of flooding, with sea-level rise leading to stronger and more frequent (**e**) … . North Sea countries, such as Denmark, are especially vulnerable, with its coastal capital of Copenhagen at particular risk. Surveys reveal that half of Danes are worried about their homes flooding.

[5] France's €30 million a year tourism industry, central to its economy, will be increasingly depressed as the temperatures warm. In the Alps and the Pyrenees, significant snow loss and a greater chance of avalanches threatens to (**f**) … the ski season and shut some resorts down altogether.

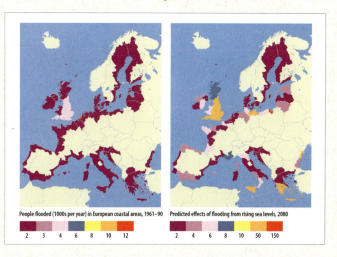

People flooded (1000s per year) in European coastal areas, 1961–90

2 3 4 6 8 10 12

Predicted effects of flooding from rising sea levels, 2080

2 4 6 8 10 50 150

[6] While a combination of geographical and economic factors mean that the developing world remains the most (**g**) … to climate change, the report hopes to highlight the fact that Europe needs to play a part in the discussion on the impacts of climate change that are already here. By focusing on the impacts of climate change across Europe, Trio hopes that the European Union (EU) can be encouraged to adopt (**h**) … targets for reducing emissions. The (**i**) … is close to meeting its 2020 target of a 20% cut in greenhouse gases, and there is a call for politicians to go beyond this before the end of the decade.

[7] The EU has released its package of climate measures for 2030, which recommend a 45% emissions reduction target. 'Climate change is causing damage to our societies, our environment and to our current and (**j**) … This damage is only going to get worse, unless we take action at the global level, but also at the European level,' says Trio. 'Europe can do much more to take effective action on climate change. Europe can lead by example and adopt more ambitious greenhouse gas emissions reduction targets for 2020.'

Adapted from www.rtcc.org

2   Scan the text and identify which of the words from Activity D3 is needed to complete each gap. Check your answers with your partner.

3   Answer the following questions. Then give your answers to your partner to check.

a   What does the report say about countries across Europe?

b   Why can Europe no longer ignore climate change?

c   Does climate change affect European countries in the same way? How do you know?

d   What reason is given for birds dying in Lithuania?

e   Why are coastal areas in Nordic Europe at a high risk of flooding?

f   Give **two** reasons why France's skiing season will be at risk.

g   What do the red areas in the second map indicate?

h   Why is the developing world still more at risk than Europe?

i   What does Wendel Trio hope will be the effect of focusing on European climate change?

j   According to Trio, what **three** things is climate change damaging?

F Writing

1   Read the following exam-style question. Decide with your partner exactly what you have to do. Do **not** write anything yet.

> Read the article about climate change (on page 159). Write a summary about the impact of climate change in Europe.
>
> Your summary should be about 100 words long (and not more than 120 words long).
>
> You should use your own words as far as possible.
>
> You will receive up to 6 marks for the content of your summary and up to 5 marks for the style and accuracy of your language.

TOP TIPS

Summary questions will usually direct you to a specific topic in the text, so it is very important that you **underline the key points** and **make brief notes** before you write your answer.

2   Re-read the text and note the points that relate directly to the summary question in Activity F1. Then make brief notes. Compare your notes with a partner's. Have you chosen the same information? Has your partner included anything that you have not?

3   Write your answer to the summary question in Activity F1, paying particular attention to the advice given in this unit. When you have written your paragraph, exchange it with your partner and check each other's writing. What exactly should you be looking for? Think about the information given in the exam-style question in Activity F1.

G 🗨 Speaking

1   Work in small groups and answer these questions.

   a   What do you use water for? On your own, make **two** lists: **eight** things you use water for **inside** your home and **four** things for **outside** your home. Compare answers as a group.

   b   Imagine that you could only have water for **half** of the things in your lists in the activity above. Which **six** would you choose? What if you could only have a **quarter** – which **three** would you choose?

   c   Does your country have enough water? Where does its water come from? How?

   d   What do you think it is like to experience a flood? How might a flood affect your daily life?

   e   Think about the water you drink. Where does it come from?

   f   Are there any restrictions on how much water you can have? If not, why not? If there are restrictions, why do they exist?

TOP TIPS
Remember that the speaking-test cards in Appendix 1 can be used to practise for your speaking test, if you are doing one. Card 4 is about climate change.

H ➕ Further practice

Write

1   Look again at the text about climate change on page 159. Write a paragraph of about 60 words, outlining what action the European Union is taking to deal with the problem.

Research and present

2   Find out as much as you can about the water supply in your country: where it comes from, how much it costs, whether it is chemically treated, and so on. Prepare a short talk of about two to three minutes to give to your group.

Design

3   Design a leaflet informing people in your area of a water shortage and advising them on how to conserve water. You may include pictures and graphics if you wish. Write 150–200 words (Extended) or 100–150 words (Core).

Make notes

4 Read the text below, then complete the notes. Write two or three notes under each heading.

<u>Results of hyponatraemia</u>
- apathy and lethargy
- ...
- ...

<u>People at risk</u>
- ...
- ...
- ...

<u>Advice about drinking water</u>
- ...
- ...
- ...

A dangerous thirst

We are told that we should drink at least 2 litres of water a day, and more if we are exercising, but what many people do not realise is that too much water can be fatal.

The result is hyponatraemia (literally 'low salt'), a condition also known as 'water intoxication'. When we sweat, we lose vital salts that the body needs to maintain its equilibrium. Excessive sweating combined with drinking dilutes the concentration of salts in the body to a dangerous level. The result is nausea, apathy, lethargy, dizziness and mental confusion; sufferers can lapse into a coma and die.

Hyponatraemia was first noticed in 1981 by a doctor in South Africa, when he treated a woman running a marathon. However, anyone is susceptible if they drink water for a prolonged period without ingesting salts.

There are four main factors that could predispose someone to suffer from hyponatraemia. Those most at risk are the very young and the very old because they are less able to regulate their thirst, and their water and salt levels, by themselves. Secondly, anyone who exercises for a prolonged period is at risk; this includes marathon and triathlon competitors. However, it is not the elite athletes who are in danger, but those who run marathons for charity, or as an occasional hobby. You do not have to be especially fit to suffer from hyponatraemia.

Thirdly, heat and humidity increase susceptibility as sweat loss rises to a litre an hour. The kind of heat at which hyponatraemia can set in is not particularly hot: 20°C. The highest number of incidents recorded at one time was when 24 runners were hospitalised during a marathon in California when the temperature was only 23°C. As it gets hotter, runners slow down, but drink more and do not replace any lost salts. Drinking more than a litre an hour for five or more hours can lead to hyponatraemia.

Lastly, people in nightclubs are also at risk because the atmosphere is hot and humid, and they tend to stay there for a long time without eating anything, but drinking excessive quantities of water. A young woman was recently admitted to hospital after drinking 10 litres of water while exercising in a gym. It took the hospital staff about two hours to diagnose her condition, by which time the young woman was unconscious. Her salt levels were found to be dangerously low and she spent four days in hospital recovering.

Of course, we should all drink water, and we need more during hot and humid conditions, but it is best to have drinks with carbohydrates in them, such as squash, and to take sports drinks when exercising.

Adapted from *The Times*.

Exam-style questions

1 Read the article about Antarctica and complete the task below.

You are going to give a talk to your school/college friends about the evolution of Antarctica. You have decided to use some information from the article in your talk. Make your notes under each heading.

a 3 billion years ago [1]

b Between 150 million and 70 million years ago [2]

c Between 4 million and 1 million years ago [2]

d 1977 to today [2]

[7 marks]

The ice land of
ANTARCTICA

The evolution of Antarctica can be traced back as far as 3 billion years ago, to an age that most of us find difficult to conceive of. At that time, Antarctica did not exist as a separate continent, but was connected to the southern continents which we now recognise as South America and Australia. A mere 150 million years ago, the separation of the continents began, and only 70 million years ago, Antarctica became isolated. This was the time when land mammals began to populate all the continents of the world.

Today, Antarctica is covered by polar ice, but fossils show that the climate and geography once supported a far wider and more abundant plant and animal life than the few seedless plants and insects which remain. About 200 million years ago, Antarctica was densely forested with trees and rainforest-type plants. During its next period of change, 80 to 100 million years ago, trees more suited to cooler temperatures began to flourish, as the continent continued its drift towards the South Pole, until about 4 million years ago, these trees slowly died out. Around 1 million years ago, Antarctica became glaciated, with the ice making the perfect environment for the fossilisation of reptiles, mammals and plants of all descriptions.

However, most of the continent's evolutionary record still lies buried deep beneath the ice, which makes up more than 95% of the surface area. Even experts have no idea what important treasures are concealed under the thick cover of ice which, in places, is as much as 2000 metres. As well as the ice, the difficult working conditions and the enormous expense of sending expeditions to the area have, for many years, restricted geological knowledge of Antarctica. More recently, great advances have been made by geologists in mapping the continent and it is now known that the continent's geology is far more complex than previously thought.

There have been no significant earthquakes in the Antarctic region, making it the 'quietest' continent in terms of earthquake movement. However, in 1977, an unusually large earth movement did take place, with a magnitude of 6.4. The centre of the tremor was in the Bellingshausen Sea to the west of Antarctica. This led geologists to believe that the region may, in fact, be more susceptible to earthquakes than had previously been thought.

163

2 Imagine that you have given your talk in Activity 1. Now your teacher wants you to follow this up with a written summary.

Look at your notes and use them to write a summary about the evolution of Antarctica.

Your summary should be about 70 words long (and no more than 80 words long). You should use your own words as far as possible.

[5 marks]

Extended

3 Read the article about Antarctica on page 163 and then complete the exam-style question below.

You are going to give a talk to your school/college friends about the evolution of Antarctica. You have decided to use some information from the article in your talk. Make your notes under each heading.

a 3 billion years ago [2]

b Between 150 million and 70 million years ago [2]

c Between 4 million and 1 million years ago [2]

d 1977 to today [3]

[9 marks]

4 Read the article about cyclones on page 165, then complete the tasks below.

Write a summary in which you include information about the wind speed and the location of cyclones.

Your summary should be about 100 words long (and not more than 120 words long).

You should use your own words as far as possible.

You will receive up to 6 marks for the content of your summary and up to 5 marks for the style and accuracy of your language.

Extreme weather
the cyclone

Cyclones form as tropical depressions above warm seawater and usually cover a huge area, often between 200 and 400 kilometres across. The majority of tropical depressions never actually reach the stage of becoming a cyclone, and simply lose their strength over a period of some days. Those that do become tropical cyclones may live for between a few hours and several weeks, but most last from five to ten days.

Wind speed

In the early stages of a tropical storm, the wind increases in strength from 'weak storm' status (65–87 kilometres per hour) to gale-force status (up to 118 kilometres per hour), which is typical of the speed of a tropical cyclone. The wind spirals towards a distinct centre, called the 'eye', which can be anything from 5 to 15 kilometres in diameter. As the wind speed of the spiral increases, atmospheric pressure drops rapidly and the diameter of the eye may increase to as much as 200 kilometres. Many tropical storms will not actually develop any further than this and, while there may be occasional wind speeds in excess of 120 kilometres per hour, the storms never actually become tropical cyclones.

Travel over land

Cyclones, which travel over a land surface, lose a considerable amount of their energy and wind speed due to the friction created with the land contours. In mountainous areas of Vietnam, most cyclones die out very quickly; however, in the flat plateau areas of Western Australia, there is little in the natural geography to create the friction necessary to reduce the strength of a cyclone. Cyclones in this area commonly travel more than 1500 kilometres. In 1969 in the United States, Hurricane Camille travelled 1800 kilometres and, while it lost much of its strength, it kept its structure.

Location

Nowadays, every cyclonic disturbance is detected by satellite. The major cyclonic areas in the North Atlantic are: south of the Cape Verde Islands, east of the Lesser Antilles, the western Caribbean Sea and the Gulf of Mexico. Water temperatures in the latter two areas rise quickly in the early summer months, causing cyclones to evolve before other areas. As water temperatures rise to 28 °C and more in late July and August, the number of cyclones across the Atlantic area increases. The storms travel west, gathering strength, and then curve back. By mid to late September, as water temperatures begin to cool, the area of cyclone origin returns to the Caribbean and the Gulf of Mexico.

Unit 15: Focus on writing skills

In this unit, we will focus on developing the skills you need to write longer pieces of continuous prose, such as an article, email, letter or report, in which you give your views or opinions.

In this unit, you will also:

- talk and read about chewing gum
- listen to a dental expert and make notes
- practise writing articles and letters
- discuss and read about foods that are bad for the planet
- research different food types
- answer some exam-style questions.

A 🗨 Speaking

1 Work in small groups and answer these questions.

   a What can you see in the pictures? What impact does discarded gum have on the environment?

   b What do you think chewing gum is made from?

   c Do you chew gum? If yes, when do you do it and why? If not, why not?

   d What do you think happens if you swallow a piece of gum? Do you think chewing gum is good for you?

2 Which of the following statements about chewing gum do you think are true? Decide in your group.

   a The ancient Greeks chewed a type of gum more than 2000 years ago.

   b The first manufactured chewing gum was available in 1870.

   c Bubble gum became available in 1928.

   d In the 1950s, the first sugarless gum was produced.

   e Powdered sugar is used to stop pieces of gum from sticking to machinery and packaging.

   f In the USA, 180 sticks of gum is the average consumption per person per year.

   g It is illegal to manufacture, import or sell gum in Singapore.

   h Turkey is the country with the most gum-manufacturing companies.

   i The Portuguese for chewing gum is *pastilka elastika*.

   j The main ingredients in chewing gum are sugar, gum base, corn syrup, softeners, flavouring and colouring.

   k When you swallow gum, it won't be digested, so it comes out in one piece. It will, however, stay inside you for a few days.

3 In fact, all of the statements above are true. Answer these questions in your group.

a What surprises you about the information in Activity A2? Why?

b Why do you think that Singapore has such strict laws about chewing gum?

c What do you think is the average consumption of chewing gum per person per year in **your** country? If you do not know, how can you find out?

d What do you think the two individual Portuguese words *pastilka* and *elastika* mean? Why do you think this? If you know Portuguese, find out how to say *chewing gum* in another language that you do not know.

4 Which do you think is more popular: gum, sweets or chocolate? Why? Look at the graph below, which shows the daily percentage confectionary intake of teenagers in Asia. Which do **you** prefer? Why?

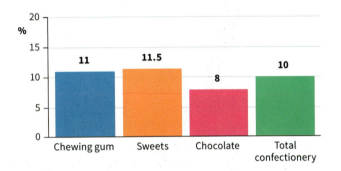

Daily percentage confectionery intake of teenagers in Asia

B ✏ Writing

1 Work on your own. Use the information in Section A of this unit to write a 'fact file' about chewing gum. Do not try to include **all** the information, only that which you consider to be the most important or interesting. Do **not** write more than 100 words. Remember to use your own words as far as possible.

2 Look at your partner's fact file. How similar or different is it to yours? Why do you think that is?

C 💬 🅐 Speaking and vocabulary

1 You are going to read an article on page 168 called *Chewing gum to chew on*. First, work with a partner and decide what you think the article will be about. Choose **one** of the following and be prepared to give reasons for your choice.

a The health dangers of chewing gum.

b The problems chewing gum causes to the environment.

c The benefits of chewing gum.

d Interesting facts about chewing gum.

2 Talk with a partner about your choice from Activity C1.

3 With the same partner, decide on the meaning of the following words taken from the text. Use paper or digital reference sources to help you.

| adheres | entrepreneur | friction | mixing vat | pliable |
| rubber bands | self-adhesive | substance | synthetic | syrup |

4 There are six paragraphs in the text, each with its own heading. Look at the headings and decide with your partner in what order they will appear.

*… and finish with viscosity   How is it made?   Let's begin with gums …
It's not just chicle   The first chewing gums   The invention of modern chewing gum*

5 Look at the headings again.

a Discuss with your partner what information you think you will find in each of the six paragraphs.

b In which paragraphs do you think the ten words and phrases from Activity C3 will appear? Why?

D 📖 Reading

1 The paragraph headings have been removed from the text. Scan it and decide which heading fits with each paragraph 1–6. Give reasons for your answers. Do not worry about the gaps in the text at the moment.

Chewing gum to chew on

[1] …

We all know gum as the **(a)** … that **(b)** … one thing to another thing and makes a sticky mess of our fingers. But chemists define gums in a different way. To them, a gum describes any thick substance of plant origin, made up of polysaccharides (multiple chains of sugar molecules), and gums have a very wide variety of applications in modern life. Gum arabic is used as a coating for **(c)** … postage stamps, while gum tragacanth is what makes toothpaste flow out of the tube. Guar gum is used to stop ice crystals forming in ice cream. Chewing gum is made from chicle and is one of the oldest sweets known to humans, beginning as a chewy sap from the Mastiche trees of ancient Greece. Across the world, even the Mayans of South America liked chewy treats.

[2] …

It was in the 1800s that **(d)** … John Curtis introduced chewing gum to the United States, with his small sticks of gum. The original sap-based gums were replaced by gums made from paraffin wax, the same substance used to make candles. So, was it like chewing candles? No! Sugar was added to these gums to give an added sweetness, but the biggest problem was that they were not chewy enough. However, a solution was found: chicle, a natural rubber sap from the Sapodilla tree of Central America, was also added. The effect was to give the gum the chewy feel that we experience today when we chew gum.

[3] …

Inventor Thomas Adams discovered that heating chicle and then mixing it with flavouring and sugar produced a new gum and soon appreciated that this was much better than paraffin-based gums. What made this sap special was that it was softer than rubber used in **(e)** … , and became even softer and more **(f)** … in the warmth of the mouth. He also discovered that freezing chicle affected it, and the rubber sap became hard. These unique properties made it the ideal choice for chewing.

[4] …

Chewing gum is made by heating gum to 115 °C, at which point it becomes thick, like a **(g)** … . This is filtered, refined and put into a **(h)** … . Then, other ingredients like sugar, corn syrup, softeners and preservatives are added. This mixture is then cooled and cut into the final bits of gum, ready to be packed and sent to stores.

[5] …

Gums from plants are expensive to make. If all gum was made out of chicle, there would not be enough of it left to make more gum. This is why it has been replaced by **(i)** … rubbers and today's gums are made of a mixture of elastomers, resins and waxes. Xanthan is a gum produced by the bacterium xanthomonas. It is cheaper than chicle, and easier to make. It can also do more things than any single gum can do and as a result it is replacing many of the older gums.

[6] …

The common property of all gums is viscosity, which describes how slowly or quickly a liquid flows. Water molecules are very tiny, and there is little **(j)** … between them as they flow, whereas polysaccharide molecules (made up of lots of sugar molecules) are huge, and flow past each other with a lot of friction. Have too much gum in the solution, and you will end up with a jelly-like material which will not flow at all.

Adapted from http://humantouchofchemistry.com

TOP TIPS

Look at these two phrases from the text you have just read:

*The **effect** was to give the gum the chewy feel …*

*He also discovered that freezing chicle **affected** it …*

The two bold words *effect* and *affected* are often confused. *Effect* is normally a noun (in some formal contexts it can be a verb). It means *result* or *change*. In the text, *The effect* means the result of adding chicle.

Affect is a regular verb and it is used to mean that one thing (*freezing chicle*) causes a change in something else (*sap*).

The expression *to have an effect on* has a similar meaning to *affect*.

*He also discovered that freezing chicle **affected** it (the sap) …*

*He also discovered that freezing chicle had an **effect** on it (the sap) …*

2 Scan the text again and complete the gaps a–j with the words from Activity C3.

3 Write your answers to the following questions.

   a How do we normally recognise gum?

   b Give **four** products from the text which use gum as an ingredient.

   c Where does chicle come from?

   d What were **two** problems with the first chewing gums?

   e What did Thomas Adams do to produce a new chewing gum?

   f Why do you think the thick syrup needs to be filtered?

   g What is **one** benefit of synthetic gums compared to natural gums?

   h What are **two** differences between water molecules and polysaccharide molecules?

   i What might stop a liquid from flowing?

4 Give your answers to Activities D2 and D3 to your partner to check. Then work together to produce the best combined answers for Activity D3.

5 Swap your answers with those of another pair. What similarities and differences do you notice? Why do you think this is?

E 🔊 Listening

1 🔊 You are going to listen to a dental expert being interviewed about chewing gum. What advice does Dr Bealing give to Thomas about gum chewing?

2 🔊 Listen again and complete the notes. Write only one or two words in each gap.

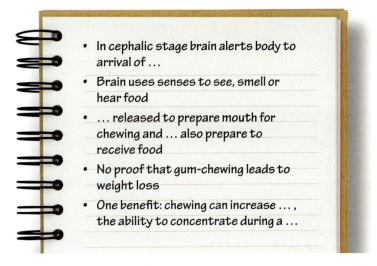

- In cephalic stage brain alerts body to arrival of …
- Brain uses senses to see, smell or hear food
- … released to prepare mouth for chewing and … also prepare to receive food
- No proof that gum-chewing leads to weight loss
- One benefit: chewing can increase …, the ability to concentrate during a …

3 Compare your answers with your partner's. Then read the audioscript on pages 201–2 to check whether your answers are correct.

169

TOP TIPS

Sometimes, you may be asked to write your opinion about something in the form of a newspaper article, or perhaps for your school newsletter or magazine. You will usually be given help, perhaps in the form of a list of ideas or other people's opinions, or sometimes pictures, but you do not have to use them in your answer. You should try to use some of your own ideas – but make sure you stick to the topic. You must show that you can use the English language for a specific purpose and that you can organise your ideas in a logical way.

LANGUAGE TIP

Make sure that your **introduction** is brief and to the point. It needs to state clearly your own opinion and should attempt to capture the reader's attention, to encourage them to continue reading.

LANGUAGE TIP

The **conclusion** needs to be a brief summary of the main arguments or points from your writing. It is also useful to restate your opinion from the introduction.

F ✎ Writing

1   Work with a partner and answer these questions.

   a   Look at this exam-style question. Decide exactly what you have to do. Do **not** write anything yet.

> Here are some views about chewing gum expressed by students you know.
>
> Chewing gum helps me concentrate when I'm studying.
>
> I chew gum when I feel hungry.
>
> Dropping gum on the street is a very dirty habit.
>
> All my friends chew gum, so I do as well.
>
> Write an article for a newspaper or magazine aimed at young people, giving your opinion about chewing gum.
>
> Your article should be 150–200 words long (Extended) or 100–150 words long (Core).
>
> The comments above may give you some ideas and you should try to use some ideas of your own.
>
> You will receive up to 10/7 marks for the content of your article and up to 9/6 marks for the style and accuracy of your language.

   b   What do you think the layout of your answer should be? How many paragraphs should it include? Do you need an introduction and a conclusion? Why, or why not?

   c   How should you organise the content of your article? What exactly should each paragraph include? Make notes about what is needed.

2   Look at these three short introductions to the question in Activity F1. Work with a partner and decide which you think is the most effective. Give reasons.

   a   I think chewing gum is not a problem. It tastes good and helps me relax when I'm concentrating on something. There are many different views on chewing gum and I'm going to discuss some of them here.

   b   Different people have different opinions about the subject of chewing gum. Some people see no problem with it, while others feel it is a bad habit. Personally, I think chewing gum is not a very good thing to do.

   c   Chewing gum can cause medical problems inside the stomach, but it can also be used as a type of medicine to help people to stop smoking. For this reason, I believe that chewing gum is a good thing for our society.

3   Look at these three short conclusions (d–f) to the question in Activity F1. Work with your partner and decide which you think is the most effective. Which conclusion goes with each introduction (a–c) in Activity F2? Give reasons.

d So, because I think the medical benefits of chewing gum described here are more important than the negative effects, I believe that chewing gum is good and we should not have a problem in letting people use it.

e Therefore, I don't see the point in banning something that is so good to eat, and which can help me to focus at school and when I'm doing my homework. It is not a problem.

f In conclusion, I can understand the need for freedom and to let people do what they want. However, chewing gum causes many problems to the environment, and so I think it is a bad habit for people.

4 Work on your own. Use your notes and ideas from the previous activities to write two paragraphs: the **introduction** and the **conclusion** to your article. Make sure that you **state your purpose** in writing the article and **restate your main opinion** about the subject at the end.

5 Read your partner's two paragraphs. What do you think? Have they given **a reason for writing** and **restated their main opinion** in the conclusion?

6 Now write the 'body' of the article. Think carefully about how many paragraphs you need to express your opinions. Remember the word limit!

7 Read as many answers from other students as possible. How are they similar or different to your answer? Why is this?

G 📖 Reading

1 Work with a partner and answer these two questions.

a What foods are bad for your health? How do you know?

b There are many foods that are bad for the future of Earth's health, as well as your own health. What do you think they are? Why?

2 Look at this list of food types.

> fast food, genetically modified (GM) foods, non-organic foods, meat, non-local food, packaged and processed food, rice, seafood, sugar, white bread

a Which do you think are bad for the future of Earth's health? Why do you think this? Consider not only what the food contains, but also **how** and **where** it is produced.

b What impact do you think food production has on our planet?

3 Match the phrases (a–f) below with **three** of the food types from Activity G2. There are two phrases for each of the three food types. Give reasons for your choices.

a … annual consumption is expanding each year by about two million tonnes

b … is an important food staple for more than half the world's population

c … is present in many products we consume every day

d … most, if not all, of this is produced in factory farms

e … uses up a lot of water, and as fresh water supplies are growing scarce, this can be a problem

f … wasteful use of wrappers, straws, bags, boxes, tomato sauce packets and plastic is the biggest source of urban litter in many countries

4 As you read the text below, fill in the gaps (a–f) with the phrases from Activity G3. Which piece of information about the three foods do you find the most surprising? Why?

Satisfying our hunger is bad for planet Earth

Nowadays, everyone has a pretty good idea about which foods are good for us and, of course, which foods are not OK to eat. And the old saying, 'Everything in moderation, nothing in excess' holds true today just as much as it did when Socrates (supposedly) said those words more than 2500 years ago. But something we need to remember is that there are many foods that are bad for Earth's health, let alone our own – mainly due to the processes used in producing them and getting them into our shops and kitchens. Some of these foods that are bad for the planet are: fast food, genetically modified (GM) foods, non-organic foods, meat, non-local food, packaged and processed food, rice, seafood, sugar, white bread.

Read about three of the main culprits.

Sugar

Sugar **(a)** … , yet we rarely give a second thought to how and where it is produced, nor to what toll it may take on the environment. More than 145 million tonnes of sugar (sucrose) is produced per year in about 120 countries and **(b)** … . Sugar production does indeed have a negative impact on soil, water and the air, especially in threatened tropical ecosystems near the equator. Sugar production destroys the natural habitats of many living creatures, to make way for new plantations. Furthermore, it uses water intensively for irrigation and pollutes the environment through excessive use of agricultural chemicals. As if those were not bad enough, the sugar-production process also discharges huge quantities of polluted waste water. Not so sweet after all, is it?

Fast food

It is not just the chemicals in fast food that affect the environment, but the whole production chain itself. One of the most common ingredients in fast food is meat, and **(c)** … . It is an unfortunate fact that factory farms contribute more to global warming than all of our cars put together. Consider also that many fast food products have to be transported long distances, further increasing their impact on air quality. But it does not end there. Fast-food products also have a negative impact on local water quality, due to the hormones, drugs and fertilisers that are used in their production. These enter groundwater, potentially causing illness to humans as well as to fish. And of course fast food outlets also use a lot of packaging. This **(d)** … . Now, do you want extra fries with your burger?

Rice

Rice **(e)** … . However, the use of chemicals, in the form of pesticides and other chemicals to treat the rice or the soil it is growing in, damages not just the pests, but it also affects the entire ecosystem in the area. It reduces the quality of the soil and harms animals and plant life in the process. Rice farming typically requires intensive irrigation. This **(f)** … . Rice farming can be made less wasteful by switching to more efficient means of irrigation, such as drip-feed irrigation. So, did you order plain or fried rice with your meal?

5 Work in groups of three for the following activities.

    a Allocate between you the three food types from the text: sugar, fast food, rice.

    b On your own, use paper or digital reference sources to find out as much new information as you can about your food type.

    c Report back to your group. Agree between you who has discovered the most interesting facts.

H 🗨 Speaking

1 How many of the foods and food types you have read about and researched in Activities G4 and G5 do you eat regularly? Are you likely to change your eating habits as a result of what you have read? Why or why not?

2 Think about your daily diet: what does it consist of? Do you think you have a healthy diet? Why or why not?

3 How does what **you** eat impact the earth?

I 🖱 Writing

1 Look at this exam-style question. Do **not** write anything yet.

You have just finished researching how the production of food impacts the environment.

Write an email or letter to a friend telling them about your findings. In your email or letter you should:

- tell your friend why you conducted the research

- explain the most interesting information you found

- describe what you are going to do as a result of your research.

Your email or letter should be 150–200 words long (Extended) or 100–150 words long (Core).

Do not write an address.

The pictures above may give you some ideas and you should try to include some ideas of your own.

You will receive up to 10/7 marks for the content of your letter and up to 9/6 marks for the style and accuracy of your language.

2 Consider exactly what you have to do and plan your answer accordingly. What are **three** important instructions that you **must** follow?

3 Write your email or letter. Give it to your partner to read and check.

TOP TIPS

Whenever you do a writing task, planning is very important: you should underline the key word/s in the question to make sure you do exactly what is asked. Write very brief notes, putting your ideas into a logical order. Check for repetition in your notes, then write your answer. When you have finished, check your spelling, grammar and punctuation.

J ➕ Further practice

Write

1   Answer the following exam-style question.

> Scientific research plays an important part in making sure we have enough food to eat. Here are some comments that you have heard on the subject:
>
> > We must use science to help us to produce more food.
>
> > If I'm hungry, I'll buy and eat anything I want.
>
> > Fewer chemicals, more flavour – what's wrong with that?
>
> > I only eat organic, locally grown produce.
>
> Write an article for your school website giving your views.
>
> Your article should be 150–200 words (Extended) or 100–150 words (Core).
>
> The comments above may give you some ideas and you should try to use some ideas of your own.
>
> You will receive up to 10/7 marks for the content of your article and up to 9/6 marks for the style and accuracy of your language.

Read and answer

2   Re-read the text *Satisfying our hunger is bad for planet Earth* on page 172 and answer the following questions.

   a   Apart from production processes, what else about food is bad for planet Earth?

   b   How many food culprits are listed?

   c   Which part of the world is particularly at risk from sugar production?

   d   Give **two** ways in which sugar production pollutes the environment.

   e   Why is fast-food transportation a problem for the earth?

   f   Other than people, what else might be affected by groundwater pollution?

   g   How many people rely on rice as part of their daily food?

   h   Identify **one** similarity between sugar and rice production.

Present

3   Most schools ban chewing gum. In the role of a teacher, give a short presentation on why it is unacceptable to chew gum in schools. Consider not only pollution and health, but also the attitude that chewing gum can convey to others.

Write

4   Television has been described as 'chewing gum for the eyes'. In other words, it keeps us entertained, but does not offer us very much else! Do you agree or disagree? Why? Write 150–200 words (Extended) or 100–150 words (Core).

Exam-style questions

1 Look at the advertisement, then answer the following question.

> **COMPETITION**
> # YOUNG SCIENTIST
> We would like you to tell us about something scientific that you have researched.
> What was the topic? How did you research it?
> What did you find out? How did you present your findings?
> Write us a short article.
> Fantastic prizes to be won!
> Best entries will appear online!

You have just read this announcement in an online newspaper and have decided to enter the competition. Write your entry.

Your answer should be 150–200 words long (Extended) or 100–150 words long (Core).

The questions in the announcement may give you some ideas and you should try to use some ideas of your own.

You will receive up to 10/7 marks for the content of your article and up to 9/6 marks for the style and accuracy of your language.

2 Some students at your school have asked for support for their campaign against using animals for medical research. Here are some different views on the subject.

> It is wrong to harm or kill animals just to help people.

> I think we should only use animals for testing things that could save human lives, not things like beauty products.

> It is essential that we test new medicines on animals before using them on people.

> If we need to test new products, we should test them on ourselves.

Write an article for your school website, giving your views.

Your article should be 150–200 words long (Extended) or 100–150 words long (Core).

The comments above may give you some ideas and you should try to use some ideas of your own.

You will receive up to 10/7 marks for the content of your article and up to 9/6 marks for the style and accuracy of your language.

In this unit, you will have the chance to practise and develop your speaking skills.

In this unit, you will also:

- read a fashion magazine interview with a designer
- discuss what fashion is
- consider different people's opinions about fashion
- make notes and write a competition entry
- talk about school uniforms.

A 🗩 Speaking

Fashion doesn't mean useful.

Fashion is a personal statement, not a style.

There are rules in fashion.

1 Work with your partner. Look at the pictures and statements, then answer these questions.

a What is fashion? Is it only clothes that are fashionable? What about furniture? Food? Mobile phones? Cafés? Opinions? Holidays? Pets?

b Does fashion affect you in a positive or negative way? How?

c What do you consider to be fashionable nowadays? Why?

d Do you follow fashion? If not, why not? Are you a fashionable person? Why, or why not?

e Which of the statements above do you agree or disagree with most? Why?

f Is fashion only for people who can afford it? Why, or why not?

2 Work in small groups and discuss these questions.

a What was fashionable when your parents and grandparents were young?

b Is there anything from those eras that you consider fashionable today?

c What types of things tend to remain in fashion?

d What do you understand by the term 'classic'? Have you seen it used in advertising?

e How do you think fashion will change in the next five years? What about in 20 years? Or even in 50 years?

3   You are going to read a magazine interview with a clothes designer. Before you read, work with a partner and decide whether you think the following statements are true or false. Give reasons.

   a   The clothing industry is backward.

   b   Clothes are made in more or less the same way as they were 2000 years ago.

   c   The Jeane Company (famous for its jeans), GHK Electrics (famous for its electronics) and Giovanni Conte (famous for his designs) are collaborating on technical clothing.

   d   The first Jeane Company jeans were sold in 1874.

   e   One day, all clothes will contain micro-computers.

4   All the statements in Activity A3 are based on the magazine interview. Do any of them surprise you and your partner? Why, or why not?

5   Look at statement c in Activity A4 again, then answer these questions with your partner.

   a   What do you think might be the result of the Jeane Company–GHK–Conte collaboration?

   b   What is technical clothing and what will technical clothing **look like**?

   c   What do you think the technical clothing will actually **do**?

B 📖 Reading

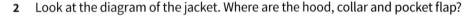

1   You will see the following words in the interview. What do they mean? Use paper or digital reference sources to help you.

| fibre spin thread weave cloth |

2   Look at the diagram of the jacket. Where are the hood, collar and pocket flap?

3   Read the questions below and identify the key word/s in each one. Decide exactly what information is being asked for. Discuss with your partner.

   a   What has changed about clothing over the years?

   b   How many basic stages are there in the clothes-making process?

   c   What roles do the three partners have?

   d   Where in the new jackets will the earphones be?

   e   What will happen when the phone rings?

   f   How are the phone and the MP3 player controlled?

   g   Where does Conte get the ideas for his clothes from?

   h   What type of garments form the majority of Conte's collection?

   i   What does Conte hope to include in his future designs?

   j   What would be the **two** benefits of face-recognition cameras?

   k   Why do you think the interviewer asks if Conte's designs will look fashionable?

4   In pairs, try to predict the answers to the questions. Compare your answers with those of other students.

TOP TIPS

Some questions may ask you to identify people's feelings and attitudes, as well as testing you on general comprehension. Make sure that you write clearly and that you include all the necessary information.

177

5   Read the magazine interview and write your answers. Check your predictions in Activity B4 and make any necessary changes.

Clothing Technology

Last week, our fashion and style reporter, Tammy Smith, spent some time with Giovanni Conte, who was last year voted the most influential designer of the millennium (so far …!). Here's what happened when they met up in the Royal Hotel …

TS: Giovanni, is it true that the clothes industry is technically backward?

GC: Most definitely! For example, although the actual fibres we use in producing materials have changed considerably over the centuries, the clothes-making process itself is basically the same: spin the fibre into thread, weave the thread into cloth, cut it into pieces and then sew it back together again to make an item of clothing. Very simple, really.

TS: But I understand all this is about to change, isn't it?

GC: That's my plan, yes, and it's incredibly exciting. I have got together with GHK Electrics and the Jeane Company to produce a range of technical clothing. We have incorporated GHK mobile-phone and MP3 technology into a range of jackets designed by me and made by the Jeane Company.

TS: But mobile-phone and MP3 technology incorporated into clothes? How does that work?

GC: Well, the jackets, which will soon be available in shops all over the world, will feature phones which can be dialled using voice-recognition technology, and a microphone and earphones built into the hood or collar.

The MP3 player automatically cuts out when the phone rings, like on an aircraft when an announcement is made. Everything is controlled via a keypad hidden beneath a pocket flap.

TS: But what happens when the jacket gets dirty?

GC: The whole range is totally machine-washable and very fast-drying.

TS: Where do you get your design ideas from?

GC: Over the years, I've collected clothes from all over the world and, in my studio in Bologna, I have built up a wardrobe of more than 50,000 garments, mostly military uniforms, which provide me with inspiration for my designs.

TS: Apart from the phone and MP3 player, what else could be incorporated into your designs?

GC: Currently, I am looking into the possibility of building in a face-recognition camera, which would provide you with information about a person when you meet them again. Parents could keep an eye on their children through miniature cameras. And all this technology would be invisible, submerged in the fabric. It won't be long before all clothes contain some sort of micro-computer.

TS: But with all this in-built technology, will clothes still look fashionable?

GC: But of course! It's very important that clothes look beautiful, so I have tried to achieve the right balance between fashion and usefulness, just as the Jeane Company first did in 1874. My designs do not look like clothes from space!

And there you have it. An extremely interesting look at what we'll all be wearing next year!

178

LANGUAGE TIP

Look at this phrase from the text:

… **although** *the actual fibres we use in producing materials have changed considerably over the centuries, the clothes-making process itself is basically the same.*

The word *although* could be replaced by several other forms, with no change in meaning:

even though   though   despite the fact that   in spite of the fact that   while   whilst

Try to use a variety of these forms in your speaking and writing, in order to sound more natural and fluent.

6   Work in groups of three (A, B and C). Together, complete the notes below by writing one or two words only in each gap. Do **not** look back at the text.

> **Technology tomorrow – the clothes industry**
>
> a   Clothes fibres have changed, but clothes-making process is same: spinning, weaving, … and … .
>
> b   Technical clothing to be produced by GHK Electrics and the Jeane Company, range of … , designed by Giovanni Conte, and soon available in shops.
>
> c   Jackets will have phones with … technology, microphone and earphones in hood or … .
>
> d   … controls everything, hidden under pocket flap.
>
> e   If dirty, jacket can be washed in … .
>
> f   Conte gets ideas from all over the world, has in excess of … items in his Bologna studio, which inspire his designs.
>
> g   Future designs could include … for face-recognition with technology … in the fabric, and therefore … .
>
> h   Clothes will still be … and will not look like clothes from … .

7   Now, **two** students (A and B) are going to be Tammy Smith and Giovanni Conte. A and B read the interview, while the **third** student (C) listens and checks the notes you made.

C   Writing

1   Look at this exam-style question. Discuss with your partner exactly what you have to do. Do **not** write anything yet.

> **Win a techno-jacket!**
>
> First prize: GHK-Jeane Company-Conte jacket with built-in phone and MP3 player!
> To enter the competition: write an article telling us WHY you would like to win the techno-jacket and HOW it would be useful to you.
> Email your entry to: technojacketcomp@ghkjcc.it

You have seen this advertisement in a magazine for a competition to win a techno-jacket. You have decided to enter.

Write an article in which you:

- give your reasons for wanting to win the jacket
- explain how you would use the technology in the jacket
- say why you deserve to win the prize.

Your article should be 150–200 words long (Extended) or 100–150 words long (Core).

You will receive up to 10/7 marks for the content of your article and up to 9/6 marks for the style and accuracy of your language.

LANGUAGE TIP

When you read your class's entries, how can you decide which one is the best? Go back to the competition information in Activity C1 and check the following. Has each student:

• given their reasons for wanting to win the jacket?
• explained how they would use the technology in the jacket?
• said why they deserve to win the prize?

Also, check if they have kept to the word limit, and look carefully at the style and the accuracy of the language they have used.

2 Work on your own. Make notes for each of the **three** sections. Remember that this is a competition, so your ideas need to be imaginative and interesting!

3 When you are satisfied with your planning, write your entry. Do not include your name! If possible, email your entry to your teacher.

4 Your teacher will give you copies of all the entries from your class. With a partner, read all the entries and decide which one should win the prize. Be prepared to say why.

D 🗨 Speaking

1 Which of the following words and phrases do you think you are likely to hear when people are talking about fashion? Work with your partner and give reasons for your choices.

a alternative styles
b being 'in'
c current fashion trends
d design and engineering

e Ferrari or Lamborghini
f pair of trainers
g sunglasses
h the latest gear

2 Look at the pictures of the six people and try to match them with the words and phrases above. Give reasons for your choices.

3 Now match the pictures 1–6 with the comments a–f below. Work with a partner and give reasons for your choices. There are no right or wrong answers.

a I think we should wear what we can afford and what we feel comfortable in.

b I will do anything to have the latest gear.

c Fashion is art, design and architecture all combined.

d It's crazy how much we parents have to spend, just because of so-called fashion!

e I'm going to have to keep dreaming for a few more years yet!

f To be honest, I hate fashion and all that it represents: money, beauty, and so on.

4 Work with your partner and do the following.

a On your own, choose **three** people from the six in Activities D2 and D3. Think about words or phrases that each person might think or say. Write down **two** words or phrases for each person, making a total of **six**. Do **not** discuss anything with your partner.

b In turns, read out **one** of your words or phrases. Your partner guesses the person and gives a reason.

5 Look at this exam-style question and answer the questions with your partner.

> Imagine you hear six people talking about fashion. For each of the speakers 1–6, choose from the list, A–G, which opinion each speaker expresses. Write the letter in the box. Use each letter only once. There is one extra letter which you do not need to use.
>
> **[6 marks]**

a How many people will you hear?

b What will they be talking about?

c How many options are there?

d Where do you put your answers?

e How many times can you use each letter?

f What do you have to do with the extra letter?

g How many marks are there for this exercise?

TOP TIPS

In some listening exercises, you have to listen to a number of short extracts and match each speaker to appropriate content. There is usually one extra piece of content that you do not need to use. Remember:

- It is important to read the question carefully and make sure you understand the topic that the speakers are going to talk about before you do anything else.
- Then read the options that you are going to match to each speaker.
- You will hear everything twice, so try to make all the matches during the first listening.
- Then check them during the second listening.

E 📖 Reading

1 Work with your partner and discuss these questions.

a Do you have to wear a uniform to school? How do feel about this?

b What are the advantages and disadvantages of wearing a uniform to school?

c Think of **at least five** jobs where a person has to wear a uniform. Why is a uniform required? Is it always for the same reason?

2 Look at these words and phrases taken from the text on page 182. Use paper and digital reference sources to check their meanings.

a create an atmosphere

b sweeping the nation

c erase their individuality

d peer-pleasing designs

e ridicule

f mandatory

3 Copy the table. Then read the article about school uniforms and complete the two columns: *reasons for* and *reasons against school uniforms.*

Reasons for school uniforms	Reasons against school uniforms
…	…

School uniforms

The introduction of school uniforms in state schools is not a new subject. Schools have a long history of using school uniforms to create an atmosphere of pride, loyalty and equality among the student population. There has always been an image of professionalism associated with having students wear a uniform. It provides for a more businesslike approach to learning, removing some of the distractions normally encountered when children feel they should possess the latest designer fashions, or follow the latest trend sweeping the nation at any given time.

School uniforms also tend to involve students more and make them part of a 'team' at the school. This is not so as to erase their individuality, but to include everyone on the same level, as far as image and dress are concerned.

Another important factor in the use of school uniforms has been cost. With fashions constantly changing from year to year, and even from season to season, parents have always felt the pressure from their children to provide them with the latest peer-pleasing designs. Uniforms reduce the cost of keeping up, since they remain the same – day after day, year after year. And their cost, in relation to fashion merchandise, is very appealing over the long term.

Wearing a uniform at school, as opposed to wearing the latest fashions, may also help the child avoid ridicule, embarrassment or abuse from others that can be caused when the 'have-nots' are compared with the 'haves'. Uniforms assist in avoiding such conflicts by removing the chance for confrontation over clothing, at least during the child's time at school.

The debate will continue. But more and more people in education – students, parents, teachers and administrators – are convinced that mandatory school uniforms lead to success. They point out that pupils in private schools, who achieve impressive academic results, have traditionally worn uniforms. As a result, most state schools have also adopted a school-uniform policy – and the trend seems set to continue.

Adapted from
www.communityonline.com

4 Write your answers to these questions.
   a What image is connected with students in uniform?
   b What does the article say about wearing a uniform and the latest design fashions?
   c How do school uniforms include everyone on the same level?
   d How does wearing a school uniform help parents to save money?
   e What do many people believe about the compulsory wearing of school uniform?

F 🗨 Speaking

1   Work in small groups and discuss the following questions.

   a   In this unit, you have read about the future of fashion. Now think back to how you responded to the question in Activity A2. Do you still think the same?

   b   Which of the six people in Section D are you most like? In what way?

   c   Give your own opinion about fashion, in the same way that the people in Section D did. Make some written notes first.

G ➕ Further practice

Write

1   Imagine that you recently visited a fashion designer.

   Write an email or letter to a friend telling them about your visit. In your email or letter you should:

   ■   describe where you went and who you met

   ■   explain what you saw and what you learned

   ■   give your opinion about their fashions compared with other modern fashions.

   Your email or letter should be 150–200 words long (Extended) or 100–150 words long (Core).

   You may use information and pictures from this unit to help you, and you should try to use some ideas of your own.

   You will receive up to 10/7 marks for the content of your letter and up to 9/6 marks for the style and accuracy of your language.

Present

2   Your entry for the competition in Section C was awarded first prize and you won the techno-jacket! Prepare a short presentation for your school in which you outline the advantages and disadvantages of owning such a jacket.

Research and write

3   Find a fashion picture in a magazine or online, then write an information leaflet about it. In the leaflet, describe the clothing and then give your opinion and ideas on its practicality and desirability. Would you want to wear an outfit like this, or be seen with someone dressed in one? Why or why not?

Design

4   Design a garment or product for the future.

   a   Label your design.

   b   Write a description giving details of the fabrics and colours.

   c   Explain the purposes and advantages of your design.

Appendix 1: Speaking-test cards

- At IGCSE level, many of you will take a speaking exam, while some of you may complete coursework tasks. Many exams will begin with a few questions, so that you can get used to each other's voices and to make you feel more relaxed. These questions will focus on your home and family life, school and perhaps your hobbies and interests as well. You are not being assessed in this part of the exam.

- Here are some examples of topic cards that may form part of the assessed part of the exam. You will be given time to think about the topic on the card and you may ask if you are unsure about anything. You are not allowed to make any written notes. When you are ready, you will have a conversation for a few minutes based on the topic.

- Remember, the topics in a speaking test will be very general and it is not a test of your knowledge about a topic. The important thing is how you use English: your vocabulary and the structure of your sentences, for example.

Card 1

Childhood memories

Many people have lots of memories from when they were young.
Discuss the topic of childhood memories with the examiner.

The following ideas **must** be used in sequence to develop the conversation:

- your earliest memory
- other events that you remember clearly
- things that have affected you later in your life
- whether people are more likely to remember good or bad things
- false memories – why some people remember things that didn't actually happen.

You are free to consider any other **related** ideas of your own.
Remember, you are not allowed to make any written notes.

Card 2

The clothes I like

Everyone likes wearing different clothes for different reasons.
Discuss the topic of 'the clothes I like' with the examiner.

The following ideas **must** be used in sequence to develop the conversation:

- whether you follow the latest fashions
- what your parents think of what you wear
- whether there are any types of clothes that you would not wear
- the influence of famous people on young people's choices
- whether young people's friends' opinions are important.

You are free to consider any other **related** ideas of your own.
Remember, you are not allowed to make any written notes.

Card 3

Changes in lifestyle

There have been many changes in the way people live in your country since the time your grandparents were teenagers.

Discuss the topic of changes in lifestyle with the examiner.

The following ideas **must** be used in sequence to develop the conversation:

- things you have, but your grandparents did not have
- your idea of a healthy lifestyle today, compared to your grandparents' lifestyles
- standards of living; income and possessions
- the way that teenagers behave
- opportunities to travel and knowledge of the world.

You are free to consider any other **related** ideas of your own.

Remember, you are not allowed to make any written notes.

Card 4

Climate change

We are seeing more and more evidence that the climate in many parts of the world is changing – sometimes with disastrous results.

Discuss the topic of climate change with the examiner.

The following ideas **must** be used in sequence to develop the conversation:

- things you already know about climate change
- the effect of climate change on you and where you live
- some examples of disasters caused by these changes
- steps taken in your country to deal with the effects of climate change
- what might be done on a worldwide basis.

You are free to consider any other **related** ideas of your own.

Remember, you are not allowed to make any written notes.

Card 5

Preparation for work

The education you have had so far (and any further education or training you intend to take) will prepare you for the world of work.

Discuss the topic preparation for work with the examiner.

The following ideas **must** be used in sequence to develop the conversation:

- subjects you are studying that might help you in a job
- skills you have developed from your hobbies that might be useful later on
- whether some of your subjects seem to have little to do with your intended career
- whether part-time work while young people are still studying might be a good idea
- other aspects of life that may help young people when they enter the world of work.

You are free to consider any other **related** ideas of your own.

Remember, you are not allowed to make any written notes.

Card 6

Studying abroad

Nowadays, many young people spend some time studying away from their home country.

Discuss the topic of studying abroad with the examiner.

The following ideas **must** be used in sequence to develop the conversation:
- what you might learn from the experience of a different country
- some of the problems you may have living and learning in a foreign country
- difficulties of settling down after a period away from home
- how study abroad might be an advantage in finding employment
- some of the problems of studying in a different education system.

You are free to consider any other **related** ideas of your own.

Remember, you are not allowed to make any written notes.

Card 7

Road accidents and road safety

There are more and more worries about the number of people who are injured in accidents on roads.

Discuss the topic of road accidents and road safety with the examiner.

The following ideas **must** be used in sequence to develop the conversation:
- your experiences of road accidents
- your opinion about why accidents happen
- who are most likely to have accidents – pedestrians, cyclists, motorists
- some consequences of road accidents
- some steps that might be taken to reduce the number of accidents.

You are free to consider any other **related** ideas of your own.

Remember, you are not allowed to make any written notes.

Card 8

Watching sport

Some people like to take part in sports, others prefer to be spectators.

Discuss the topic of watching sport with the examiner.

The following ideas **must** be used in sequence to develop the conversation:
- sports that you go to see or would like to see
- your thoughts about extreme sports and what young people think about them
- what it is about sport that makes it interesting to watch
- the difference between watching on television and actually being there
- whether some sportsmen and women get paid far too much money.

You are free to consider any other **related** ideas of your own.

Remember, you are not allowed to make any written notes.

Card 9

Happiness

We all like to be happy, but what does that mean to each of us?
Discuss the topic of happiness with the examiner.

The following ideas **must** be used in sequence to develop the conversation
- happy moments you have had in your life
- what might make you unhappy
- how you would define happiness
- what might make someone unhappy
- the idea that as we get older we expect to be less happy
- whether it is true that 'Happiness is a state of mind'.

You are free to consider any other **related** ideas of your own.
Remember, you are not allowed to make any written notes.

Card 10

The police

A police force is necessary to enforce the law, but how strict should it be?
Discuss the topic of the police with the examiner.

The following ideas **must** be used in sequence to develop the conversation
- any experience you have had with the police
- what you would do if you were head of the police force
- the characteristics needed to be a good police officer
- reasons why the police might be criticised
- how much power the police should have.

You are free to consider any other **related** ideas of your own.
Remember, you are not allowed to make any written notes.

Card 11

Young children

Some young children need to be constantly busy and require a lot of attention.
Discuss the topic of young children with the examiner.

The following ideas **must** be used in sequence to develop the conversation
- your experience of being with young children
- activities you think young children enjoy
- the challenges of being a teacher of young children
- how young children might be treated differently in different societies
- situations where young children have to 'grow up' very quickly.

You are free to consider any other **related** ideas of your own.
Remember, you are not allowed to make any written notes.

Unit 1: D Speaking Activity 1 Track 2

Maria: Hi Christos, how are you?

Christos: Hey Maria, I'm really great, what about you?

Maria: Everything's fine! <u>Why don't we go</u> to the shopping centre later? I want to see if I can get some new trainers.

Christos: Yes, we could do that, but <u>I'd rather go</u> at the weekend. Can you wait until then?

Maria: I suppose so, but why?

Christos: Well, I get paid for my part-time job tomorrow, so I'll have some money to spend.

Maria: Fair enough! So <u>let's go</u> at the weekend instead. But what are we going to do today?

Unit 3: E Speaking Activity 1 Track 3

Anna: <u>I strongly believe that</u> fast food restaurants are here to stay.

Terry: <u>I honestly don't agree with that</u>. I am sure that people are beginning to realise how unhealthy fast food is.

Anna: But it's so convenient! <u>I can't imagine</u> people giving that up.

Terry: <u>I'm not so sure about that.</u>

Unit 4: A Speaking and listening Activity 7 Track 4

Speaker 1

Well, of course, we had booked everything well in advance, because in Britain these services get full very early, and we didn't want to be disappointed. Anyway, we got to the terminus in central London in plenty of time and we stood on platform 13E for Edinburgh. It was a beautiful summer's day. There was me, my wife Julia and the three children. They were still quite young then: three, six and eight, I think. We were supposed to leave at 8.30 in the morning and, as it got closer to our departure time, we all began to get quite excited. By 8.30, we had started to get a little bit anxious because the platform was completely empty, apart from us five with all our luggage. At 9.00, Julia told me to go and find out what was happening, so off I went to the booking office to make enquiries. And yes, you can guess what was wrong – we were 12 hours early! Our departure time was 8.30 p.m., not a.m. I had misread the time on the tickets.

Speaker 2

They call it an airport, but it's really just a field. My sister had booked me a flight as a treat for my 13th birthday, which was May 20th, three years ago, and I must admit that I was absolutely dreading it! I've never really enjoyed flying, and the thought of going up in the air for 30 minutes in a basket really didn't appeal to me. I couldn't understand how the thing was driven and steered, and I think that's what put me off. But once we got up in the air, at 9 o'clock in the morning, it was spectacular – the most beautiful views of the hills, fields and villages below, with the sun sparkling on the river. We didn't want to come down!

Speaker 3

I had investigated all the different options available to me and, in the end, this was by far the cheapest, at only $275. Of course, it wouldn't be nearly as fast as going by plane, but the cost was far less and I would be able to see something of the countryside. Some friends had travelled the same route the previous year and had said how brilliant it had been, so I wasn't really worried. What they hadn't told me was how uncomfortable these vehicles are when you've been in one for almost two days. It's very difficult to sleep, and there are no toilets or washing facilities, so you've got to hang on until the scheduled stops, usually every four to five hours. When I finally arrived in the south of Spain, after nearly 48 hours on the road, I slept for over 19 hours!

Speaker 4

We set off in the afternoon, as the sun was starting to drop, and with it the temperature, although it was still incredibly hot and humid. We knew the journey would take about two hours, so we had time to reach the oasis before dark, and before the temperature plummeted. With me was my twin teenager sister, Amelia. She was used to riding horses, so this wasn't as difficult for her as it was for me. Even so, she said that riding without a saddle was very uncomfortable, and I had to agree with her! She also complained about not having a riding hat, but I told her she'd look pretty silly if she did! We moved at a leisurely pace – these wonderful animals won't be rushed – and we had time to be amazed by the beautiful scenery all around us and, as dusk fell, in the sky as well. We arrived, made camp, ate and fell into a deep sleep under the stars.

Unit 4: B Speaking and listening
Activity 2 Track 5

For many years, *boda-bodas* have been called Uganda's silent killers. *Boda-bodas*, our country's ubiquitous motorbike taxis, snake through traffic jams, navigate potholed roads and provide much-needed employment for young people. They are also injuring and killing thousands every year, monopolising hospital budgets and destroying livelihoods. Since they appeared on the streets of Uganda in the 1960s, the number of *boda-bodas* has swelled. One recent news report estimated that there were more than 300,000 bikes operating in the capital, Kampala.

As a result, the number of motorbike accidents has increased dramatically. According to the Injury Control Centre, there are up to 20 *boda-boda*-related cases at Mulago National Referral Hospital in Kampala every day and the strain on the country's limited health budget is growing. About 40% of trauma cases at the hospital are from *boda-boda* accidents. The treatment of injured passengers and pedestrians accounts for almost two-thirds of the hospital's annual surgery budget.

While *boda-bodas* are helping to reduce youth unemployment – one recent study estimated that 62% of young people in Uganda are jobless – the impact of a serious injury can be catastrophic for riders and their families. Ali Niwamanya, 25, a *boda-boda* driver, spent three months in Mulago hospital and another five at home recovering after a collision with a car in the capital in September. Niwamanya is now in debt after taking out a 3 million Ugandan shilling loan (that's about 1200 US dollars) for a new bike.

While the human impact of the *boda-boda* craze is evident in the packed hospital wards, the strain that road fatalities could have on the economy is worrying politicians. The death toll on Uganda's roads is twice the average across the rest of Africa. There were 3343 road deaths in 2011, but the World Health Organization believes the figure could be more than double that. Some people are warning that, in the very near future, the death toll from Uganda's roads will be higher than that from diseases such as malaria.

Some measures are being taken to try to halt the problem. Last month, the government announced that more money would be available to improve and maintain roads. Even though road safety measures were not specifically included within the budget, the government is establishing a national agency to run campaigns and manage roads. In Kampala, the Capital City Authority is introducing regulations, including registration of drivers, first-aid training, reflector jackets and helmets, and a monthly fee of 20,000 Ugandan shillings paid by the city's 250,000 motorbike taxis.

Other initiatives are also springing up. The Global Helmet Vaccine Initiative is holding a one-day workshop for 100 riders, part of a national scheme under which it has trained 1800 *boda-boda* riders in basic road safety. On completion, each participant receives a yellow helmet bearing the slogan: 'Your life is your wealth.'

Adapted from www.theguardian.com

Unit 4: D Speaking   Activity 1   Track 6

Male teenager: The thing that surprised me more than anything was the number of *boda-bodas* on the roads.

Female teenager: What surprised me most was the number of injuries and deaths.

MT: I couldn't believe how long Ali Niwamanya was in hospital for.

FT: I had no idea about the rate of unemployment.

Unit 4: E Listening   Activity 3   Track 7

A

Woman: Good morning, Mega Music Store, how can I help you?

Gregory: Hi, I'd like to know if I can order something from you.

W: Yes, of course – we can help you with DVDs and MP3 downloads, as well as other software and tablets, and so on.

G: Actually, I don't want any of those; I just want to order a power cable. The product number is CD39 dash 2BK. Can you do that?

W: Certainly. Let me take your details …

B

Here is the weather forecast for tomorrow for your local area. There will be some light rain overnight, turning to sunny spells in the early morning and there will be high clouds by the end of the morning. Heavy showers are forecast for the late afternoon and evening. The top temperature is expected to be 18 degrees Celsius.

C

Marina: Hello, could I have some information about your evening classes, please?

College secretary: Of course. Are you interested in anything in particular, or do you want details of everything we offer?

M: I'm interested in learning a new language. I want to learn Italian!

CS: If you look over there, behind those bookshelves, you'll find leaflets about all our evening classes, or you could use one of the computers to check online.

D

Thank you for calling the Health and Fitness Sports Centre, the home of tennis, squash, badminton, futsal and swimming. The Sports Centre management has just introduced new prices for using the tennis facilities, so for non-members a weekend court will now cost €12 an hour, while during the week, the daytime price is €8 and €10 after 6 p.m. For members, the price is €9 at any time during the week, and €11 at the weekend.

Unit 4: F Further practice Activity 3
Track 8

Modern-day Turkey covers an area that has stood at the crossroads of history for thousands of years, leaving it with an incredible number of fantastic sights for visitors to explore. With so many options, selecting the top tourist attractions in Turkey is tough. However, I've put together a selection of some of Turkey's most famous attractions, along with a couple of gems that I feel you really should know about. No matter what you're looking for in Turkey, whether it's a relaxing beach holiday, a city-break or a journey into the country's ancient past, something or somewhere will inspire you.

Firstly, and probably the most famous tourist attraction in Turkey, the Hagia Sophia is one of the best-preserved ancient buildings in the world. Built in the 6th century CE by the Byzantine Emperor Justinian, the building was converted to a mosque with the Turkish conquest and today operates as a museum.

Turkey is awash with ancient cities, making it tough to select just one. However, the most popular of these attractions is Ephesus near the modern town of Selcuk. It contains some of the best-preserved Greek and Roman ruins in the world. Impressive attractions at Ephesus include the Library of Celsus, the Temple of Hadrian and the ancient theatre.

If you've had enough history, the Istanbul Dolphinarium presents you with a unique chance to explore the fascinating world of sea mammals. Here, by taking a closer look at these magnificent creatures, you will get to know them better and realise their importance. You can watch the marine mammals' exciting show, swim, interact or scuba dive with the dolphins. Also, there are individual dolphin-therapy sessions for the kids with special needs.

Finally, there are many reasons why you should visit the Princes' Islands. For starters, all of the islands are car-free, and you can rent a bike and cycle around the islands, without fear of getting knocked over. If you go in the spring, you'll enjoy fresh air and green space, while in the summer, think about bringing your swimming things as the weather will be warm enough to think about having a dip in the sea.

Enjoy Turkey!

Adapted from www.historvius.com, www.tripadvisor.co.uk and www.travelsavvymom.com

Unit 4: Exam-style questions Track 9

Question 1

And now for the prices and opening times at the Star Cinema. All tickets are priced at $10 for adults and $6.50 for students and children. Our weekend opening time is two o'clock in the afternoon and on weekdays we open one hour later, at three.

Question 2

Daniela: Do you sell street maps?

Shopkeeper: Well, yes, we do, but I'm afraid we've sold out.

D: Do you know where I can get one?

S: Try the newsagent's on the other side of the park. Or the shop at the bus station will have plenty.

D: Isn't there anywhere closer than the bus station?

S: Let me think … Oh yes, the supermarket across the road from here.

Question 3

Jason: Excuse me! Sorry to trouble you but I'm completely lost! This is my first day working here and I can't find where I need to go!

Woman: You must be the new part-time helper, right? Don't worry, you'll soon find your way around. This is the staff room. But where do you want to go?

J: I'm trying to find the supervisor's office. I need to give him my contact details.

Woman: Well, you're not too far away. Look, you see the lift over there? Go up to the second floor and when you get out of the lift, turn left and left again at the end of the corridor. The supervisor's office is the first door on the right.

J: Thanks so much.

Question 4

Welcome aboard our city sightseeing bus. First, let me tell you about the tour. We're going to travel through the most historic parts of the city for about an hour, with lots of opportunities for you to take photos, or just admire the wonderful buildings and scenery. Then we'll drop you off near the market place. You can visit the museum, which is very interesting, or why not buy some fruit and cheese from the market and have a snack in the park next to the museum? But please please please come back promptly to the bus after one hour – we can't wait for any latecomers! Now for some safety information … .

Unit 5: D Speaking Activity 3 Track 10

If I were you, I'd …

I think it would be better …

It might be a good idea …

Why don't we … ?

I don't think she should …

I strongly advise you …

My advice would be …

Unit 6: D Speaking Activity 1 Track 11

Sipho: What do you think about this cosmetic scientist career?

Tendani: Well, you know me, I love biology and chemistry … .

S: Yes, I do too, but I'm not sure it's something that I want to do.

T: OK, but if I were you, I'd think seriously about it.

S: Why?

T: Well, for one thing, there are so many job possibilities.

S: Yes, you're right, but how do I know if it's the right thing for me?

T: You ought to speak to the careers advisor at school.

S: Yes, I know, I have done, but she always asks me the same question: 'What do you want to do when you leave school?'!

T: Why don't you make a list of ideas before you see her?

S: Hmmm, good idea! I should, shouldn't I?

T: What about speaking to your parents? I'm sure they could help.

S: Yes, absolutely. I'll speak to them tonight and then make a list! You know something, Tendani? You should be a careers advisor!

Unit 6: E Listening and speaking
Activity 3 Track 12

Baruti Ngwani: Welcome to this week's show. Today we're going to talk about careers and, in particular, one career which some of you may believe is only for men: working for NASA, the National Aeronautics and Space Administration in the USA! My guest is Kagiso Abaka, a careers advisor for NASA, based here in Joburg. Welcome!

Kagiso Abaka: Hi, Baruti.

BN: So, what does a young woman need to do in order to work for NASA?

KA: The same as a young man, of course! For anyone who likes finding out how things work, solving puzzles and problems, or creating and building things, then why not consider a career in science, technology, engineering or maths? Within NASA, women work in all of these areas, and there is information available on careers and how you can prepare for them.

BN: Interesting … . But what is an engineer? What does an engineer actually do?

KA: Good question! Engineers are the people who make things work, using power and materials. Engineers have moved the world into skyscrapers, high-speed cars, jets and, of course, space vehicles. They make our lives interesting, comfortable and fun. Everything in our daily lives relies heavily on the work of engineers: computers, television, satellites … .

BN: Is there just one type of engineer, then?

KA: No, there are many types, including aerospace, chemical, civil, computer, electrical, industrial, mechanical, and so on. Obviously each type specialises in a particular area.

BN: Hmmm, I see. So is an engineer a scientist?

KA: Not really. Scientists are knowledge seekers, who are always searching out why things happen. They are inquisitive, which means that they are always asking questions. Nature, Earth and the universe are what fascinate the scientist. The scientist questions, seeks answers and expands knowledge.

BN: What career options are available for people like this?

KA: There's an amazing variety. Careers are available in both the life and physical sciences.

BN: For example?

KA: For example … becoming a biologist, medical doctor or nutritionist would all require studies in life sciences, whereas a job as an astronomer, chemist, geologist, meteorologist or physicist would all involve studying the physical sciences.

BN: OK, I see. I've also heard about technicians. What do they do? Is it different from engineers and scientists?

KA: Technicians are an important part of the NASA team. They work closely with scientists and engineers in support of their research. Their skills are used to operate wind tunnels, work in laboratories, construct test equipment, build models and support many types of research.

BN: Most of our listeners are still at school, studying hard, so what should their focus be, if these types of careers are interesting to them?

KA: Well, obviously, education is a critical requirement. Mathematics and science are the basis for most NASA careers and the decisions you make in school can affect your future career possibilities.

BN: And after high school?

KA: It can seem like a long journey, but a career as a scientist or engineer requires four to seven years of college study after high school. A bachelor's degree requiring four years of study is the minimum necessary. Colleges and universities also offer graduate programmes where students can obtain master's and doctoral degrees. The master's programme usually takes two years. An additional two to four years is needed to earn a doctorate.

BN: And for anyone who likes the idea of a career as a technician?

KA: Well, technicians typically earn a two-year Associate of Science degree. Some may continue for two additional years and obtain a bachelor's degree in engineering technology. Others may earn a bachelor's degree in engineering or one of the physical sciences.

BN: So for those of you who want to think about a career with NASA, it may seem a long way off, but study hard and who knows? One day one of you might be walking on the moon!

Adapted from http://spaceflightsystems.grc.nasa.gov

Unit 7: C Speaking and listening
Activity 4 Track 13

Fatima: OK, Abdullah, let's do some practice for our speaking exam.

Abdullah: Good idea, Fatima. You go first – what's your presentation about?

F: Come on, Abdullah, you should know by now that we don't have to do a presentation or give a speech in the exam.

A: Really? I thought that's what we have to do. So what is it then?

F: We have a discussion with the examiner about a topic. It lasts about 10 to 15 minutes, I think.

A: Great! I'm going to talk about fast-food restaurants and I guess you would choose animals or becoming a vet.

F: Unfortunately, we don't get to choose our topic, Abdullah. The examiner has a set of topic cards and we have to talk about the one he or she chooses for us.

A: But what if I don't know anything about the topic? I won't be able to say anything! Fatima, that's mean!

F: But it's not a test of knowledge about the topic. The topic is just to give us something to talk around. We are being tested on how well we can communicate in English.

A: OK, fair enough. What happens when we see the topic card? Can we make written notes?

F: No, but there are some ideas on the topic card which we can use and we have a couple of minutes to prepare. We should use that time properly, to think and plan for the discussion.

A: And then what happens? We start talking about the topic, right?

F: Yes, that's right. The examiner will ask us some questions, too, about the topic.

A: Do I lose marks if I get the answers wrong?

F: No, Abdullah, there are no right or wrong answers – the examiner just wants to hear you speaking in English. Try to use expressions like: *In my opinion … , I believe … , On the other hand … , On the whole … ,* and so on.

A: Hmmmm, so answering with 'yes' or 'no' is probably not a good idea, right? We need to use 'because' as much as possible.

F: Right! We need to explain ourselves with more ideas and reasons.

A: What happens if I don't understand something? Maybe the examiner will think I'm not very good.

F: Come on, Abdullah! Just tell the examiner if you don't understand, or you could ask them to give you an example, or say something like: *Do you mean … ?*, or ask the examiner to repeat something

A: Like: *Sorry, could you say that again, please?*

F: Exactly!

A: OK, so let's have a look at one of these topic cards, then, so we can practise.

F: There are plenty in the back of our Coursebook, Abdullah …

Unit 8: B Listening Activity 1 Track 14

Pablo Selles: We are very lucky to have in our studio today Janine Mesumo, who works as a careers advisor at an international school in Madrid. Her main role is to advise students who have recently completed their IGCSEs, AS and A Levels on what they should do next. Part of this is giving them advice on writing their first CV. Have I got that right, Janine?

Janine Mesumo: Absolutely, Pablo. Actually, a great deal of my time is spent in helping students draw up their CV, which can be quite problematic when you haven't yet had any work experience.

PS: What areas should first-time CV writers include?

JM: I think the key here is not to try to include too much. Prospective employers need to be able to get a quick overview, rather than a detailed biography of someone's life – that can come at the interview. However, there needs to be enough information, so that the employer can decide whether or not to call the applicant for an interview.

PS: Hmm, I see. So what information would you say is essential?

JM: Start with personal details: name, address, contact details. You'd be surprised how many people forget to put their telephone number and email address on their CV! Then, education and qualifications. Some people recommend combining these two areas; so, for example, you might say '1999–2001, International School, Madrid, six IGCSEs in Maths, English …', and so on, rather than listing the qualifications in a different section.

PS: That's an interesting idea – I like that! What comes next?

JM: Well, this is where some students become rather worried, because usually the next section is work experience.

PS: But often students don't have any work experience!

JM: Exactly, and so they worry about leaving a blank. But as a school- or college-leaver, nobody is going to expect you to have an employment history, so there really is no need to worry. However, it is worth mentioning weekend or after-school jobs, or any work for charities, or voluntary work.

PS: OK, and after that? What about hobbies and interests?

JM: Yes, it is important to include leisure interests, but a common mistake is simply to list things, for example: 'reading, football, music'.

PS: So what should our listeners do?

JM: Instead of simply giving a list, explain in what way these things interest you or what skills you have developed through them. For example, if you put reading, give details about what you like to read …

PS: … and if you list music, what types of music you like listening to.

JM: Exactly, but also, music might mean playing an instrument, so give that information as well. Or if you're the captain of a sports team, include that information as it demonstrates leadership skills.

PS: Any other sections that need to be included?

JM: Well, two really. The first should include any skills which have not been mentioned before, such as IT skills, proficiency in other languages (don't just put 'French'!), and details of any organisations or clubs which you belong to. And finally, give the names, addresses and contact details for two referees.

PS: Which are what?

JM: A referee is a person who would be willing to write about you in a positive way! Always check with the person before you put their name on your CV.

PS: Janine, we're coming to the end of our time. Thank you very much for a very informative chat. If any listeners would like more information on writing their CV, just go onto our website and you'll find everything you need.

193

Unit 8: D Listening Activity 3 `Track 15`

Interviewer: Good morning, Miss Gupta. Please take a seat.

Abha Gupta: Thanks.

Int'er: Did you have any problems getting here?

AG: Nope, I found the address very easily. I checked it out yesterday.

Int'er: I see. Now, you've just left school with four IGCSEs. Is that correct?

AG: Yeah.

Int'er: And the subjects?

AG: Oh, right, err, let me think now … Science, English, Art and Music.

Int'er: Thank you. Which of those was your favourite subject at school?

AG: I didn't really like any of them. The teachers were not very interesting. I must've been really lucky to pass them.

Int'er: And which school did you attend?

AG: The new one, behind the park at the start of the motorway.

Int'er: I see. Now, tell me something about your interests, the things that you do in your free time.

AG: Well, not much really. I like riding my bike. That's why I think this job would be good for me.

Int'er: Because you like riding a bike?

AG: Er, yeah. The job's to do with sport, isn't it?

Int'er: Yes, Miss Gupta, it is. Have you had any work experience yet – for example a weekend job?

AG: Well, yes, I had a job with my brother washing cars. We used to do it in our free time. We got loads of money to spend on clothes and DVDs, or for going to the cinema and other things.

Int'er: What personal qualities do you think you could offer us here at Winning Sports?

AG: Well, like I told you, I like sports, especially riding my bike, and every weekend I go to the match, if they're playing at home, of course. What else do you want to know?

Int'er: I think that's all for the time being, Miss Gupta.

AG: Is that it?

Int'er: Yes, thank you very much, Miss Gupta. That's all. Goodbye.

AG: Did I get the job?

Int'er: I'll be in touch. Goodbye.

Unit 8: D Listening Activity 4 `Track 16`

Int'er: Did you have any problems getting here?

Int'er: Now, tell me something about your interests, the things that you do in your free time.

Int'er: Have you had any work experience yet – for example, a weekend job?

Int'er: What personal qualities do you think you could offer us here at Winning Sports?

Unit 8: E Listening Activity 1 `Track 17`

Part A

Lan Huang: Hello, have a seat. My name's Lan Huang. And you are … Mr Hairilombus Papachristofer *[hesitantly]*, is that correct?

Bambos: Hello, pleased to meet you. Actually, the pronunciation is Haralambous Papachristoforou. Most people call me Bambos, for short. I'm Greek, on my father's side.

LH: Really? How interesting! Did you have any trouble finding our office, ummm … Bambos?

B: Not at all, Ms Huang. I came yesterday to make sure I knew exactly how to find you, and to check how much time I would need. And today I used Google maps on my smartphone, just in case. I arrived two hours early!

LH: That shows good initiative! Now, what is it about the job that interests you?

B: Well, first of all, I visited your website when I saw the advertisement, and discovered more about the format of *Teen Weekly*, and that really interested me.

LH: It did? Why?

B: Basically, I just love writing. Ever since I was a child, I've been writing stories and trying to write poems too. I've also won three writing competitions.

LH: Congratulations! Is there anything else that demonstrates your love for writing?

B: Well, I've been editor of our online school webzine for two years, and I also publish my own monthly blog.

LH: Excellent! Now, obviously our readership is teenagers, young people who are still at school. What do you think are the main interest areas for your age group?

B: I guess for many teenagers, myself included, the most interesting topic is celebrity gossip and stories about film stars and musicians, sports people, important people – where they are, what they are doing, and so on.

But not just gossip. I think many teens are interested in their society and culture, as well as global issues like the environment.

LH: Good. Anything else?

B: Well, for many teenagers, becoming an adult is a scary thought, and they often want to discuss their future education and careers.

LH: Thank you, Bambos. Now, is there anything you would like to ask me?

B: Well, yes, Ms Huang, I have some questions. I made a note on my phone – can I check them?

LH: Please, go ahead …

Unit 8: E Listening Activity 4 Track 18

Part B

Bambos: OK, firstly, what is the commitment in terms of time? I assume it's a part-time position, as I'm still at school?

Lan Huang: Yes, of course. It's very part-time, so only 20 hours per month.

B: Great. Secondly, would I be able to work from home?

LH: Absolutely! In fact, we prefer you to do that. We would probably need you here for a meeting once every two to three months.

B: Perfect. Umm … thirdly, the advertisement mentions 'competitions'. What type of things do you ask your readers to do for these?

LH: Good question! To be honest, this is a new idea and something that we want the successful applicant for the job to consider.

B: Really? That's awesome. OK, finally, is the salary paid weekly or monthly?

LH: As it's a part-time job, based on monthly hours, the company pays at the end of each calendar month.

B: Thank you. That answers all my questions.

LH: Thank you, Bambos. It was a pleasure meeting you.

Unit 8: H Further practice Activity 3
Track 19

Speaker 1

My home country, Nigeria, can be very hot at times, but nothing like the temperatures here in Dubai. I'm not sure I will ever get used to it! Thank goodness that everywhere has air conditioning, but even that doesn't help in the really hot summer months, when it is almost impossible to be outside during the heat of the day. At least the heat forces me to stay indoors to study, and that's the real reason why I'm here – to study and get my degree. I just wish I'd chosen somewhere a little cooler!

Speaker 2

Dubai is so cosmopolitan – it doesn't matter what you like or what you want to do, you can find it here somewhere. It's impossible not to be active doing something every minute of every day because there is just so much to entertain you. My biggest problem is making a choice! When I've done enough studying, it's time to think about which shopping mall to meet my friends at, or which café to go to for some much-needed relaxation. Now that's a challenge!

Speaker 3

My family told me that, in this digital age, I would never be apart from them when I came on my own to study in Dubai. Yes, we chat online every day, and send each other instant messages constantly, and I'm forever downloading photos of my sister's new twin babies, but it's not true – I am alone, and I miss them so much. I've made some friends, it's true, but at the weekends I don't go out much. I just think about my family and how much I miss them all.

Speaker 4

I thought studying here in Dubai would be much easier than back home in Sweden, but you know something? I've never studied so much in all my life! We have so much to read and so many assignments to complete every month, and there always seems to be yet another quiz or test to prepare for. I know it will all be worthwhile in the end, don't get me wrong, and I'm not afraid of hard work, but I'm still young and I want to enjoy this experience as much as possible. There never seems to be enough time for anything apart from studying. And do you know something? I haven't even been to the top of the Burj Khalifa yet, and I've been in Dubai for nearly two years!

Speaker 5

My reason for choosing Dubai as a place to study is mainly because of its location. I thought about a college in Europe, probably the UK, because obviously I speak English, but I decided against it. Not only is it difficult and expensive to travel outside Europe from there, but also the weather is awful! I'm from Brazil, remember?! So, now that I'm here in Dubai, it's easy to travel either east or west. I've already been to Egypt, but next trip I want to go east, maybe to the Maldives, or perhaps further. I'm not sure yet, but the sky is the limit!

195

Speaker 6

I tried at high school to start learning Arabic because I find the language and culture so incredibly interesting, but I failed miserably. It was so difficult to find a good teacher and to meet up with other people trying to learn Arabic so that we could practise together. I almost gave up. But then my dad suggested that I could combine learning Arabic with studying abroad, and that's how I ended up here in Dubai. At first I didn't want to leave home and, unfortunately, being in an international university means that nobody here uses much Arabic. But at least there are plenty of good teachers readily available, and there are plenty of opportunities to practise. An excellent choice I think! Now I love living and studying in Dubai, and my Arabic has really improved.

Unit 8: Exam-style questions Track 20

Interviewer: There used to be more than 20,000 tigers in India, but today, despite heroic efforts by conservationists to protect these great wild cats, there are fewer than 2000 left, in remote areas south-west of Delhi. Sanjit, why is this?

Sanjit Roy: Well, we have managed to deal with hunters who kill tigers for their wonderful fur, but we are now faced with a much greater problem. Cosmetics manufacturers in the West are struggling to meet the demand for products made from talcum powder, and this is bringing the Indian tiger to the point of extinction.

Int'er: So does talcum powder come from tigers?

SR: No, not at all. This white powder comes from marble and other stones, and is used in beauty products, such as eye make-up, lipstick, soap and deodorant. The global market for these products is worth literally billions of dollars to the cosmetics industry.

Int'er: But I still don't see the connection with tigers. Surely these products are harmless.

SR: Oh, yes, the products themselves are harmless. The problem is that the marble which talcum powder is made from is found in the tigers' last natural habitat. This habitat is being destroyed as the marble is extracted.

Int'er: Now I understand, Sanjit. So how serious is the problem?

SR: I predict that, within ten years, the Indian tiger will be no more. It will be lost forever. And all because of our desire to look and smell more beautiful.

Int'er: But surely the tigers could be moved to a sanctuary or a reserve before it's too late. Aren't these protected by environmental laws?

SR: Oh, yes, they certainly are. However, you should not underestimate the impact of the processes used to get marble for talcum powder. Dynamite is used to blast open the ground which borders the tigers' habitat. Great towers of waste are left to litter the landscape. And large areas of forest are destroyed to make way for the mining operations.

Int'er: So what does this loss of habitat actually mean for tigers?

SR: It means that the tigers don't have enough food and water because their hunting area has been drastically reduced in size. Remember also that the territory of an adult male tiger can be anything up to 100 square kilometres.

Int'er: Sanjit, what can be done to save the Indian tiger?

SR: Probably very little. Some of the world's biggest cosmetics manufacturers purchase their talcum powder from India and they are not easily convinced of the damage they are doing to the environment, and to the Indian tiger in particular. However, the Indian government has started to investigate the mining of marble and has begun to order the closure of several mines. But we need more action, and we need it now, before it's too late for the tiger.

Int'er: Sanjit, thank you.

Unit 9: D Speaking Activity 2 Track 21

Student 1

I really think Scott was a hero because of the incredible difficulties that he faced. Firstly, during his attempt to return home after reaching the South Pole, he and his team had very little food and no oil for burning. Also, the weather was extremely cold and Scott was forced to stay in his tent, even though it was only 11 miles to base camp. Can you imagine how that must have felt? Eventually Scott and his team all died in the tent, unable to move outside. They all showed great courage, strength and bravery, but it was such a tragic ending.

Student 2

For me, Scott was not a hero because what he did was simply a hobby for him. I think a hero is someone who shows special qualities when doing something which is not a leisure activity, like a firefighter, for example. I believe what Scott did was hard work – and it was certainly dangerous – but he did it because he wanted to and he enjoyed it. Just think about it: there was no pressure on him and his team to suffer in the way that they did. Sure it was a tragedy, but they did not need to die in such a terrible way, or put other people's lives in danger.

Unit 10: G Listening and speaking
Activity 1 Track 22

Khardung La Pass is at an altitude of 5359 metres and is 39.7 kilometres from Leh. The drive from Leh to Khardung La is about three hours up on a winding road, interrupted by minor landslides and avalanches. Higher up, the mountains are covered with snow that melts slowly into slush and mud. The army maintains this road throughout the day.

The pass is an important gateway to the Nubra and Shyok Valleys, as well as to Siachen Glacier. Construction work for the pass began in 1976 and was first opened 12 years later. Today, it is a two-way road. Though motorable road came late, it has long been navigated by traders. A caravan of about 10,000 horses and camels navigated this road annually on their way to Kashgar in Central Asia.

Hundreds of bikers take this road daily. Some more adventurous travellers drive up to Khardung La and peddle back on their bicycles. The idea of conquering the highest motorable road seems to be on many people's agenda while traversing this pass. Travellers often stop to have their photo taken along with the signpost that proclaims Khardung La Pass to be the highest motorable pass in the world. The pass cuts through the mountain peak and so it offers amazing views of Leh and mountains surrounding the valley.

Adapted from www.mapsofindia.com

Unit 11: C Listening Activity 4 Track 23

Kigongo Odok: Hello, my name is Kigongo Odok. Welcome to another edition of 'Youth Uganda'. Today I am very happy to welcome Namono Alupo, the Project Coordinator for the HARP project here in Uganda. Welcome, Namono!

Namono Alupo: Thank you so much for inviting me, Kigongo!

KO: Namono, adolescents can be a very vulnerable group of people as they make the transition to being an adult. But what exactly is an adolescent?

NA: Good question! Well, neither children nor adults are adolescents: they are young people in the years where their bodies and minds are changing and growing very quickly. Because of this, adolescents are often overlooked by existing health programmes.

KO: Is it the same for *refugee* adolescents?

NA: It's often worse, I'm afraid. The child–adult transition is made even harder for refugee adolescents because of living in a new place, where they may have no family to give them support and guidance.

KO: I guess also that some refugees may have witnessed violent situations, or had to live in poor conditions?

NA: Yes, that's very often the case. Unfortunately, some refugees not only witness, but also experience, violence themselves. Furthermore, their health may have been compromised by poor living conditions, a lack of knowledge about where to go and seek help, and the limited number of health workers able to provide adequate services.

KO: Are there specific problems that adolescent refugee *girls* face?

NA: Yes, of course. It's known that they are often subject to the same problems as their adult counterparts …

KO: Such as?

NA: Well, preferential feeding practices discriminate against girls and women, and food aid frequently neglects the special nutritional requirements of girls and women.

KO: I see. What else?

NA: Well, health services are often inaccessible to women and adolescent refugees, family violence is prevalent, and we need to be aware of safety while seeking water. On top of all that, neither animal feed nor cooking fuel is always readily available – and basic sanitary protection and soap are often unavailable.

KO: So what is HARP doing to help these vulnerable adolescent girls?

NA: HARP provides education on a range of health issues, such as nutrition, physical and emotional changes through adolescence, hygiene, preventing disease, and self-esteem. Refugee girls and young women learn about these topics through the use of Girl Guide and Girl Scout methods. So they create posters, songs, poems and role plays, whatever they feel happy and confident to do. They also create a flipbook, which contains drawings and explanations of the topics.

KO: And how does HARP deal with different ages?

197

NA: There are three curricula for different age groups and, once the girl has completed the curriculum, she gains a badge. Leaders from the local refugee community are trained to be able to deliver the HARP programme.

KO: So how do the girls help their communities?

NA: Well, the second part of the project then challenges each girl to take the messages they have learned out to the local community through peer education …

KO: Meaning … ?

NA: Meaning that they use the flipbook and the songs, poems and role plays that they have created to teach their friends about the topics they have covered. Each girl is challenged to reach 25 of her peers. This peer education earns them bronze, silver and gold certificates. So, through the network of peer educators, the health messages have the potential to reach tens of thousands of adolescent girl refugees.

KO: It really is an amazing project that you are involved in. I'm sure all our listeners join me in wishing you continued success with HARP.

NA: Thank you!

Adapted from www.wagggsworld.org

Unit 12: A Speaking Activity 6 Track 24

Paramedics provide an immediate response to emergency medical calls. They are usually the first senior healthcare professional on the scene, and they are responsible for assessing the condition of a patient and providing treatment and care prior to hospital admission. A paramedic will attend emergencies, including minor injuries, sudden illness and casualties arising from road and rail accidents, criminal violence, fires and other incidents. They are usually in a two-person ambulance crew, with the other crew member being an ambulance technician or emergency care assistant who helps them. Some will work alone, however, using an emergency response car, motorbike or bicycle to get to a patient.

Adapted from www.prospects.ac.uk

Unit 12: B Listening Activity 4 Track 25

John: Dr Mary, what can you tell us about Florence Nghtingale's early years?

Dr Mary Winterson: Well, Florence Nightingale was born in Italy on 12th May 1820 and was named Florence after her birthplace. Her parents, Fanny and William, were wealthy and spent a considerable amount of time touring Europe.

J: How did she do at school? Did she get good grades?

MW: Yes, she did. As a schoolchild, Florence was academic and rarely had problems with her studies. She was attractive and the expectation was that she would marry and start a family.

J: But that didn't happen, did it?

MW: No, it didn't. Florence had different ideas. As a teenager she became involved in the social questions of the day, making visits to homes for sick people in local villages, and she began to investigate hospitals and nursing.

J: How did her parents react to this?

MW: Not very well, I'm afraid! Her parents refused to allow her to become a nurse as, in the mid-19th century, it was not considered a suitable profession for a well-educated woman. Because of the conflict which arose between Florence and her parents, it was decided to send her to Europe with some family friends, Charles and Selina Bracebridge.

J: Not such a bad punishment! Where exactly did they go?

MW: The three of them travelled to Italy, Greece and Egypt, returning to England through Germany in July 1850. While in Germany, they visited a hospital near Dusseldorf, where Florence returned in the following year to undergo a three-month nurse training course. This enabled her to take a post at a clinic in London in 1853.

J: Wasn't Britain at war around this time? With Russia?

MW: Yes, you're absolutely right. In March 1854, Britain was at war with Russia. While the Russians were defeated in the autumn of that year, British newspapers criticised the medical facilities for the soldiers wounded during the fighting. In response to the criticism, the government appointed Florence Nightingale to oversee the introduction of female nurses into British military hospitals in Turkey and, on 4th November 1854, she arrived in Scutari with a group of 38 nurses.

J: What an amazing story! What happened when they got to Scutari?

MW: Well, initially, the doctors did not want the nurses there because they felt threatened but, within ten days, many more casualties arrived and all the nurses were needed to cope with this sudden influx of wounded soldiers.

J: So the doctors were forced to accept the female nurses? Were the nurses successful?

MW: Yes! The introduction of female nurses in military hospitals was an outstanding success, and the nation showed its gratitude to Florence Nightingale by honouring her with a medal in 1907. Throughout her life, she continued tirelessly to campaign for better conditions in hospitals and for improved health standards.

J: When did she die?

MW: She died on 13th August 1910, having been a complete invalid herself and totally blind for 15 years. She was a national heroine. Her far-sighted reforms have influenced the nature of modern health care, and her writings continue to be a resource for nurses, health managers and planners.

J: Yes, she was certainly an inspiring woman.

Unit 12: E Listening Activity 1 `Track 26`

Marianna Milutinovic: Today we welcome Alvaro Solomou, one of the 1200 relief workers with the Red Cross, the ICRC, who is going to talk to us about the ICRC's approach to giving assistance. Welcome to the programme, Alvaro.

Alvaro Solomou: Hello, Marianna, and thank you for inviting me.

MM: Alvaro, can you tell us about how the ICRC assists victims of famine and drought and other natural disasters?

AS: Well, we should remember that, all too often, natural disasters happen in areas where there is already some other sort of problem, such as an economic crisis, or a period of political instability. Put the two together and the people involved become even more insecure and desperate.

MM: I imagine that different contexts also create extra problems, don't they?

AS: Yes, geographic context, as well as ethnic, political and economic, all translate into different needs and, therefore, the response the ICRC makes must be adapted to suit the context.

MM: How is that done?

AS: We use what is called the 'Assistance Pyramid'. This establishes that preference must be given in any relief situation to the foundations of the pyramid – in other words, to food, water and essential goods – before anything else is done.

MM: What about healthcare? Isn't that a priority?

AS: Hygiene and medical care take second and third places in the pyramid. Obviously, if a person is starving and thirsty, it does not matter how good the healthcare is.

MM: I see. Does the ICRC only assist when there is a crisis?

AS: No, not at all. In fact, in recent years, it has been the policy to provide help in developing countries once a crisis has passed, or even before one has occurred.

MM: How is that actually done?

AS: Well, for example, the ICRC assistance programmes have been extended, so that they now include seed and tools distribution, and the provision of veterinary care. The ICRC identifies priorities in a region, in order to provide the best possible assistance.

MM: Going back to the issue of water for a moment, isn't it true that millions of people across the world have difficulties gaining access to water? What can the ICRC do about this?

AS: Oh yes, that's absolutely true and, of course, in many places the water that is available is actually extremely unhealthy and may carry waterborne diseases, such as cholera and typhoid. The ICRC has a programme of assistance, which includes construction, engineering and providing access to water, along with hygiene and environmental protection, thus ensuring that water is clean and safe to use.

MM: Is it dangerous working for the ICRC?

AS: Well, in any crisis situation there are dangers, but all of us are strongly motivated by humanitarian work, and hopefully we can all cope with the stress and the pressures which are bound to exist.

MM: Alvaro, thank you for giving us such an interesting insight into the work of the ICRC.

Unit 12: Exam-style questions
`Track 27`

Part A

The world's transport crisis has reached such catastrophic proportions that road-traffic accidents now kill more people each year than malaria. I predict that by 2030, 2.5 million people will be killed on the roads in developing countries each year and 60 million will be injured. Even today, 3000 are killed and 30,000 seriously injured on the world's roads every day.

These are really frightening statistics, but, of course, it isn't only road-traffic accidents which concern me.

Air pollution from traffic claims 400,000 lives each year, mostly in developing countries, and some 1.5 billion people are exposed every day to levels of pollution well in excess of World Health Organization recommended levels.

We need to be aware of this because the damage being caused to people now, and especially youngsters, will follow them through until later life, and directly affect not only their health, but also their economic potential, and the health budgets of already strained national administrations.

Research shows us that the problems of the world's poor are multiplied by the car. It's a simple basic fact. Deaths and injuries take place mainly in developing countries and mainly to pedestrians, cyclists, bus users and children. The poor suffer disproportionately. They experience the worst air pollution and are deprived of education, health, water and sanitation programmes because the needs of the car now soak up so much national income. Advances in vehicle, engine and fuel technology are more or less irrelevant in Asian and African cities, where the growth of car and lorry numbers is dramatic and where highly polluting diesel is widespread.

Fortunately, I can report that in certain places, such as in parts of South America, something is being done. Transport budgets have been reallocated to improve the quality of life of poorer citizens and the results have been staggering. Bicycle- and pedestrian-only routes were planned, and cars were banned from certain areas. Parks were built on derelict land and car-free days implemented. This policy was radical and has improved the quality of life for the poor. This needs to be repeated all over the world.

Part B

Male teenager: Didn't that guest speaker give an interesting talk about traffic problems yesterday? It will really help us with that school project we have to do this term.

Female teenager: Yes, she was very interesting and she gave me some good ideas for our project too. I've already done some research.

MT: Since yesterday morning? Wow, that was quick!

FT: Well, I found out from my aunty, who's a police captain, that in the UK, the number of people killed in road accidents has fallen dramatically since 2000.

MT: Really? By how much? Maybe we can use the data?

FT: Well, in 2000, 3409 people died, including pedestrians, cyclists, motorcyclists and all vehicle users, but last year that had dropped to less than 1800.

MT: That's incredible! That's nearly a 50% drop. I read somewhere that the annual death rate from road accidents in the UK is about five per 100,000.

FT: So for every 100,000 people, five die? That doesn't seem very high, even though, of course, it should be 0. I know that in some countries in Africa, it's more than 40 per 100,000.

MT: I think we could design a graph for our project – a line graph – showing how the death rate from road traffic accidents has changed over the past ten or 15 years.

FT: And we need to make it clear that nearly half of people killed are pedestrians, cyclists or motorcyclists – my aunty told me they are called 'vulnerable road users'.

MT: So they are more at risk because a car or a lorry gives you more protection. And we know that in South America even more 'vulnerable road users' are killed …

FT: … Yes, I spoke to the speaker yesterday and she told me the figure is nearer to 70%.

MT: I think we could put some focus on the effectiveness of bicycle- and pedestrian-only routes, and what happens when cars and other vehicles are banned from certain roads.

FT: Good idea. I know that locally more and more people are using their bikes to get to and from school and work, using the new cycle paths …

MT: … and that new pedestrians-only area downtown has really increased the number of shoppers. Banning cars has to be the way ahead.

FT: I agree. Well, I think we have enough to be going on with. Let's Skype later and discuss how to proceed. Bye!

MT: Great, talk later …

Unit 13: G Further practice Activity 1
Track 28

Roland: Welcome to this week's 'Science Chat Show'. My guest today is Lefteris Christou, an expert on mobile-phone technology, who is based in Athens. Welcome, Lefteris!

Lefteris Christou: Hello, Roland, great to be with you.

R: I've been reading that the smartphone of the future will be a device that stays in our pockets, and it will act as a server for devices which we wear, such as a watch, glasses, a heart-rate monitor or other health-related sensor, or even a microchip in your brain! Is this really true, Lefteris?

LC: Yes, Roland, it is. These wearable devices will become like personal assistants, anticipating your every need, but they will be powered by your smartphone. And this solves the big issue with wearable technology right now, which is the challenge of meeting the power requirements of these small devices without sacrificing battery life and affordability.

R: I think I understand …

LC: Look … by offloading the processing and connectivity issues to the smartphone, the wearable device can be small and inexpensive. Problem solved!

R: So, in the future, my smartphone will be the brain of my various wearable devices?

LC: Exactly! It will provide the power, storage and the data connection. Your wearable device won't need cellular connectivity because your phone will provide that. Your wearable device will connect to your phone via Bluetooth or Wi-Fi and you will be able to connect to the Internet, or call friends and actually speak to them, via that connection.

R: That's amazing!

LC: Another really important feature provided by your smartphone will be its ability to accurately understand and transcribe your voice input. You won't be able to type on that screen.

R: Because it's too small, right? And it's in your pocket too!

LC: That's right, Roland. Wearable technology is forecast to make a big impact over the next few years and, as that technology evolves, so will our smartphones. They will have to race to keep up! The battle of the smartphones will no longer be about the size and resolution of the screen, but the way your watch, glasses or other devices communicate with it.

R: So, might there come a time when our wearable devices no longer need our smartphone to be the server in your pocket? And could there be a not-too-distant future when our wearable devices connect directly to the network around us without piggybacking off our phones?

LC: I think the answer is 'yes'! The race among smartphone manufacturers right now is to make bigger and better screens, so it seems contradictory that we would start to move towards even smaller screens.

R: Is there a possibility to send information to a different screen? I mean, not the screen on our phone?

LC: That's a very good question! Right now, when we get a message on our iPhone, we can also see it on our Macs and our iPads. The next screen outlet for the data that we currently check on our smartphone could be the television in the living room or the kitchen. When we

no longer need the server in our pocket, the need for the smartphone may diminish.

R: It really is incredible technology and it's coming our way very soon! Thank you, Lefteris, and we hope to welcome you back one day soon … .

Adapted from www.pcadvisor.co.uk

Unit 15: E Listening Activity 1 Track 29

Thomas Sampson: Welcome to our weekly programme on health issues for young people. Today I have with me in the studio Dr Maria Bealing, a dental expert. Hello, Dr Bealing.

Dr Bealing: Hello, Thomas, and thank you for inviting me.

TS: Dr Bealing, people have been chewing gum since the ancient Greeks used the bark from mastic trees as a breath freshener. And today, gum is chewed for many more reasons, such as when we feel hungry, or to get a nicotine hit if you're trying to give up cigarettes. But is chewing a stick of gum actually harmful to the body?

DB: Well, the moment a person unwraps a piece of gum and tosses it into their mouth, the brain is alerted that the digestive process is about to begin, and bells start ringing up there! During what's called the cephalic stage …

TS: Sorry, the what?

DB: The cephalic stage … c-e-p-h-a-l-i-c … this is when the body anticipates the arrival of food and …

TS: Sorry to interrupt again but how does the brain know that food is on its way?

DB: Through the senses: we either see the food, in a cupboard or in the supermarket fridge, or smell it in a restaurant, or hear someone chopping it up in the kitchen, or hear a gum wrapper being opened, and so on.

TS: OK, I understand.

DB: And then the brain releases saliva to help us chew whatever is coming.

TS: That's why we use the expression 'mouth-watering'? It means that our saliva, the juices in our mouth, is ready to receive food?

DB: Exactly. And this gets our stomach juices excited too. But because no real substance is ever delivered, some people argue that gum chewing tricks the brain, which upsets the stomach.

TS: I've heard that people can lose weight through gum-chewing. Is that correct?

DB: Scientific studies haven't successfully proven that gum can stave off hunger and lead to weight loss. Chewing gum jump-starts the digestive process and so it may, in fact, increase hunger, and this may, in turn, lead to weight gain.

TS: So are there any benefits in gum chewing?

DB: Well, researchers have found a benefit. Recent studies have shown that chewing gum during a task can increase cognitive function. In other words, chewing while doing can help some people concentrate.

TS: I must admit that I'm a bit of a gum-chewer, so should I stop, or can I carry on?

DB: My advice, if you really want to chew, is to try sugarless gum, but only after a meal. The saliva it helps to produce will clean your teeth and the minty or fruity flavour of the gum will sweeten your breath and possibly satisfy a sweet tooth.

TS: Thank you doctor, that sounds very sensible to me!

Acknowledgements

The author and publishers are grateful for the permissions granted to reproduce texts in either the original or adapted form. While every effort has been made, it has not always been possible to identify the sources of the all materials used, or to trace all copyright holders. If any omissions are brought to our notice, we will be happy to include the appropriate acknowledgements on reprinting.

p. 17 adapted from http://www.esrb.org/ratings/ratings_guide.jsp, courtesy of the Entertainment Software Ratings Board; p. 18 adapted from an advertisement in *The Independent*, 8th June 2003, copyright *The Independent* 2003; p. 19 adapted from an article in *The Independent Review*, 20th August 2003, copyright *The Independent* 2003; p. 23 adapted from www.denver.org/what-to-do/attractions/denver-teen-activities; p. 25 adapted from www.financialized.ca/how-much-pocket-money-is-enough; p. 27 adapted from 'The Kuala Lumpur Experience', *Weekender Bahrain*, November 2013; p. 29 © English Heritage; p. 31 adapted from *Actually Factually, Mind-Blowing Myths, Muddles and Misconceptions*, pages 110–12, Buster Books, 2009 and www.factmonster.com/ipka/; p. 33 adapted from an '13+ things your fast food worker won't tell you' by Michelle Crouch, *Reader's Digest*, November 2012, www.rd.com/slideshows/13-things-your-fast-food-worker-won't-tell-you, customer_service@readersdigest.co.uk; p. 35 adapted from www.reuters.com/article/2013/01/09/us-mcdonalds-italy-idUSBRE9080SE20130109; p. 39 adapted from 'Hospitality with dates', *Ahlan Wasahlan*, November 2013, © *Ahlan Wasahlan* Magazine, 2013; p. 40 Adapted from 'Marketing the mollusc' by Dr Karen Millson, *Tribute*, 1990, © Apex Press and Publishing, Oman; p. 47 adapted from www.garda.ie/Controller.aspx?Page=10707&Lang=1, An Garda Siochana; p. 49 adapted from http://think.direct.gov.uk/cycling.html, courtesy of The Department for Transport; p. 58 adapted from www.dailymail.co.uk/health/article-402925/Why-teenagers-morning.html#ixzz2sowACIvl; p. 64 adapted from http://chemistscorner.com/how-to-become-a-cosmetic-chemist/; p. 68 adapted from www.livestrong.com/article/370326-females-in-athletic-training/; p. 71 adapted from www.arabnews.com/news/486921; pp. 72–3 adapted from 'Indian camel breeders lament Pushkar fair's downfall', *Arab News*, 16th November 2013; p. 76 adapted from www.vocabulary.co.il/why-is-learning-to-spell-important/; p. 92 adapted from http://bestcareerlinks.com/jobsforteens.html; p. 99 adapted from http://edition.cnn.com/2012/07/24/sport/olympic-strangest-events/; p. 104 adapted from www.dailymail.co.uk/news/article-1240463/Hero-teenager-saves-children-trapped-burning-house.html#ixzz2tTwKmz5S; p. 106 adapted from http://kidshealth.org/teen/asthma_center/treatment/asthma_triggers.html#, © The Nemours Foundation/KidsHealth. Reprinted with permission; p. 109 adapted from http://en.wikipedia.org/wiki/Eus%C3%A9bio, Creative Commons ShareAlike License; p. 111 adapted from www.independent.co.uk/news/uk/home-news/im-the-fat-beggar-kids-companys-camila-batmanghelidjh-reveals-why-the-fight-for-funds-for-vulnerable-children-never-ends-9171790.html, © Nick Duerden/*The Independent*; p. 115 adapted from an article in *Gulf Life*, December 2031, pp. 50–52, Al Nisr Publishing LLC; p. 118 adapted from news.bbc.co.uk, 31st December 2007, courtesy of BBC News; p. 119 adapted from 'Impressed? It's even better underwater …' by Adam Dudding, *The Independent on Sunday*, 19th May 2002; p. 120 adapted from *Culinaria Italy*, 2000; p. 134 adapted from www.nhscareers.nhs.uk/explore-by-career/ambulance-service-team/careers-in-the-ambulance-service-team/paramedic/; p. 142 adapted from 'Twitter overtakes Facebook' by Alex Greig, *Mail Online*, 24th October 2013, www.dailymail.co.uk/news/article-2475591/Twitter-overtakes-Facebook-popular-social-network-teens-according-study.html; p. 145 adapted from www.pcadvisor.co.uk/opinion/mobile-phone/3466728/future-of-smartphones/, courtesy of PC Advisor (2013); p. 156 adapted from www.telegraph.co.uk/earth/earthnews/9907789/Shipping-lanes-could-open-over-the-North-Pole-due-to-climate-change.html, © NI Syndication Ltd, 2000; p. 159 adapted from www.rtcc.org/2013/12/04/europe-already-feeling-climate-change-impacts-report/, courtesy of Sophie Yeo, RTCC, www.rtcc.org; p. 162 adapted from *The Times*, 28th August 2001; p. 168 adapted from http://humantouchofchemistry.com/fun-facts-about-chewing-gum-to-chew-on.htm; p. 182 adapted from www.communityonline.com, 16th January 2008; p. 189 adapted from www.theguardian.com/global-development/2013/aug/13/uganda-motorbike-deaths-road-safety-boda-bodas, © Amy Fallon/the guardian.com; p. 190 adapted from www.historvius.com/features/tourist-attractions-in-turkey, www.tripadvisor.co.uk/Attraction_Review-g293974-d1787137-Reviews-Istanbul_Dolphinarium-Istanbul.html and www.travelsavvymom.com/blog/five-favorites/istanbul-turkey-5-family-favorites/; pp. 191–2 adapted from http://spaceflightsystems.grc.nasa.gov/girlscouts/gsusa_careers.html; p. 197 adapted from www.mapsofindia.com/india-tour/jammu-and-Kashmir/is-khardungla-pass-the-highest-motorable-road-in-the-world/; pp. 197–198 adapted from www.wagggsworld.org; p. 198 adapted from www.prospects.ac.uk/paramedic_job_description.htm; pp. 200–201 adapted from: http://www.pcadvisor.co.uk/opinion/mobile-phone/3466728/future-of-smartphones/, courtesy of PC Advisor (2013).

Picture credits

p. 6 jsbdueck/Shutterstock; p. 7 (1) Stockbyte/Thinkstock; p. 7 (2) moonboard/Thinkstock; p. 7 (3) Intellistudies/Shutterstock; p. 7 (4) cdrin/Shutterstock; p. 7 (bl) Dragon Images/Shutterstock; p. 7 (br) Ariwasabi/Shutterstock; p. 8 (l) silroby80/Shutterstock; p. 8 (r) AFP/Getty Images; p. 11 (l) Pica82/Thinkstock; p. 11 (m) Oramstock/Alamy; p. 11 (r) Photothek via Getty Images; p. 12 (l) Hemera Technologies/Thinkstock; p. 12 (r) Jack Hollingsworth/Thinkstock; p. 16 (t) Przemyslaw Skibinski/Shutterstock; p. 16 (b) Paula French/Shutterstock; p. 17 logos courtesy of ESRB; p. 18 Peter Jarvis/Alamy; p. 19 MadrugadeVerde/Thinkstock; p. 20 (1) Nasib Bitar/GNU Free Documentation License/Wikimedia; p. 20 (2) Andrey_Popov/Shutterstock; p. 20 (3) Digital Vision/Thinkstock; p. 20 (4) CBS via Getty Images; p. 20 (5) FOX via Getty Images; p. 23 Arina P Habich/Shutterstock; p. 25 Jupiterimages/Thinkstock; p. 27 anharris/Thinkstock; p. 29 vencavolrab/Thinkstock; p. 32 (1) Anna Kurzaeva/Shutterstock; p. 32 (2) Moreno Novello/Shutterstock; p. 32 (3) highviews/Shutterstock; p. 32 (4) baibaz/Thinkstock; p. 35 (t) Ingram Publishing/Thinkstock; p. 35 (b) grafvision/Shutterstock; p. 39 (l) Atid Katib/Getty Images News/Thinkstock; p. 39 (r) Olgakr/Thinkstock; p. 40 JPL Designs/Shutterstock; p. 42 (1) vichie81/Thinkstock; p. 42 (2) Bplanet/Shutterstock; p. 42 (3) nitinut380/Shutterstock; p. 43 (4) IvonneW/Thinkstock; p. 44 Barbara Gonget/G&B Images/Alamy; p. 49 Getty Images; p. 50 jackmalipan/Thinkstock; p. 52 Top Photo Group/Thinkstock; p. 53 (1) XiXinXing/Shutterstock; p. 53 (2) bikeriderlondon/Shutterstock; p. 53 (3) Black Rock Digital/Shutterstock; p. 54 Andrew Fox/Alamy; p. 57 Monkey Business Images/Shutterstock; p. 62 (1) Jupiterimages/Thinkstock; p. 62 (2) Monkey Business Images/Thinkstock; p. 62 (3) Fuse/Thinkstock; p. 62 (4) Andresr/Shutterstock; p. 62 (5) Tyler Olson/Shutterstock; p. 64 James Steidl/Hemera/Thinkstock; p. 67 Ablestock/Thinkstock; p. 68 Dennis MacDonald/Alamy; p. 72 sabirmallick/Thinkstock; p. 74 (1) scyther5/Shutterstock; p. 74 (2) Nagel Photography/Shutterstock; p. 74 (3) Maridav/Thinkstock; p. 74 (4) mihalec/Shutterstock; p. 74 (5) M. Unal Ozmen/Shutterstock; p. 74 (6) AFP/Getty Images; p. 74 (7) Voronin76/Shutterstock; p. 76 Fuse/Thinkstock; p. 77 Christian Science Monitor/Getty Images; p. 81 (t) Brian A. Jackson/Thinkstock; p. 81 (b) Digital Vision/Thinkstock; p. 83 (t) Fuse/Thinkstock; p. 83 (b) omgimages/Thinkstock; p. 86 (1) Jupiterimages/Thinkstock; p. 86 (2) Antoine Juliette/Oredia/Oredia Eurl/SuperStock; p. 86 (3) Sergi Lopez Roig/Shutterstock; p. 86 (4) Universal Images Group/SuperStock; p. 86 (5) Dmitry Kalinovsky/Shutterstock; p. 87 Photofusion Picture Library/Alamy; p. 90 Photofusion Picture Library/Thinkstock; p. 92 Monkey Business Images/Thinkstock; p. 94 Sophie James/Shutterstock; p. 95 Colette3/Shutterstock; p. 96 Monkey Business Images/Thinkstock; p. 97 (1) thobo/Thinkstock; p. 97 (2) Faith Saribas/Reuters/Corbis; p. 97 (3) Andrew Woodley/Alamy; p. 99 Olha Insight/Shutterstock; p. 102 Time & Life Pictures/Getty Images; p. 104 John Hanley/Shutterstock; p. 105 Pixelbliss/Shutterstock; p. 106 federicocandonifoto/Shutterstock; p. 108 (1) Concord Productions Inc./Golden Harvest Company/Sunset Boulevard/Corbis; p. 108 (2) Getty Images for Burda Media; p. 108 (3) AFP/Getty Images; p. 108 (4) AFP/Getty Images; p. 109 Universal/TempSport/Corbis; p. 111 Getty Images; p. 115 SerenityPhotography/Shutterstock; p. 118 courtesy of Elyse Schein; p. 119 Rich Carey/Shutterstock; p. 120 Shaiith/Thinkstock; p. 121 (1) Rich Carey/Shutterstock; p. 121 (2) David de Lossy/Thinkstock; p. 121 (3) Purestock/Thinkstock; p. 121 (4) Mikadun/Shutterstock; p. 121 (5) Digital Vision/Thinkstock; p. 122 (l) Tanya Puntti/Thinkstock; p. 122 (r) cienpies/Thinkstock; p. 123 TP/Alamy; p. 127 Alexander Mak/Shutterstock; p. 130 (1) Giambra/Shutterstock; p. 130 (2) bikeriderlondon/Shutterstock; p. 130 (3) Christian Science Monitor/Getty Images; p. 131 (t) Anneka/Shutterstock; p. 131 (b) Wikipedia; p. 134 Candyboximages/Thinkstock; p. 135 Ton Koene/age footstock/SuperStock; p. 136 AFP/Getty Images; p. 140 Nik Merkulov/Thinkstock; p. 142 Christin Gilbert/age footstock/SuperStock; p. 144 KPG_Payless/Shutterstock; p. 145 Arman Zhenikeyev/Fuse/Thinkstock; p. 149 racorn/Shutterstock; p. 150 (l) Yu Lan/Shutterstock; p. 150 (r) Rich Carey/Shutterstock; p. 153 (1) Hung Chung Chih/Thinkstock; p. 153 (2) guentermanaus/Shutterstock; p. 153 (3) mycola/Thinkstock; p. 153 (4) Vladimir Melnik/Shutterstock; p. 154 erandamx/Thinkstock; p. 156 Raldo Sommers/Thinkstock; p. 159 satori13/Thinkstock; p. 160 WhiteTag/Shutterstock; p. 163 vau902/Thinkstock; p. 165 Stocktrek Images/Thinkstock; p. 166 (1) Matthew Collingwood/Thinkstock; p. 166 (2) Purestock/Thinkstock; p. 166 (3) Ziga Cetrtic/Thinkstock; p. 168 Ecelop/Shutterstock; p. 172 (l) Hoang Cong Thanh/Shutterstock; p. 172 (r) Yelena Yemchuk/Thinkstock; p. 176 (1) zkruger/Shutterstock; p. 176 (2) Art Konovalov/Shutterstock; p. 176 (3) evgeny freeone/Shutterstock; p. 176 (4) Marko Poplasen /Shutterstock; p. 180 (1) Getty Images; p. 180 (2) WhiteTag/Thinkstock; p. 180 (3) Moodboard/Thinkstock; p. 180 (4) David Davis/Thinkstock; p. 180 (5) WavebreakMedia/Thinkstock; p. 180 (6) Fotoluminate LLC/Shutterstock; p. 182 stockyimages/Shutterstock.

Produced for Cambridge University Press by White-Thomson Publishing
+44 (0)843 208 7460
www.wtpub.co.uk

Project editor: Sonya Newland
Designer: Kim Williams, 320 Media
Illustrators: Peter Bull Art Studio